The Ninth Amendment and the Politics of Creative Jurisprudence

Marshall L. DeRosa

The Ninth Amendment and the Politics of Creative Jurisprudence

Disparaging the Fundamental Right of Popular Control

Routledge
Taylor & Francis Group
LONDON AND NEW YORK

An earlier version of chapter 6 was published in *Perspectives on Political Science*, vol. 22, no. 2 (Spring 1993), 52-60. Reprinted with permission of The Helen Dwight Reid Educational Foundation; published by Heldref Publication. © 1993.

Published 1996 by Transaction Publishers

Published 2017 by Routledge
2 Park Square, Milton Park, Abingdon, Oxon OX14 4RN
711 Third Avenue, New York, NY 10017

First issued in paperback 2017

Routledge is an imprint of the Taylor and Francis Group, an informa business

Library of Congress Catalog Number: 95-37023

Library of Congress Cataloging-in-Publication Data

DeRosa, Marshall L., 1955-
The Ninth Amendment and the politics of creative jurisprudence : disparaging the fundamental right of popular control / Marshall L. DeRosa.
p. cm.
Includes bibliographical references and index.
ISBN 1-56000-233-6 (alk. paper)
1. United States—Constitutional law—Amendments—9th. 2. People (Constitutional law)—United States. 3. Federal government—United States. I. Title.
KF4558 9th.D47 1995
342.73'085—dc20 95-37023
[347.30285] CIP

ISBN 13: 978-1-138-51650-2 (pbk)
ISBN 13: 978-1-56000-233-8 (hbk)

To Mary, my best friend and sensational wife

Contents

Preface

The enumeration in the Constitution of certain rights shall not be construed to deny or disparage others retained by the people (Ninth Amendment, 1791).

Our form of government may remain notwithstanding legislation or decision, but, as long ago observed, it is with governments, as with religions, the form may survive the substance of the faith (Chief Justice Melville W. Fuller, Champion v. Ames *[1903]).*

This book focuses attention on the inherent tension between judicial review and popular control in the articulation of unenumerated rights. As has been the case with most of the other aspects of our partly federal and partly national republic,[1] this area of jurisprudence may prove to be very instrumental in the ongoing transition from the traditional model of federalism in which the States had meaningful public policy prerogatives within their respective jurisdictions, to a model of nationalism in which the States are merely administrative extensions of the United States Government. Within the context of American federalism, this book proceeds to address the diminishing relevance of the *original* Ninth Amendment to the meaningful rule of law in the articulation of unenumerated rights. As the wisdom of the framers—Federalists and Antifederalists—attests, what is at stake is the diminution of a principal component of our constitutional heritage, the fundamental right to be self-governing citizens within the context of constitutionally quasi-sovereign States.

To make my case I have tracked the Ninth Amendment in its traditional and evolving forms. This does not mean that the Ninth Amendment is unique in the articulation of nationalized rights; the corpus of constitutional law manifests the importance of other constitutional elements, such as congressional commerce powers, the due process and equal protection clauses, and the various penumbras and emanations from other constitutional provisions. But the Ninth Amendment does provide us with a constitutional platform from which to view significant developments in the ongoing nationalization of unenumerated constitutional rights; from the vantage point of the Ninth Amendment we can survey juridical developments that have and probably will continue to significantly alter American constitutionalism in the public policy area of unenumerated rights, the 1994 Republican party's electoral success notwithstanding. Toward that end, chapter 1 analyzes the current debate over Ninth Amendment rights; chapter 2 utilizes the privileges and immunities clauses as instructive about the traditional relationship between the states' police powers and unenumerated fundamental rights; chapter 3 analyzes the critical role of academia in the first half of the twentieth century and its impact on jurisprudential developments; chapters 4 and 5 concentrate on national and state case studies; chapter 6 analyzes an enumerated fundamental right and its modification by creative jurisprudence; chapter 7 contrasts mutually exclusive theories of two contemporary scholars, thereby making clear two distinct tracks future constitutional developments may take; and chapter 8 offers a prop to the collapsing federal constitutional structure.

Note

1. See *The Federalist Papers* #39, ed. Clinton Rossiter (New York: New American Library, 1961).

1

The Promise of Judicial Federalism

I

As we approach the close of the twentieth century and prepare to embark on the twenty-first, it behooves us to determine the relevance of American federalism in the high conflict and high salient public policy area of unenumerated rights. The cardinal principle of our political culture, that "Governments are instituted among Men, deriving their just Powers from the Consent of the Governed,"[1] was not to be suspended in the articulation of unenumerated rights; qualified yes, suspended no. By evaluating Ninth Amendment constitutional law developments, we can discern the extent of unenumerated rights public policy conformity with this cardinal principle. Of course, the U.S. Supreme Court is the institution at the center of this analysis due to its constitutional responsibility for authoritatively adjudicating rights controversies, which in turn necessitates determinative decisions about the role of the states in the federal system and the manner and extent of popular control over the articulation of unenumerated rights.[2]

There currently is substantial confusion about what the role of the states is and should be, as is evidenced by a lack of scholarly consensus on the relevance of American federalism. One scholar contends that "federalism has fallen on hard times. It has lost its meaning in American politics not only as a result of centralizing tendencies in government but also as a result of the failure of scholars to nourish the idea of it."[3] Another maintains that the demands of national commerce necessitate the end of historical federalism.[4] Some have gone so far as to issue postmortems on American federalism, maintaining that American federalism does not merit scholarly attention because reference to it is illusory.[5] Claims such as these are cause for concern because of the inherent value of a viable federal system in maintaining constitutional government grounded in the popular control and consent of the governed.[6]

Remarkably, scholarship about judicial politics presents us with a somewhat more positive picture of federalism's future: "State constitutional law has been *reemerging* for the last twenty years. The once new *judicial federalism*—as the increased constitutional activism of state courts employing independent state law has felicitously been styled—has been welcomed, promoted, and urged as an antidote to the U.S. Supreme Court's retrenchment in civil rights and liberties in the Burger-Rehnquist era."[7] Moreover, "since the early 1970s, state courts of last resort have issued a growing number of decisions in which provisions of state constitutions have served either as independent grounds or as the only grounds for ruling on questions of individual rights and liberties.... Since 1977, state high courts have rendered at least 217 rights-affirming decisions based upon provisions of their state constitutions—approximately a 131 percent increase in the number of such decisions over the 94 decisions issued during 1950–1977."[8]

Such statistics are facially encouraging for advocates not necessarily of federalism, but rather a liberal state court response to what is perceived to be a conservative leaning U.S. Supreme Court. However, citing such data verges on the nondescript. The U.S. Supreme Court's willingness to permit state courts to adjudicate state cases involving rights is not synonymous with permitting the states to deviate from national standards.[9] Other explanations are more credible, such as the practical attempt to reduce the federal courts' case loads by channeling cases to the state courts.[10] But what is significant is that the U.S. Supreme Court has not tolerated substantive state deviations from its vision of unenumerated rights and the application of its vision on the states through the Fourteenth Amendment.[11] Thus, claims of a reinvigorated judicial federalism are premature, superficial, and inconsistent with pronouncements that either anticipate or declare the final days of American federalism. By focusing our attention on Ninth Amendment jurisprudence, we can better discern just how promising the new judicial federalism is in particular, and the long-term prospects for American federalism in general.

II

There are two important historic postulates relevant to Ninth Amendment jurisprudence: first, that the Ninth Amendment was *originally* designed to reaffirm a federal approach to the articulation of unenumerated rights, and second, the *original design has been displaced* with a nationalized approach in the jurisprudence of unenumerated rights. Consequently, the Ninth Amendment is integral to American federalism and can be utilized to either support or undermine it. Moreover, nationalistic and federal paradigms of unenumerated rights are not necessarily compatible, and may at times be mutually exclusive. Procedurally the U.S. Supreme Court's willingness to write its understanding of unenumerated rights into the Ninth Amendment is incompatible with a federal model of the Ninth Amendment through which the states could exercise prerogatives in the articulation of unenumerated rights within their respective jurisdictions; precluding such state prerogatives by nationally defined unenumerated rights is inconsistent with the states functioning as quasi-sovereign entities in exercising their Ninth Amendment prerogatives.[12] It is beyond dispute that the nationalization of unenumerated rights presents a diminutive impact on the role of the states in the federal system.[13] In other words, national uniformity and state diversity are conversely related.

The U.S. Constitution was designed to accommodate degrees of diversity among the states and between the state and the national governments. Publius forewarned that "the State governments will too naturally be prone to rivalship with that of the Union, the foundation of which will be the love of power."[14] Implicitly Publius was acknowledging that there would be diverse interests among the states and between some states and the national government; the federal arrangement was designed to accommodate such diversity by sanctioning public policy diversity. In the absence of this federal model, the framers would ask, how can public policy be grounded in popular control and popular consent? This does not mean that when public opinion culminates in a national consensus that a federal approach to public policy should be preempted by national uniformity with, I might add, the blessings of the national branches of government, particularly the U.S. Supreme Court, even though the national policy in question is, for the time being, grounded in popular consent and control. Because public opinion waxes and wanes, the extent to which political power is exercised by the national or state governments should not depend on the current political climate and the issue(s) in question, but rather on constitutional *terra firma*. The framers would remind us that political power has an encroaching nature and one should not expect the power distribution between national and state governments to be static in some areas of public policy while nationally aggrandizing in others. For example, expanding congressional commerce powers have been very difficult to contain to strictly issues of commerce.[15]

Overall, in post-World War II America the national government has been acquiring vast powers at the expense of the states. True, some states initiate innovative policies independent of national control, such as health, welfare, and environmental reforms,[16] but only as long as the U.S. Congress acquiesces in these state experiments. Moreover, because the acquisition of national power has been incremental and—until the 1994 Republican takeover of the Congress—unchallenged, there is the expectation that the nationalizing trend will culminate in most significant areas of public policy; the articulation of unenumerated rights is no exception. Accordingly, when the national government extends its policy jurisdiction into the realms of unenumerated rights (both economic and cultural[17]) of citizenries of the respective states, it is easy to loose sight of the fact that the national government's gain is the states' loss, and that the latter increasingly concede the capacity to be self-governing in those areas of public policy taken over by the national government. Even the Republican-controlled Congress has not conceded its authority over the states; the Republicans' preference for the states is grounded in a cost-benefit analysis of balancing the national budget, in contradistinction to reestablishing traditional federalism.

In spite of the accolades for the U.S. Supreme Court for its role in promoting national supremacy,[18] especially in those areas of public policy where the states have apparently fallen short, such as *de facto* and *de jure* racial segregation, which obviously provide grist for the nationalizing mill, the displacement of meaningful autonomous participation of the states in the federal system does have serious consequential costs attached. The most significant cost is the denigration of the critical role of the states in providing essential checks on the national government. According to Publius, "It may safely be received as an axiom in our political system that the State governments will, in all possible contingencies, afford complete security against invasions of the public liberty by the national authority."[19] The states' responsibility to function as external checks on the national government, thereby making the latter accountable to the people, was intended to be an integral part of the American scheme of checks and balances. The framers' interest in this function of the states is obvious when one considers that the debate surrounding federalism was the most contentious issue at the Philadelphia Convention and the ensuing ratification processes. They refused to centralize political power in a unitary national government, being cognizant that the scope of national power was very problematical for their overall commitment to a republican form of government premised upon the consent of the governed.[20]

Accordingly, if the U.S. Supreme Court clears the way for national unenumerated rights public policy, as it did with economic policy, then the collateral impact on republican government—as supported by a model of federalism with quasi-sovereign states—will be, if not neutralized, at a minimum dealt a serious setback. The U.S. Supreme Court has been incrementally constructing the Ninth Amendment into an instrument of rights nationalism, thereby removing a significant external check on the abusive use of national governmental power. At the core of this juridical development is the court's emphasis on higher law doctrines.[21]

III

Influenced by, but distinct from, the English Common Law tradition, the early American process for articulating rights was incremental, tied to legal precedent and, to a greater extent than was the case in England, contingent upon popular control. The framers[22] acknowledged as much by subjecting the status of nationally recognized rights to modification through a cumbersome amendment process, while simultaneously leaving intact state recognized rights in state constitutions and statutes. Such a system may or may not have had the most desirable results, but designing a process most conducive to achieving a just system of rights has been the perennial problem of political philosophy and none of the framers was naive enough to assume that the problem of political justice was finally resolved in 1787, nor were they prepared to allow national scheme of rights to be easily imposed upon the states in order to achieve national uniformity. Thus, integral to the framers' commitment to popular control of public policy is the integrity of the states in the federal system,[23] a commitment that the framers would not—and politically speaking could not—have abandoned because states failed to conform to some national standard. Moreover, the prospect of the U.S. Supreme Court imposing its version of unenumerated rights on the states would have been readily recognized as a violation of the unenumerated right to be self-governing, as that right was contingent upon the states functioning as effective checks on the national government.

The tension between state-based popular control over unenumerated rights and U.S. Supreme Court managed Ninth Amendment unenumerated rights should not be dismissed as trivial.[24] Of the numerous rights included in the body of the text and its subsequent amendments, there is no mention of subordinating the state constitutions and statutes to higher laws as defined by the U.S. Supreme Court. All constitutionally recognized rights are subject to modification through a political process, namely the amendment process described in Article V. Only four provisions of the Constitution even hint at limiting the amendment process. Three of these provisions are found in Article V, which (1) protect the importation of slaves until 1808; (2) prohibit capitation and other direct taxes levied by the national government upon individuals; (3) protect equal state suffrage in the U.S. Senate, and less directly; (4) Article VI, which states that "no religious Test shall ever be required." Other than these four instances,[25] the amendment process is an open conduit for state participation in the definition of nationally recognized rights, and that participation is premised upon the fundamental right to be self-governing within a federal framework. Conversely, according to one recent commentator, the Ninth Amendment answers in the negative the fundamental question of "whether the Framers intended the Constitution to protect a limited list of individual rights, freezing forever the political and social mores of eighteenth century America."[26] According to this view, the Ninth Amendment is at the disposal of the federal courts, serving as an open constitutional window through which judicially sponsored political and social change can blow. However, such emphasis on the Ninth Amendment for political and social change is misdirected; historically it has been the legislative and amendment processes of the nation and states that have functioned as the engines of governmentally protected individual rights, in contradistinction to the Ninth Amendment serving as a grab bag of unenumerated rights for the U.S. Supreme Court. To the extent that the Ninth Amendment is interpreted by the U.S. Supreme Court as a conduit of innovative political and social mores, to the same extent states are required to concede popular control over the effected areas of public policy.

When the Constitution is kept distinct from the Declaration of Independence, popular control over rights policies within the states becomes clearer. Unlike the Declaration, which is committed to the proposition that "all men are created equal,"[27] the Constitution is committed to the right of the people to be self-governing within the federal framework.[28] Unlike the Declaration, the U.S. Constitution is primarily nomocratic, that is, "characterized, not by objectives, but rather by its mode of operation and devotion to a body of laws which codified that mode."[29] The Constitution delineates the processes through which the people are to govern themselves. Thus, the U.S. Supreme Court poses a serious threat to the constitutional order designed to facilitate self-government when it claims that the U.S. Constitution, or higher law as incorporated into the Ninth Amendment, inherently guarantees to every citizen certain rights, which members of the bench believe to be requisite to civilization, progress, humanity, or standards of decency, and then proceed to incorporate their understanding of these otherwise unspecified rights into constitutional law.[30] This higher law incorporation is sanctioned by a teleocratic view of the Constitution, which "has come into fashion only during the last few decades and has all but destroyed the original Constitution." According to Forrest McDonald:

> This is the notion that the design of the Constitution was to achieve a certain kind of society, one based upon abstract principles of natural rights or justice or equality or democracy or all of the above. It holds that the specific provisions of the document are of secondary importance or none at all; what counts are the "principles" it supposedly embodies, usually principles based upon the Declaration of Independence or Lincoln's Gettysburg Address, neither of which has any standing in law.[31]

Of course, higher law has and does influence American law and court procedure, but it was not the intent of the framers to permit innovative U.S. Supreme Court higher law doctrines to displace the constitutionally sanctioned state prerogatives regarding rights. The U.S. Supreme Court's reliance on higher law doctrines, as a rationalization for voiding state policies, is problematical because it runs counter to Article VI, which stipulates that "this Constitution, and the Laws made in Pursuance thereof" are supreme. In conjunction with a proper understanding of the Ninth and Tenth Amendments,[32] it is evident that a U.S. Supreme Court judicial transfusion of higher law into American constitutional law, which strikes down state statutes that establish parameters of rights inconsistent those U.S. Supreme Court preferred higher law standards, is in effect subordinating American republicanism to juridical abstractions.

IV

In the original American federal system the sorting out of rights was the responsibility of the respective states' political processes and the national amendment process. Nevertheless, the U.S. Supreme Court has a critical function in the articulation and enforcement of rights, and certainly the Court's performance can be evaluated along the lines of social and legal principles and praised or criticized accordingly. However, any short-term advantages based upon social and legal arguments in a particular case (or cases) may have important long-term consequences detrimental to popular control and its facilitator the American federalism. Accordingly, the merits of a particular case should not be considered in a political, social, or legal vacuum, but placed in the larger theoretical context of American federalism, at least until the following fundamental theoretical (and, I might add, recurring) question is satisfactorily resolved: In what manner and to what extent should the U.S. Supreme Court's preemption of the popular control basis of rights be tolerated?

There are several perspectives from which this question should be addressed. The first involves the constitutional prerogatives of the people within their respective states to be self-governing. It is problematical for a viable federal system when the public policies of a state violate rights that are essential to meaningful participation in the democratic process. As Justice Stone maintained in *United States* v. *Carolene Products Co.* (1938), these procedural participatory rights have privileged judicial protection; as a result, the Supreme Court's nullification of state policies that unconstitutionally limit access to political participation is certainly within the purview of judicial review.[33] This is a significant Court responsibility. If public policy is to be the product of a self-governing people, then it is essential for the channels of political participation[34] to be open to all "qualified" citizens,[35] irrespective of majority or minority status. The Supreme Court's authority for such intervention is grounded in Article IV, section 4, which stipulates that "The United States shall guarantee to every State in this Union a Republican form of Government." The republican form of government the framers had in mind was grounded in popular control through a scheme of representation.[36]

In the event that entrenched interests detract from or usurp popular control, the U.S. Supreme Court has a constitutional responsibility in reinstating it, due to the fact that certain constitutional provisions (i.e., Article IV, section 4,[37] and amendments XV, XVII, XIX, XXIV, and XXVI) and the theoretical underpinnings of the national and state constitutions provide for government accountability through popular control of the governmental process.

Second, if the federal courts were to adopt a hands-off policy on unenumerated rights, there is the nagging question as to whether state majorities would confer rights responsibly. This was a critical issue during the 1787 Convention and the subsequent drafting of the Bill of Rights. Fortunately, it need not concern us here. It is a philosophical question, decided in the affirmative by the American framers on the side of the states. Of course, state majorities are subject to a system of internal and external checks and balances, but in the final analysis sovereignty constitutionally resides in the people and not in the judiciary, and unless stipulated otherwise, as in Article I, section 10, and the Fourteenth Amendment of the U.S. Constitution, state majorities do have public policy prerogatives in the policy area of rights. Therefore, to tolerate judicial intervention on the basis that state majorities are incompetent to justly govern their respective communities, not only turns the Constitution on its head, but runs the serious risk of becoming a self-fulfilling prophesy by substituting majority rule with lawyerly elitism, in which the legal profession (as represented in the federal courts) dominates the articulation of rights. Such deference to the modern equivalent of Platonic legal guardians is contrary to the letter and the spirit of American constitutionalism. Furthermore, there is no constitutional basis for the Court's version of fundamental rights to supplant popular control, but there is a fundamental right to succeed and/or fail within the parameters of constitutionalism in the exercise of self-government.

Third, there exists the problem of a workable demarcation between national and state governments regarding public policy jurisdictions. At one time it was imagined that the U.S. Constitution embodied a judicially enforceable demarcation, but the document has been subject to such juridical contortions over the last several decades that, for all intents and purposes, the term *federalism* verges on the anachronous. A case in point is *Garcia* v. *San Antonio Metropolitan Transit Authority* (1985), in which the Court majority placed the status of state sovereign immunity vis-à-vis the commerce powers of Congress not on any particular constitutional provision, such as the nature of Congress' delegated powers and the states' reserved powers of the Tenth Amendment, but at the political discretion of Congress. Choosing to ignore the diversity of regional interests, Justice Blackmun wrote on behalf of the Court that "the political process ensures that laws that unduly burden the states will not be promulgated."[38] Summarizing the implications of this reasoning, the dissenters charged that "these changes may well have lessened the weight Congress gives to the legitimate interests of states as states. As a result, there is now a real risk that Congress will gradually erase the diffusion of power between state and nation on which the Framers based their faith in the efficiency and vitality of our republic."[39] If the dissenters are correct, then through the machinations of the U.S. Congress and the U.S. Supreme Court the states can be reduced to administrative extensions of the national government, fulfilling this or that public policy function as the U.S. Congress deems convenient or appropriate. Based upon the model of federalism inherent in *Garcia,* Congress could enact national standards of unenumerated rights through the exercise of its commerce powers, thereby trumping the various state standards with national standards, the Ninth and Tenth Amendments notwithstanding.

These perspectives alert us to the important practical fact that the states' roles in the process of delimiting Ninth Amendment unenumerated rights is contingent upon the U.S. Supreme Court recognizing and protecting the constitutional role of the states. What I undertake to adumbrate below is that, should the U.S. Supreme Court insist on applying higher law Ninth Amendment standards to the states, standards that do not have their basis in states' popular control, but rather in juristic abstractions such as natural rights, common law, and the like, the end result will be the subordination of the public policy prerogatives of the states to a national unenumerated rights paradigm, with lethal consequences for constitutional federalism.

V

As written, the original intent of the Ninth Amendment's framers is historically discernible, but if taken out of its historical context its wording is open to various plausible interpretations.[40] Much of the current confusion regarding the amendment could have been avoided if the framers would have specified that the "other" rights are those retained by the people of the states, and not simply the people.[41] Of course, that would have left in doubt the status of the rights of the people in the territories (Article IV, section 3) and the people residing in the seat of the national government (Article I, section 8). Nevertheless, the status of the Ninth Amendment did not become problematical until its incorporation into the Fourteenth Amendment and its subsequent application to the states. Until the 1960s the Ninth Amendment served as a precautionary reminder that there were limits to the national government's powers that were not explicitly stated in the Constitution, and these unenumerated rights were, indeed, retained by the people in their respective states. Even the staunch nineteenth-century nationalist Justice Story conceded that "this clause was manifestly introduced to prevent any perverse or ingenious misapplication of the well-known maxim, that an affirmation in particular cases implies a negation in all others; and, *e converso,* that a negation in particular cases implies an affirmation in all others."[42] Prior to its incorporation the Ninth Amendment, as did the Bill of Rights in general, restricted the National Government and not the states. The states had their own constitutions and bills of rights.[43] However, as a component of American fundamental law applicable to both the national and state governments it can potentially qualify many of the statutes with which it comes into contact by either curtailing their enforcement or negating them altogether on the basis that the governmental power being exercised is in violation of an unenumerated right. For example, if the Court is serious about the fundamental right to privacy, then state laws that prohibit polygamy could be interpreted as an infringement on the unenumerated right to privacy among the polygamists, not to mention the First Amendment's free exercise clause. Other examples abound, such as laws prohibiting prostitution, the recreational use of hallucinogens, euthanasia, bestiality, and even consensual cannibalism. Of course, these examples lack the necessary political support to be seriously considered on the bench or in the halls of Congress, however the long-term impact of unenumerated rights debates among academicians and jurists[44] may incrementally bypass popular control over these and other policy issues.

For the past three decades the significance of the Ninth Amendment has incrementally increased due to its utility in limiting governmental power, especially state power. The basis of this elevation is its close association with an undefined but pervasive notion of higher law and its protégé, natural rights. This in and of itself is not problematical. What does present a problem of major proportions is the manner and extent to which natural law theories are displacing state popular control over social policy.

The issue should not be reduced to what are natural rights (or just social policy), but rather what procedures are constitutionally sanctioned to make authoritative and binding determinations establishing rights policy? This procedural question must be distinguished from the substantive question regarding the content of such determinations. In his influential but specious 1955 treatise on the subject, Bennett B. Patterson, in a chapter titled "What Are The Unenumerated Rights?" advocated that the federal courts make better use of the Ninth Amendment, thereby combining the procedural and substantive questions into one neat package of judicial activism:

> We are content if we have established the Ninth Amendment as embodying a living philosophy, and helped the law of human rights to be given an opportunity to grow as other sciences have grown. We believe that the law should grow, and our constitution should be *interpreted* in the light of current history.... There must be some unenumerated rights. The amendment must be given some meaning. Its value and meaning should not be lost through disuse. The amendment can only be saved by our courts.[45]

Patterson's real concern is that the constitutional expansion of individual rights is not keeping pace with the "intellectual and spiritual growth" of human progress; his hope is that judicially defined Ninth Amendment rights will close the gap:

> Our thesis is that human rights which are not enumerated in the Constitution will be revealed and become apparent in the future, and it is within the spirit of the Constitution, and the letter of the Ninth Amendment, that these rights should be recognized and protected.[46]

Consider his treatment of the unenumerated right to privacy:

> If there is such a right, it is difficult to classify it under any right that is enumerated in the Constitution.... While the courts seem to feel that it should exist, there is a great timidity and lack of forthrightness in the protection of this right, because its existence is not to be found in the written and enumerated law.[47]

Patterson's argument is that even though the right to privacy is not to be found in the Constitution, the U.S. Supreme Court should follow its better instincts and judicially extend the document to protect such an important right under the cover of the Ninth Amendment.

Moreover, Bennett's version of judicial enforcement of unenumerated rights is not necessarily deferential to national borders. A case in point, after invoking Patterson one commentator suggested that all domestic laws be tested against international standards of justice, because such standards embody a consensus on higher law natural rights. In reference to the United Nations Charter of Rights, he wrote:

> With a comprehensive perspective, the courts could more easily and more rationally discover the content of rights which are not specifically enumerated in the Constitution but which are, nevertheless, rooted in the expectations of the people and in documented policy.... In a sentence, the courts can use a wider juristic focus to regain the original constitutional construct and to utilize international human rights as an interpretive aid for proper application of the ninth amendment and the universal implementation of human rights as called for by the United Nations Charter.[48]

Not only does incorporation of international standards of justice into the Ninth Amendment assume that the former are superior to domestic standards, but it also elevates the U.S. Supreme Court to a national star-chamber of internationally recognized rights, while risking, on the rails of treaties and international agreements, moving the adjudication of rights controversies to international courts of justice. Either way, there would be little tolerance for state participation in the articulation and protection of rights when state policies run counter to nationally and internationally established norms.

VI

Popular control over the articulation of unenumerated rights is the bulwark against which nationalization aims. Within the context of the American political tradition the people are sovereign, a sovereignty that is qualified by a scheme of republicanism, separation of powers, a system of federalism, and written constitutions.[49] Thus, it is a fundamental tenet of the American political process that not only are there certain constraints placed upon the people and their agents in government, but that these constraints are essential, otherwise the numerical majority will oppressively exercise political power over numerical minorities, at both the national and state levels. An important function of written constitutions is to secure the rights of numerical minorities from oppressive majoritarian government by establishing limits to the exercise of political power, but within the context of popular sovereignty and not by judicial guardians. As stated by Publius:

> When a majority is included in a faction, the form of popular government, on the other hand, enables it to sacrifice to its ruling passion or interest both the public good and the rights of other citizens. To secure the public good and private rights against the danger of such a faction, and at the same time to preserve the spirit and the form of popular government, is then the great object to which our inquiries are directed.[50]

Such "inquiries" led to the conclusion that an important institutional mechanism designed to balance the "public good and private rights" within the "spirit and form of popular government" is judicial review. What Publius meant by the words "spirit" and "form" is unclear and certainly suspect if taken out of context; suspect in the sense that preserving the spirit and form of popular government is not necessarily the same as preserving substantive popular government. For example, in the event that the majority sacrifices to its "ruling passions or interests," the public good and the rights of other citizens, the courts are obliged to protect the constitutional rights of minorities. Presumably, such intervention would be justified on the grounds that the majority passed legislation contrary to some provision(s) of the Constitution. Checking the majority is accomplished procedurally by the courts articulating through constitutional law the acceptable parameters of popular control over public policy. Hence, the U.S. Supreme Court preserves the spirit and form of popular government by keeping majorities within the parameters of constitutional powers they initially approved. But the type of judicial avant-gardism advocated by Patterson and like-minded commentators makes shambles of the spirit, the form, and substance of popular government, because they advocate that judges, and not the constitutional political processes, should determine what constitutes an acceptable exercise of political power by majorities, state and national; under this schema judicial review is the vehicle of social change with U.S. Supreme Court justices at the controls.

The constitutional mechanism designed to protect the majority's constitutional public policy preferences from an oppressive minority is the electoral process. According to Publius:

> If a faction consists of less than a majority, relief is supplied by the republican principle, which enables the majority to defeat its sinister views by regular vote. It

> may clog the administration, it may convulse the society; but it will be unable to execute and mask its violence under the forms of the Constitution.[51]

The operational phrase is "regular vote"; the electorate's indirect control through the presidential nominating and the senatorial confirming processes does not provide effective and timely popular control over federal judges and justices with life tenure. The U.S. Supreme Court and the federal judiciary in general are not susceptible to a "regular vote" and therefore pose a special problem for government premised upon the consent of the governed, especially when federal judges intentionally behave factiously. Under the leadership of Chief Justice John Marshall,[52] the U.S. Supreme Court justices acquired the role of recognized gatekeepers of constitutional government through the exercise of judicial review.[53] It is assumed that the motivations of justices as they demarcate constitutional limits are more reliable than their executive and legislative counterparts. Judicial motivations are ideally fueled by the pursuit of a constitutional order, rather than catering to special interests as public officials tied to an electoral process are and should be. However, the constraints on judicial review (such as court appointments and packing, modifications of their appellate jurisdiction, and constitutional amendments) have minimal influence on judicial behavior.[54] As long as the federal judiciary maintains the spirit and form of popular government it has little to fear from a political or electoral backlash to their jurisprudence, even when they are undermining, albeit *sub rosa,* popular control through judicial higher law doctrines.

Due to training and the practical need for political legitimacy the justices have ample opportunities to dress extraconstitutional higher law jurisprudence—whether the liberal or conservative variety—in constitutional garb.[55] That being the case, the heightened interest in the Ninth Amendment, and by implication the higher law natural rights doctrines discovered therein,[56] provide the federal judiciary with a greatly expanded wardrobe that facilitates the ability of judges and justices to masquerade as jurists while actually performing legislative and even executive functions, thereby substituting their policy preferences for those established as a result of popular control in the respective states. This type of judicial dysfunction[57] is facilitated by a public respect for the U.S. Supreme Court that has not been substantially undermined, due in large measure to a politically passive public that has not scrutinized the evolving machinations of the U.S. Supreme Court.[58]

To reiterate, problematical for American federalism is the association of the Ninth Amendment with higher law doctrines and its incorporation into the Fourteenth Amendment, thereby making the Ninth Amendment's unfolding penumbra applicable not only to the national government but also to the states. Justice Iredell expressed the essence of the dilemma for the American system of law as early as 1798:

> If any act of Congress, or of the legislature of a state, violates those constitutional provisions, it is unquestionably void; though, I admit, that as the authority to declare it void is of a delicate and awful nature; the court will never resort to that authority, but in a clear and urgent case. If on the other hand, the legislature of the union, or the legislature of any member of the union, shall pass a law within the general scope of their constitutional power, the court cannot pronounce it to be void, merely because it is, in their judgment, contrary to the principles of natural justice. The ideas of natural justice are regulated by no fixed standard; the ablest and the purest men have differed upon the subject; and all that the court could properly say, in such an event, would be, that the legislature (possessed of an equal right of opinion) had passed an act which, in the opinion of the judges, was inconsistent with the abstract principles of natural justice.[59]

Justice Iredell makes three pertinent observations. First, judicial review should be exercised only in clear and urgent cases. Issues that are transient and/or ambiguous are political and beyond the scope of the U.S. Supreme Court's nullifying power. Second, opinions about the principles of extraconstitutional natural justice are just that, opinions subject to debate, with the Court lacking any privileged intellectual or constitutional role in having their opinions prevail over those of legislators and executives accountable to the people. Third, the proper role of the Court is that of elevating the level of debate by informing and admonishing legislatures, but by no means has it the constitutional authority to replace the legislatures' policies on rights with its own.

The U.S. Supreme Court's willingness to supersede legislatures in this area of law is not so much an attack on legislatures per se as it is an attack on the sovereignty of the people. Early in the twentieth century the push to displace the sovereignty of the people from its preferred political theory pedestal began to gain momentum by establishing natural rights as the primary basis of political obligation. That basis is not the consent of the governed, but rather higher law as articulated by the elites within the legal and academic communities. In 1930 one influential advocate optimistically wrote that

> if the sovereign be made subject to a developing body of rules of law in both private and public law, the theory of an absolute sovereign has ceased to have its former all-inclusiveness. Older theories of sovereignty which still retain feudal and monarchal characteristics are apparently in need of revision. A certain tendency to discredit the state is now abroad. The forces which combine to spread this tendency are various. There is the old doctrine of natural rights, which lies behind most of the contemporary movements that advocate resistance to the authorities of the state.[60]

In the American system the "authorities of the state" are the people, insofar as government officials are their agents. Hence, resistance to authorities of the state—resistance facilitated by a recourse to higher law doctrines—is in the final analysis a ruse to thwart popular control over public policy.

Obviously, this reliance upon higher law is not new. It is as old as American constitutional government itself and extends back to the English Common Law tradition. In fact, Justice Iredell was responding to Justice Chase's reliance on "general principles of law and reason."[61] Contemporary judicial reliance on the Ninth Amendment has taken on a similar task, namely augmenting the much relied upon substantive "due process" and "equal protection" conduits for higher law into American constitutional law.

VII

The current debate regarding the proper model of judicial interpretation has been so far removed from its proper federal context that descriptive words such as *interpretivism* and *noninterpretivism* have become almost cliché. When one factors in the Ninth Amendment such distinctions verge on the nondescript, because with few exceptions[62] Ninth Amendment interpretivists are few and far between. Justice Black admitted to discussing "the due process and the Ninth Amendment arguments together because on analysis they turn out to be the same thing—merely using different words to claim for this Court and the federal judiciary power to invalidate any legislative act which the judges find irrational, unreasonable, or offensive."[63] There can be little doubt that some laws are irrational, unreasonable, or offensive, but nevertheless constitutional. The bottom line is that the Court, through their extrapolation of unenumerated rights from the Ninth Amendment, can easily incorporate into constitutional law their notions of rational, reasonable, and agreeable laws, thereby circumventing the political processes of the states. Because Judge Bork questioned the legitimacy of Ninth Amendment activism, his detractors included both conservatives and liberals.

Professor Kurland acknowledged:

> My concern is very much that by providing as narrow a construction of the Constitution as possible with regard to individual rights and liberties, Judge Bork would be denying the essence of the purpose behind the Constitution's origins 200 years ago, which was the preservation of all the liberties that the English legal tradition had created and were in the process of creating and were expected to continue to create. (Comm. Print Draft, Vol. 3, at 1390)

Similarly, Professor Tribe testified:

> He [Judge Bork] reads the entire Constitution as though the people who wrote and ratified it gave up to government all of the fundamental rights that they fought a revolution to win unless a specific reservation of rights appears in the text.... I am proud that we have...a 200-year-old tradition establishing that people retain certain unspecified fundamental rights that courts were supposed to discern and to defend. (Comm. Print Draft, Vol. 2, at 6-7)[64]

What Bork's critics fail to thoughtfully address is that within the context of American federalism the fundamental issue is not simply the quality of the laws per se, but the institutional mechanisms that authoritatively make such determinations.

Objectivity about constitutional means as opposed to desirable political outcomes is muddled in the current political climate, because in large measure "rights" debates are actually skirmishes in a broader phenomenon that can be descriptively called *kulturkampf*.[65] The U.S. Supreme Court is viewed as the institution through which various factions can successfully bypass popular control when the prospects for success at the legislative levels are remote; furthermore, a juridical policy agenda is very effective in that regard, because when a public policy controversy ends up in the U.S. Supreme Court's judicial lexicon of unenumerated rights, the legislative decision making process is made to acquiesce to juridical notions of constitutionality, in effect negating popular control.

Admittedly, the specter of majority tyranny is problematical if the U.S. Supreme Court were to take Justice Iredell's and Judge Bork's position that unless explicitly protected in the Constitution, unenumerated rights controversies are nonjusticiable and consequently to be decided in legislative processes. But U.S. Supreme Court activism in resolving unenumerated rights issues—thereby overturning the public policy products of state popular control—raises a specter of another sort, government by a minimally accountable elite. Should the Ninth Amendment irrevocably develop into another weapon in the U.S. Supreme Court's arsenal to place substantive limits on state popular control, to that extent state popular control of public policy will continue to be supplanted by an unelected and electorally unaccountable national judiciary in the critical public policy area of unenumerated rights.[66] As was the intent of the framers, a viable federalism is requisite to having the national government premised upon the consent of the governed; furthermore, federalism was designed to serve as a major obstacle to a nationally imposed cultural hegemony. Within the context of federalism, the Ninth Amendment acknowledges that there are, indeed, unenumerated rights, but the articulation and protection of those rights were originally tied to popular control of citizens in their respective states.

VIII

The belief that the Rehnquist Court will be increasingly receptive to the new judicial federalism is grounded more in optimism than fact. Consider the grounds for such optimism:

> Thus, today, under what has been called "the new federalism," U.S. Supreme Court interpretations of the U.S. Bill of Rights establish minimum national standards, or floors, of protection. States cannot fall below the floor, but they can elevate rights above the floor and may also lay floors where the U.S. Supreme Court or federal statutes have not provided protection. Reliance on the 50 state bills of rights and the U.S. Bill of Rights, therefore, now helps, in ways not quite true in the past, to promote that "double security" of "the rights of the people," of which James Madison spoke (*Federalist* 51) with respect to the federal system as a whole.[67]

A judicial federalism that is premised on "floors" upon which the states can only add to and not detract from the rights edifice misses the point. A viable judicial federalism is not simply one in which the states merely have the option of expanding U.S. Supreme Court sanctioned unenumerated rights; an authentically viable judicial federalism is one in which the respective state courts adjudicate unenumerated rights controversies based upon their respective state constitutions, which in turn are the products of their respective constitutionally established political processes.

There is adequate precedent for deference to the states, as is evidenced by the privilege and immunities clause of Article IV, section 2. This provision has been overlooked too long by Ninth Amendment scholarship.[68] As chapter two makes clear, the privileges and immunities clause provides much needed insight into the constitutional function of the states in the articulation of unenumerated rights.

Notes

1. See paragraph two of The Declaration of Independence.
2. This is not to say that the Supreme Court is omnipotent in the area of rights public policy; but then again, this is not to say that it is not very powerful, especially when it exercises judicial review over the states. Professor Dahl was correct when he described the Supreme Court as particularly effective in keeping otherwise deviating states within the policy objectives of the national governing coalition (see Robert Dahl, "Decision-Making in a Democracy: The Supreme Court as a National Policy-maker," *Journal of Public Law* 6 [1957], 279—95). For example, from 1789 to 1992 the number of federal laws declared unconstitutional by the Supreme Court numbered 128, whereas state and local laws declared unconstitutional numbered 1,204 (*Vital Statistics On American Politics,* 4th ed., Harold W. Stanley and Richard G. Niemi, eds. [Washington, D.C.: CQ Press, 1994], 308). The 1,204 can be misleading; it is significant that for every state or local law declared unconstitutional, all similar actual or potential laws are thereby voided, which if tabulated would increase the number substantially.
3. Thomas R. Dye, *American Federalism: Competition Among Governments* (Lexington, Mass.: Lexington Books, 1990), 3.
4. There must be a national policy regarding many aspects of interstate commerce—a policy that is nonparochial and, moreover, uniform throughout the country—if that commerce is to retain its national character and not be balkanized. Consequently, there must be a national policymaking body to fashion that policy, and, incident thereto, to supervise state regulations adversely affecting interstate commerce to determine whether such regulations are consistent with the requirements of national commerce... ultimate supervisory authority falls to the Congress... [but] it has fallen to the judiciary, and hence to the Supreme Court, to attend to the details and determine whether local laws brought before it are consistent with the demands of national commerce." (Michael J. Perry, *The Constitution, The Courts, And Human Rights: An Inquiry into the Legitimacy of Constitutional Policymaking by the Judiciary* [Yale University Press, 1982], 39)

   Perry proceeds to rationalize noninterpretive judicial review over human rights in chap. 4, 91-145, even in light of his acknowledgment that "there is no plausible textual or historical justification for noninterpretive [judicial] review" (ibid., 92). Following his argument for uniformity of interstate commerce policy, Perry advocates noninterpretive activism to bring uniformity to an otherwise fragmented system of American human rights (ibid).
5. See William H. Riker, "Six Books in Search of a Subject-Or Does Federalism Exist and Does It Matter?" 2 *Comparative Politics* 135 (1969), cited in Harold M. Hyman, "Federalism: Legal Fiction and Historical Artifact?" Brigham Young University Law Review (1987), 905.

6. For our purposes the inherent value of American federalism is a given. This is not meant to imply that American federalism is a perfect system, but rather that it is integral to government accountability to the governed. This very issue was debated at length during the constitutional convention in Philadelphia and the subsequent state ratifying debates. See Gordon S. Wood, *The Creation of the American Republic, 1776–1787* (Chapel Hill, N.C.: University of North Carolina Press, 1969); Forrest McDonald, *Novus Ordo Seclorum: The Intellectual Origins of the Constitution* (Lawrence, Kans.: The University Press of Kansas, 1985); and Donald S. Lutz, *Popular Consent and Popular Control: Whig Political Theory in the Early State Constitutions* (Baton Rouge, La.: LSU Press, 1980).
7. Vincent Martin Bonventre, "Beyond the Reemergence-Inverse Incorporation And Other Prospects For State Constitutional Law." Albany Law Review, vol. 53 (Winter, 1989), 403-04; citations omitted.
8. Collins, Galie, and Kincaid, "State High Courts, State Constitutions, and Individual Rights Litigation Since 1980: A Judicial Survey," *Publius: The Journal of Federalism* 16 (Summer 1986), 141-42. The statistics cited are misleading if not compared to the overall increase in state and federal litigation and the fact that federal and state civil rights legislation actually bolstered such increases.
9. There is scant evidence that the Rehnquist Court may stop, or actually reverse, the nationalizing trends of the Warren era regarding Ninth Amendment issues. The prospects of such a development is considered *infra*. Claims that "The ongoing civil liberties exchange between the federal and state courts underscores the importance of federalism as a means of securing rights even in a post-incorporation world" are premature to say the least (Collins and Galie, "Models of Post-Incorporation Judicial Review: 1985 Survey of State Constitutional Individual Rights Decisions," *Publius* 16 (Summer 1986), 111-12.
10. This is accomplished through recourse to a relatively new judicial procedure, referred to as the abstention doctrine (see Charles Alan Wright, *The Law of the Federal Courts* [St. Paul, Minn.: West Publishing Co., 1983], 302-20); see Stanley and Niemi, *Vital Statistics On American Politics,* 301-306, for data on federal courts' caseloads.
11. One of the sacred cows of modern jurisprudence is the theory of selective incorporation; nevertheless, it also is a judicial innovation (see Raoul Berger, *The Fourteenth Amendment and the Bill of Rights* [Norman: University of Oklahoma, 1989]).
12. By *quasi sovereignty* I mean state jurisdiction over a particular area of public policy that is recognized by law and/or precedent. This is to be distinguished from Publius's political monster *imperium in imperio,* whereby the recognition of which government—state or national—has what authority is ambiguous to the point of resulting in destabilization and eventually conflict; see *The Federalist,* #15.
13. There has been and continues to be legitimate concern over the willingness and/ or capability of the States to consistently and without deviation protect the fundamental rights of their respective citizens. However, and this is an important qualification to be discussed *infra,* the framers resolved this constitutional—as opposed to political—dilemma.
14. *The Federalist,* #25, 163.
15. See Heart of Atlanta Motel v. United States, 379 U.S. 241 and Katzenbach v. McClung, 379 U.S. 294 (1964) in which the Civil Rights Act of 1964 was sanctioned under congressional commerce powers, as opposed to section 5 of the Fourteenth Amendment.

16. See David Osborne and Ted Gaebler, *Reinventing Government: How the Entrepreneurial Spirit is Transforming the Public Sector* (Reading, Mass.: Addison-Wesley Publishing Company, Inc., 1992); especially chap. 9, "Decentralized Government: From Hierarchy to Participation and Teamwork," 250–79.
17. For a discussion on the evolution of the "double standard" between economic and cultural rights, see Henry J. Abraham, *Freedom and the Court: Civil Rights and Liberties in the United States,* 5th ed. (New York: Oxford University Press, 1988), 11–37.
18. The modern U.S. Supreme Court has blazed the trail for this expansion of national power. In the wake of the *Brown* (1954) decision, "the Supreme Court won much new prestige by attempting to rectify a clearly indefensible and intolerable situation. This new status enabled it to assume a new role in the American system of government, as the accelerator of social change. The *Brown* decision proved to many people—including many judges—that judges were better at setting policy than the elected representatives of the people" (Lino A. Graglia, "Judicial Activism: Even on the Right Its Wrong," *Public Interest* 95 [1989], 57, 59–60).
19. *The Federalist,* #28: 181.
20. The framers were in search of a workable balance of power between their simultaneous commitments of establishing an effective national government and keeping intact the states. See Publius's discussion about the "extended republic" (ibid., #10: 81-84).
21. In way of clarification, the Supreme Court interchangeably uses higher law, natural law, natural rights, English Common Law, standards of justice, and so on. The context of usage can modify the meaning, but references to these phrases in this book connote standards that are superior to state and national constitutional and statutory laws.
22. References to the framers include both the Antifederalists and Federalists, at the national and state conventions.
23. One should keep in mind the preamble to the U.S. Constitution, which reads, "We the People of the United States, in order…" originally read, "We the People of the States of New-Hampshire, Massachusetts, Rhode-Island and Providence Plantations, Connecticut, New York, New Jersey, Pennsylvania, Delaware, Maryland, Virginia, North-Carolina, South-Carolina, and Georgia, do ordain, declare and establish the following Constitution for the Government of Ourselves and our Posterity" (Max Farrand, ed., *The Records of the Federal Convention of 1787,* 4 vols., 1: 565). In the final version the states were not individually named because of the uncertainty surrounding which states would and which would not ratify the document and become part of the union; the minimum was nine states (Article VII). Nevertheless, this practical editorial change by the Committee of Style does not substantively detract from the Preamble's emphasis on the "people" within the states and their right of self-government.
24. There are numerous instances of the Court speciously imposing its views of what constitutes a fundamental right, views that implicitly fly in the face of popular control. For example, in *Rochin* v. *California* (1952), the plaintiff's stomach was forcibly pumped to recover contraband drugs. After Rochin was convicted according to state law, and the conviction was affirmed by two higher state courts, the U.S. Supreme Court concluded that the state's conduct violated the fundamental rights of the plaintiff. Claiming the need for progress and change, and that the state's conduct "shocks the conscience," the Court overturned the conviction on due process grounds (342 U.S. 165). True enough, many may find such police

conduct to be unacceptable, but what is of constitutional significance is that in 1952 the majority of Californians supported such police conduct, as evidenced by their state criminal code and reaffirmed by their state courts.

25. Of course, time expired on the first, the second was negated by the Sixteenth Amendment, and the fourth is still in effect, even though its linkage to Article V is more remote.
26. Lawrence E. Mitchell, "The Ninth Amendment and the 'Jurisprudence of Original Intention,'" *The Georgetown Law Journal,* vol. 74 (1986), 1719, 1725.
27. For a traditional view of what the Declaration's "equality" means, see Willmore Kendall, "Equality: Commitment or Ideal?" *The Intercollegiate Review: A Journal of Scholarship and Opinion,* vol. 24, no. 2 (Spring 1989), 25-33.
28. See Willmore Kendall and George Carey, *The Basic Symbols of the American Political Tradition* (Baton Rouge, La.: LSU Press, 1970), *passim.*
29. M. E. Bradford, "Changed Only A Little: The Reconstruction Amendments And The Nomocratic Constitution of 1787," *Wake Forest Law Review,* vol. 24, no. 3 (1989), 573. The Preamble to the U.S. Constitution does state some objectives, but more precisely it justifies the union of states, "in Order to form a more perfect Union, establish Justice, insure domestic Tranquility, provide for the common defence, promote the general Welfare, and secure the Blessings of Liberty to ourselves and our Posterity." But there is neither historical nor textual evidence that these ends were designed to supplant the decision making processes premised upon popular control. Moreover, the preamble to the U.S. Constitution closely resembles Article Three of the Articles of Confederation: "The said states hereby severally enter into a firm league of friendship with each other for their common defence, the security of their liberties, and their mutual and general welfare; binding themselves to assist each other against all force offered to, or attacks made upon, them, or any of them, on account of religion, sovereignty, trade, or any other pretense whatever." Once again, a justification for entering a firm league of friendship" with other states, without authorizing the national government to, for example, pursue the "general welfare" independently of the states. Bradford's constitutional scholarship is discussed in detail in chap. 7.
30. For example, in defiance of two constitutional provisions, the Fifth and Fourteenth Amendments, and the laws of at least thirty-five states, which variously sanctioned capital punishment, Justice Thurgood Marshall wrote in his dissenting opinion: "But if the constitutionality of the death penalty turns, as I have urged, on the opinion of an *informed* citizenry, then even the enactment of new death statutes cannot be viewed as conclusive. In *Furman,* I observed that the American people are largely unaware of the information critical to a judgment on the morality of the death penalty, and concluded that if they were better informed they would consider it shocking, unjust, and unacceptable" (Gregg v. Georgia, 96 S.Ct. 2909, 2973 [1976]). In short, Justice Marshall was attempting to impose his version of morality on the majority of people who held contrary views, views constitutionally sanctioned.
31. Bradford, *Original Intentions: On The Making And Ratification Of The United States Constitution* (Athens: The University of Georgia Press, 1993), McDonald's foreword, xii.
32. Bradford, *Original Intentions,* 573–98; see Berger, *Federalism, The Founders' Design* (Norman, Okla.: University of Oklahoma Press, 1987), for a definitive account of the nature of American federalism. Essentially, the Tenth Amendment reserves to the states those powers not delegated to the national government,

whereas the Ninth Amendment is a reminder to the Supreme Court that the rights mentioned in the U.S. Constitution are not inclusive; the Ninth Amendment's command "shall not be construed" is obviously directed to the federal courts to take cognizance of rights unique to the states. In short, it is a rule of construction directed towards the federal courts.

33. See United States v. Carolene Products Co. 304 U.S. 144 (1938) and Smith v. Allwright, 321 U.S. 649 (1944). This is not meant to imply that *Carolene Products* was simply decided on, or was subsequently restricted to, the procedural right to participate in elections.
34. This is a restrictive view of the political participation that the courts should protect, one primarily of access to the electoral process. This restrictive view is to be contrasted with John Hart Ely's position, in a chapter titled "Clearing the Channels of Political Change," where he maintains that "virtually everyone agrees that the courts should be heavily involved in reviewing impediments to free speech, publication, and political association" (*Democracy and Distrust: A Theory of Judicial Review* [Cambridge: Harvard University Press, 1980], 105). True enough, the channels of political change should be open, but open for popular participation in the selection of decision makers who make public policy, and not for the court, *fait accompli,* to make public policy. Having the Court "heavily involved" in First Amendment issues regarding the acceptable forms of political expression can be problematical. Consider the question: Are pornography and flag burning really requisite to meaningful political participation? (See Miller v. California 413 U.S. 5 (1973) and Texas v. Johnson 491 U.S. 397 [1989].)
35. One should expect some qualifications, such as restrictions placed upon children, the mentally incompetent, residency requirements, and convicted felons, to name a few.
36. See *The Federalist* #10: 81-84 and Donald Lutz, *Popular Consent and Popular Control* (Baton Rouge, La.: LSU Press, 1980) for the Federalists' and Antifederalists' views on representation.
37. Article IV, section 4 stipulates that "the United States shall guarantee to every State in this Union a Republican Form of Government." In *Luther* v. *Borden,* 48 U.S. 1 (1849), the Supreme Court concluded that this clause was nonjusticiable and therefore a political question to be decided by the legislative and executive branches. However, as stated in his *Baker* v. *Carr* concurring opinion, Justice Douglas was correct in concluding that "the statements in Luther v. Borden... that this guaranty is enforceable only by Congress or the Chief Executive is not maintainable.... It is indeed contrary to the cases discussed in the body of this opinion—the modern decisions of the Court that give the full panoply of judicial protection to voting rights" (Baker v. Carr 369 U.S. 186, 243 [1962]). For all intents and purposes, *Luther* is at odds with *Baker,* and the results in *Baker,* and subsequent companion cases, are at odds, in significant ways, with Article IV, section 4. See Justice Frankfurter's opinion in *Colegrove* v. *Green* 328 U.S. 549 (1946).
38. Garcia v. San Antonio Metropolitan Transit Authority, 105 S.Ct. 1005, 1020 (1985).
39. Ibid., 1035.
40. It is not the intent of this paper to place the Ninth Amendment in its historical context, but rather to demonstrate its contemporary impact on American federalism. Admittedly, an understanding of the historical context is important, insofar as it makes manifest the political context into which the amendment has been

placed. For a concise and useful essay on the amendment's historical origins, see The Honorable Joseph L. Call, "Federalism and the Ninth Amendment," *Dickinson Law Review*, vol. 64 (1960), 121-31.

41. The Confederate framers attempted to make explicit what the U.S. framers left implicit. Their version of the Ninth Amendment reads: "The enumeration, in the Constitution, of certain rights, shall not be construed to deny or disparage others retained by the people *of the several States.*"
42. Ironically, quoted by Justice Goldberg in Griswold v. Connecticut (85 S.Ct. 1678, 1685) to expand the rights for which the national government is responsible vis-à-vis the states. He wrote that "the Ninth Amendment simply lends strong support to the view that the 'liberty' protected by the Fifth and Fourteenth Amendments from infringement by the Federal Government or the States is not restricted to rights specifically mentioned in the first eight amendments" (ibid., 1686).
43. See Barron v. The Mayor and City Council of Baltimore, 8 L.Ed. 672 (1833). For a succinct discussion of the "selective incorporation theory" see Berger, *The Fourteenth Amendment and the Bill of Rights* (Norman, Okla.: University of Oklahoma Press, 1989).
44. Chapter three considers the impact of academic debate on rights jurisprudence.
45. Bennett B. Patterson, *The Forgotten Ninth Amendment: A Call For Legislative and Judicial Recognition of Rights Under Social Conditions of Today* (Indianapolis: The Bobbs-Merrill Company, Inc., 1955), 56 (emphasis added).
46. Ibid., 55.
47. Ibid., 55.
48. Jordon J. Paust, "Human Rights and the Ninth Amendment: A New Form of Guarantee," *Cornell Law Review*, vol. 60 (1975), 236-37. Paust concedes that guidelines such as the ones he recommends would have a pervasive impact on the legislative process. He approvingly acknowledges that, "as a prominent international jurist declares, 'it is increasingly recognized that there is a human rights dimension to every human interaction and every authoritative decision.' Again, action or inaction by the courts will have its effect" (ibid., 260; notes omitted).
49. *The Federalist*, #10: 81-84; #51: 320-25; #39: 240-46; and #78: 464-72.
50. Ibid., #10: 80.
51. Ibid., #10: 80.
52. See Marbury v. Madison 2 L.Ed. 60 (1803).
53. For an early alternative view see Justice Gibson's opinion in Eakin v. Raub, 12 Sergeant and Rawle (Pennsylvania Supreme Court) 330 (1825).
54. See William Lasser, *The Limits of Judicial Power: The Supreme Court in American Politics* (Chapel Hill: The University of North Carolina Press, 1988). Lasser correctly maintains that "despite all the controversy and criticism of the past thirty years, the Court is as powerful and effective today as at any time in its history. Its unprecedented activism, far from endangering its place in American politics, seems to have given the Court more power. Its critics have been unable to reverse outright even one of the Court's controversial decisions, and the Court shows no signs of retreating from its activists approach to constitutional decision making. The justices, having ignored all the advice proffered to the Court, have been rewarded instead of punished" (ibid., 5).
55. Judge Richard Neely maintains that there are two systems of government in America, the myth and the operational systems. The courts are especially called upon to perpetuate this duality, otherwise they could not fulfill their indispensable tasks of addressing the practical extraconstitutional duties thrust upon them

by the governing process (see Richard Neely, *How Courts Govern America* [New Haven, Conn: Yale University Press, 1981], 12–13).

56. According to Professor Corwin, the Ninth Amendment makes the U.S. Constitution complete by recognizing transcendental justice. Moreover, the Constitution is subordinate to "higher law" with or without the Ninth Amendment, laws which are to be discovered and which bind and control (see Edward S. Corwin, *The "Higher Law" Background of American Constitutional Law* [Ithaca, New York: Great Seal Book, 1961], 4–5).
57. By "judicial dysfunction" I do not mean to imply that this is either inadvertent or that there is not a conscious attempt to mislead the public; this is discussed at length in chapter 3 *infra*.
58. One is tempted to say that the public has been effectively duped. For example, when Justice Douglas's retirement opened the way for a Ford Administration's appointment to the bench, John Hart Ely cautioned the Administration that "should the Court over time come to be viewed as just another political branch, America will have lost something that is entirely unique and extremely valuable." It is crucial, he insisted, "that the process of selection be one that is structured, and, at least as important, that it be *perceived* by the public, as not primarily political" (cited in David M. O'Brien, *Storm Center: The Supreme Court in American Politics,* 2nd ed. [New York: W.W. Norton & Company, 1990], 63 [emphasis added]). See Planned Parenthood v. Casey for a discussion on "the principles of institutional integrity" between the justices (112 S.Ct. 2791 [1992]).
59. Calder v. Bull 1 L.Ed. 648, 654 (1798).
60. Charles Grove Haines, *The Revival of Natural Law Concepts* (Cambridge, Mass: Harvard University Press, 1930), 333 (citations omitted). For more recent theories along these same lines see Thomas C. Grey, "Do We Have an Unwritten Constitution?" *Stanford Law Review,* vol. 27 (1975), 703; "The Uses of An Unwritten Constitution," *Chicago-Kent Law Review,* vol. 64, no. 1 (1988), 211; and Sotirios A. Barber, "The Ninth Amendment: Inkblot Or Another Hard Nut To Crack," *Chicago-Kent Law Review,* vol. 64, no. 1 (1988), 67.
61. See Calder v. Bull, 887.
62. One notable exception is former Supreme Court nominee Robert H. Bork; see "Nomination Of Robert H. Bork To Be An Associate Justice Of The United States Supreme Court." Report of the Committee on the Judiciary, United States Senate, 100th Congress, 1st Session, Exec. Rept. 100-7, 13 October 1987, 8-45, and Robert H. Bork, *The Tempting of America: The Political Seduction of the Law* (New York: The Free Press, 1990); however, as discussed *infra,* even Bork's jurisprudence falls short of an originalist model of federalism.
63. Griswold v. Connecticut, 381 U.S. 479, 511 (1965); cited in John Hart Ely, *Democracy and Distrust: A Theory of Judicial Review* (Cambridge, Mass: Harvard University Press, 1980), 38.
64. U.S. Senate, Report of the Committee on the Judiciary, 20.
65. See James Davison Hunter, *Culture Wars: The Struggle To Define America* (Basic Books, 1991), especially 52-106. James Q. Wilson wrote that "we are engaged in a cultural war, a war about values. It is not a new war; it has been going on for centuries as part of a continuing struggle at national self-definition. Once the issues were slavery, temperance, religion, and prostitution; today they are divorce, illegitimacy, crime, and entertainment" (*The Moral Sense* [New York: The Free Press, 1993], xi). However, as Samuel Francis explains, there is more to cultural/ideological conflicts than meets the eye; they are part and parcel of power

politics. See his "Equality As a Political Weapon," in *Beautiful Losers: Essays on the Failure of American Conservatism* (Columbia: University of Missouri Press, 1993), 208-21.

66. See Berger, *Government By Judiciary: The Transformation of the Fourteenth Amendment* (Cambridge: Harvard University Press, 1977).
67. John Kincaid, "The State and Federal Bills of Rights: Partners and Rivals in Liberty," in *Intergovernmental Perspective*, vol. 17, no. 4 (Fall 1991), 33; also see W. John Moore, "In Whose Court?" *National Journal* (5 October 1991), 2396.
68. For example, in approximately a thousand pages of discussions about the Ninth Amendment, there is not a substantive analysis of the relevance of the privileges and immunities clauses; see *The Rights Retained By The People: The History and Meaning of the Ninth Amendment*, 2 vols., ed. Randy E. Barnett (Fairfax, Va.: George Mason University Press, 1989 and 1993).

2

Privileges and Immunities and the States' Police Powers: Two Sides of the Same Federal Coin

I

The privileges and immunities clauses of the U. S. Constitution are integral to understanding the original American federal systems of rights. The American *systems* of rights is distinguishable from a *system* of rights, due to the federal arrangement that contains multidimensional classifications of citizenship and political obligation, state and national; moreover, unlike a unitary system, a federal system heightens the probability of disparity in the recognition of rights among the states and between a state and the national government. The privileges and immunities clauses were designed to cope with policy disparities by facilitating comity between the states within the American federal context. This was necessitated by the historic reality that the original federal arrangement respected the prerogatives of the states to articulate their respective definitions of rights for their respective citizens in relation to citizens from other states, while at the same time attempting to bind the states together into a national community, or in the words of the Preamble to the Constitution, "to form a more perfect Union."[1]

The framers of the U.S. Constitution included the privileges and immunities clause in an attempt to promote comity among the states within the federal framework. Article IV, section 2 of the U.S. Constitution stipulates that "the Citizens of each State shall be entitled to all Privileges and Immunities of Citizens in the several States."[2] In the absence of this provision the status of citizens domiciled in one state but temporarily in another would be tenuous and potentially detrimental to the development of an integrated national economy. Scholarship has lost sight of the importance of this clause and its close relationship to American federalism, assuming it to be a constitutional anachronism, while others have seized the opportunity to reshape it into something quite different from its original function, attempting to convert it into a judicial tool for dismantling the federal basis of rights in order to make way for a national one. Nevertheless, its inclusion in the Constitution is evidence that the framers acknowledged the prerogative of the states to establish privileges and immunities distinct from one another. Judge Robert Bork's contention that "the privileges and immunities clause remains largely unknown, was given a limited construction by the Supreme Court and has since remained dormant"[3] signifies a lack of juridical appreciation for this important clause. Bork's equating limited construction with dormancy is misleading. To the contrary, if the provision has not resulted in a steady flow of U.S. Supreme Court controversy, this could be evidence of the consensus surrounding its place and significance in the American constitutional scheme, rather than its dormancy or irrelevancy.[4] John Hart Ely, on the other hand, acknowledges the importance of privileges and immunities guarantees, but his acknowledgment is based upon a misunderstanding that would fundamentally alter the federal arrangement. Ely concedes that, "needless to say, there is not a bit of legislative history that supports the view that the Privileges and Immunities Clause was intended to be meaningless. Yet the *Slaughter-house* interpretation persists to the present day." Endorsing Justice Field's dissent in the 1873 case, Ely approvingly quotes the Justice: "What the clause in question [i.e., Article IV's privileges and immunities] did for the protection of the citizens of one State against hostile and discriminating legislation of the other States, the fourteenth amendment [privileges and immunities clause] does for the protection of every citizen of the United States against hostile and discriminating legislation against him in favor of others, whether they reside in the same or in different States."[5] Following Field's lead, Ely maintains that the Fourteenth Amendment nationalized Article IV's privileges and immunities, a nationalization that strips the states of their prerogatives to establish their own standards of rights.

American federalism is premised upon the dual citizenship of Americans, state and national. To test state policies against national standards (that is, national privileges and immunities in contradistinction to state-based standards), significantly detracts from the states' constitutional prerogatives[6] to regulate the health, safety, morals, and general welfare of their respective citizens, thereby negating the constitutional arrangement that the privileges and immunities clauses were designed to perpetuate. The balance between state and national standards is difficult to maintain, consequently even the most watchful scholarship over judicial interpretation of the Constitution has stumbled over this provision:

> With Justice Harlan, I agree that the "privileges or immunities" clause was "expected to be the primary source of substantive protection; the Equal Protection and Due Process Clauses were relegated to a secondary role..." Nevertheless, in the *Slaughter-house Cases* (1872) the Supreme Court virtually deprived the clause of meaning, and in the more than one hundred years that have elapsed, that judgment has been left standing.[7]

These three representative interpretations falter on the rocks of historical analysis. Obviously, the states do not have *cartes blanches* in the exercise of their respective public policy prerogatives. The U.S. and state constitutions place limits on the exercise of state powers, but because the privileges and immunities clauses were designed to accommodate states' rights prerogatives within the federal framework, and not to obliterate them, prudence is needed when construing the privileges and immunities of state and U.S. citizens. The positions of Bork, Ely, and Berger make evident the confusion surrounding current debate about the meaning of "privileges and immunities" as that clause is found in Article IV and the Fourteenth Amendment. However, Ely's position is the most problematical for American federalism, not simply because he advocates utilizing the clause as an instrument of nationalization, but because he takes such advocacy to new heights. But Ely is just part of a chorus that dates back to the early nineteenth century. In 1833 Justice Joseph Story set the tone for the current debate when, in reference to the privileges and immunities clause, he opted for national—as opposed to state—standards: "The intention of this clause was to confer on them, if one may so say, a general citizenship; and to communicate all the privileges and immunities, which the citizens of the same state would be entitled to under like circumstances."[8] As implied by Justice Story, the debate is essentially about the determination of rights in the American federal system; this debate about rights is thrusting the privileges and immunities clause toward a fundamental transformation, a transformation that gained momentum during the postbellum debates about fundamental rights for African Americans. In order to comprehend the importance and nature of that transformation, especially as it impacts upon a system of rights premised upon the consent of the governed, a historical analysis of the provision is necessary.

II

The privileges and immunities clause of Article IV did not fortuitously find its way into the U.S. Constitution in 1787. It not only had precedence, but the expectation was that the clause would be an important component of the federal structure. Nine years earlier, the framers of the Articles of Confederation included its precursor in Article IV of that document. The wording is instructive:

> The better to secure and perpetuate mutual friendship and intercourse among the people of the different states in this Union, the free inhabitants of each of these states—paupers, vagabonds, and fugitives from justice, excepted—shall be entitled to all *privileges and immunities* of free citizens in the several states.[9]

As the wording indicates, the intention of the clause was to facilitate interstate activity by protecting citizens engaged in interstate travel from discriminatory state legislation. In the absence of this provision discriminatory state legislation was a distinct possibility in a confederacy in which each state retained "its sovereignty, freedom, and independence, and every power, jurisdiction, and right, which is not by this Confederation expressly delegated to the United States in Congress assembled."[10] The legislation that was prohibited was primarily of a commercial nature. The remainder of Article IV addresses that specifically:

> and the people of each state shall have free ingress and regress to and from any other state, and shall enjoy therein all the *privileges of trade and commerce,* subject to the same duties, impositions, and restrictions, as the inhabitants thereof.[11]

In both instances Article IV of the Articles of Confederation conformed to the reality that the citizens in their respective states have distinct processes for establishing the privileges and immunities of their respective citizens, in contradistinction to a uniform national standard for the entire United States.[12] The intent of the article was to prevent the states from setting up legislative barriers that would adversely affect citizens from other states. The article limits the states from legislating in such a way that "ingress and regress to and from any other state" was officially obstructed. Once within the jurisdiction of the state, the interstate citizen was entitled to the same privileges and immunities, neither more nor less than the citizens of that state, but perhaps more or less than citizens in other states—an important *federal* qualification.

The citizens in their respective states determined what the privileges and immunities would be within their states' jurisdiction, with the exception that they should not discriminate against citizens from other states, but they did have the option of discriminating against noncitizens and their own citizens. Accordingly, an English subject who was entitled to all the privileges and immunities of English Common Law was not entitled to the guarantees of Article IV of the Articles of Confederation. It is important to note the word "citizens." One had to be a citizen of some other state within the United States; noncitizens, domestic and international, were not entitled to these protections because they were not part of a state citizenry. Thus, the rights conferred were exclusive, in contradistinction to universal; exclusive in the sense that a person was required to be a member of a state's citizenry in order to be entitled to the privileges and immunities of the other states.

The state citizenship requirement is integral to the fundamental principle of establishing government upon the consent of the governed through popular sovereignty. Each state constituted a sovereign community. The relationships among the individuals of the community and between the community and the government were regulated by the constitutional and statutory laws, which were a product of the political process in which the citizens made their preferences known and, if in the political majority, enforced. These same state laws articulated the privileges and immunities to which the people were entitled. Because noncitizens were outside this consensual political process, they were not by right entitled to the privileges and immunities of the community, in this case the community of states formed by the Articles of Confederation. This did not exclude the community of citizens from conferring rights on noncitizens, according to their own discretion within their own state jurisdictions, it simply means that the privilege and immunities clause did not force the states to do so.

Unlike their English counterparts, the citizens in their respective states were primarily guided by written constitutions, and not unwritten common law: "In the American constitutional tradition, what *replaced* common law was a new political technique, the written constitution. No matter how important common law was for the operation of the American legal system, the written constitution that framed the system sprang from ideas, principles, and practices evolved primarily in America."[13] Significantly the origins of written constitutions, political covenants and compacts, are uniquely American: "We cannot say, therefore, that these covenants and compacts derived from English common law or the British constitution. Nor can we say that what is recognizably American in these documents was an eighteenth-century synthesis of European Whig and Enlightenment thinkers."[14] As the American reliance on written constitutions evolved, popular sovereignty, the basis of that reliance, became increasingly important by the 1780s. Professor Lutz correctly observes that "there was nothing else in Europe to compare with the American practice of popular sovereignty. Nor was this a recent phenomenon in America. For all the resonance with Locke's ideas, many of the principles and assumptions of American constitutionalism were operative before Locke published his *Second Treatise on Civil Government*. In temporal terms, it makes more sense to call Locke an American than it does to call America Lockean."[15] Such being the case, to infuse the privileges and immunities clause with English Common Law theories thereby detracting from the importance of state-based popular sovereignty, is ahistorical and inaccurate. The privileges and immunities of the inhabitants of a particular state were determined first and foremost by the political processes of the state and not the English Common Law. State political processes discriminately conferred privileges and immunities, variously utilizing distinctions based upon state citizenship, property, race, religion, residency, and longevity of residency. The key to understanding the American bases of rights is the political process; it was such processes that established state constitutions, and it was state constitutions that established the processes for formulating statutes, both (state constitutions and statutes) of which delineated the conventional rights of their inhabitants, in contradistinction to some abstract universal rights of man that lacked the imprimatur of the state nomocratic political processes.

Furthermore, the historical evidence indicates that the phrase "privileges and immunities" was primarily associated with interstate commerce in two respects, in contradistinction to a fountainhead of nationally guaranteed higher law fundamental rights: (a) flow of commerce between the states; and (b) the role of the national government in facilitating that flow. Consider that in response to the debate surrounding the Congressional power to regulate interstate commerce during the 1787 Philadelphia Convention, delegates Daniel Carroll and Luther Martin (both from Maryland) voiced the concerns of their constituents that this congressional power could be used to favor some state ports over others. In the attempt to qualify that congressional power, they moved that the following clause be adopted:

> The legislature of the United States shall not oblige vessels belonging to the citizens thereof, or to foreigners, to enter or pay duties or imposts in any other state than to that to which they may be bound...nor shall any *privilege or immunity* be granted to any vessel on entering or clearing out, or paying duties or imposts in one state in preference to another.[16]

This provision was eventually adopted in the following form: "No Preference shall be given by any Regulation of Commerce or Revenue to the Ports of one State over those of another."[17] But it is clear from the language of the motion that "privileges and immunities" pertained to commerce. Just as the flow of commerce between the states was not to be inhibited by Congress giving preference to certain ports, the same was to be accomplished by the privileges and immunities clause in Article IV, section 2, which prohibited the states from statutorily penalizing citizens from other states conducting business therein.

III

The rationale behind these provisions was to minimize obstructive barriers to interstate commerce, while simultaneously leaving to the states the ample latitude to manage their own internal affairs. True, Congress was delegated the power regulate commerce with foreign nations, among the several states, and with Indian tribes,[18] but not to the extent that the federal model was to be transformed into a unitary one. The connection between the privileges and immunities clauses and Congressional commerce powers fluctuates as the U.S. Congress increases or decreases its power to regulate commerce. The national judiciary was an important institutional mechanism through which this division of powers between the national and state governments over commerce was to be maintained, with the privileges and immunities clauses as necessary backdrops to state policy prerogatives.

Due to the expectation that most legal disputes involving privileges and immunities would involve interstate parties, the national judiciary was the logical forum for adjudication unless, notably, a state was the defendant in a suit.[19] To a significant extent the viability of what was then an experimental integrated commercial union rested upon the states' compliance with the constitutional mandate to respect the privileges and immunities of interstate citizens. In the absence of such compliance the union would become increasingly commercially balkanized. Publius maintained that

> it may be esteemed the basis of the Union that "the citizens of each State shall be entitled to all the privileges and immunities of the citizens of the several States." And if it be a just principle that every government *ought to possess the means of executing its own provisions by its own authority* it will follow that in order to [*sic*] the inviolable maintenance of that equality of privileges and immunities to which the citizens of the Union will be entitled, the national judiciary ought to preside in all cases in which one State or its citizens are opposed to another State and its citizens. To secure the full effect of so fundamental a provision against all evasion and subterfuge, it is necessary that its construction should be committed to that tribunal which, having no local attachments, will be likely to be impartial between different States.[20]

Publius maintained that the "privileges and immunities" clause is the basis of the Union and because of its importance noncompliance should not be left to the state courts; leaving the adjudication of disputes to the state courts could result in conflict between the states, thereby disrupting the integration of the states' economies into a prospering national economy: "It is worthy of remark that not only the first, but every succeeding Congress, as well as the late convention, have invariably joined with the people in thinking that the prosperity of America depended on its Union."[21] Consequently, "whatever practices may have a tendency to disturb the harmony between the States are proper objects of federal superintendence and control."[22] States' discriminatory commercial policies against interstate travelers have such a tendency.

IV

The federal judiciary's most notable pre-Fourteenth Amendment jurisprudence on privileges and immunities is embodied in *Corfield* v. *Coryell* (1823).[23] Riding circuit, Supreme Court Justice Bushrod Washington wrote the court's opinion.[24]

The facts of the case include the seizure of the Philadelphian plaintiff's vessel while dredging for oysters in waters that were reserved by New Jersey for its citizens. The sixth section of New Jersey's 1820 oyster law was at issue. It stipulates that "it shall not be lawful for any person who is not at the time an actual inhabitant and resident in this state, to rake or gather clams, oysters, or shells, in any of the rivers, bays, or waters in this state, on board of any canoe, flat, scow, boat, or other vessel, not wholly owned by some person, inhabitant of, and actually residing in this state; and every person offending herein, shall forfeit and pay $10, to be recovered, &c.; and shall also forfeit the canoe, flat, &c."[25] The state statute discriminates against state residents who are not citizens of New Jersey. The court upheld the state statute on technical grounds and entered judgment for the defendant.[26] However, in the course of deciding the case Justice Washington addressed the question: "What are the privileges and immunities of citizens in the several states?"[27] It is worthwhile to analyze Justice Washington's many-times-quoted but misunderstood answer to this question:

> We feel no hesitation in confining these expressions to those privileges and immunities which are, in their nature, fundamental; which belong, of right, to the citizens of all free governments; and which have, at all times, been enjoyed by the citizens of the several states which compose this Union, from the time of their becoming free, independent, and sovereign. What these fundamental principles are, it would perhaps be more tedious than difficult to enumerate. They may, however, be all comprehended under the following heads: Protection by the government; the enjoyment of life and liberty, with the right to acquire and possess property of every kind, and to pursue and obtain happiness and safety; *subject nevertheless to such restraints as the government may justly prescribe for the general good of the whole*. The right of a citizen of one state to pass through, or to reside in any other state, for purposes of trade, agriculture, professional pursuits, or otherwise; to claim the benefit of the writ of habeas corpus; to institute and maintain actions of any kind in the courts of the state; to take, hold and dispose of property, either real or personal; and an exemption from higher taxes or impositions than are paid by the other citizens of the state; may be mentioned as some of the particular privileges and immunities of citizens, which are clearly embraced by the general description of privileges deemed fundamental: to which may be added, the elective franchise, *as regulated and established by the laws or constitution of the state in which it is to be exercised.*[28]

The italicized portions of the quotation (*supra*) are essential to Justice Washington's opinion. Inherent in his response are four notable qualifications. First, there are fundamental and nonfundamental privileges and immunities. Second, the origin and application of the privileges and immunities are positive, rather than abstractly universal. Their origins are the free, independent, and sovereign states, and the application is to the citizens of those governments. Third, the general categories of the privileges and immunities are: (a) protection by government; (b) enjoyment of life and liberty; (c) the right to acquire and possess all types of property; (d) the right to pursue and obtain happiness and safety; (e) the right to ingress and regress from state to state for commercial purposes; (f) the right to access the courts and habeas corpus; (g) the right to an equitable tax burden in the course of interstate trade; and (h) the right to the elective franchise, subject to state regulation. Fourth, all of these privileges and immunities are subject to state regulations for the general good. The state regulation of rights extends to citizens and noncitizens of the states, with the former in control of the policy making process. In reference to the "privileges and immunities" clause Justice Washington unambiguously stated that "we cannot accede to the proposition which...under this provision of the constitution, the citizens of the several states are permitted to participate in all the rights which belong exclusively to the citizens of any other particular state, merely upon the ground that they are enjoyed by those citizens."[29]

Within the context of American federalism, Justice Washington stipulated that the purpose of the privileges and immunities is not to establish a national standard of rights for all Americans, but to better "secure and perpetuate mutual friendship and intercourse among the people of the different states of the Union."[30] The fourth qualification makes this clear by acknowledging that the general good of the respective states takes priority over those individual rights that are not constitutionally enumerated; that is, the states must extend the privileges and immunities they do recognize to citizens from other states in their jurisdiction, unless to do so is contrary to the general good of the particular state. For example, just as the elective franchise can be regulated, so too can the pursuit of trade. Justice Washington reasoned that "it would, in our opinion, be going quite too far to construe the grant of privileges and immunities of citizens, as amounting to a grant of co-tenancy in the common property of the state, to the citizens of all the other states.... The oyster beds belonging to a state may be abundantly sufficient for the use of the citizens of that state, but might be totally exhausted and destroyed if the legislature could not so regulate the use of them as to exclude the citizens of the other states from taking them."[31] Explicit in Justice

Washington's reasoning is the acknowledgment that citizens in one state, New Jersey, may have privileges and immunities that citizens from another, Pennsylvania, lack, even though the Pennsylvanian temporarily resides in New Jersey. According to the court, this dichotomy is acceptable because it is a reasonable approach to protect citizens of a particular state from "serious public inconvenience and injury" that may result as a consequence of their membership in the federal union, in this particular case depleting the community's supply of oysters. This deference to the states is significant, in light of the explicit language of Article IV, section 2, which stipulates "The Citizens of each State shall be entitled to *all* Privileges and Immunities of Citizens in the several States."[32]

The significance of Justice Washington's reasoning should not be overlooked. He concedes that there are individual fundamental rights, such as "the right to acquire and possess property of every kind," but these fundamental rights do not take priority over the community's responsibility to "avoid serious public inconvenience and injury," or to express it more descriptively, the public welfare of the state is to be promoted by the state policies, to the extent that state policy can reasonably deny a citizen from another state *all* the privileges and immunities that its own citizens enjoy. The privileges and immunities clause is neither designed to detract from state popular sovereignty by nationalizing rights nor the public welfare of the people living within the jurisdiction of the respective states. The privileges and immunities clause is designed to promote the national good by economically integrating the states into a national economy; nevertheless, as important as national economic integration was to the framers, it was not their intent to displace the public welfare of the particular states as defined by the states' constitutional policy making processes.

This does not mean that constitutional deference to the states' prerogatives in the policy areas impacting privileges and immunities is not devoid of significant constitutional restrictions. The substantive U.S. constitutional limits placed on the states are to be found primarily in Article I, section 10. The privileges and immunities clause of Article IV is an extension of those constitutional limitations on the states, and in this particular instance state policy toward interstate citizens. The establishment of a national community of states and the national citizenship that resulted altered the nature of the state political communities in two important ways. First, the enhanced dichotomization of community into national and state components, which is the essence of federalism; and second, nationalizing the process through which persons achieve dual citizenship in both the national and state communities.

For example, Article I, section 8, confers upon the Congress the power "to establish an uniform Rule of Naturalization, and uniform Laws on the subject of Bankruptcies throughout the United States." The states' prerogatives to exercise these powers were not viewed as contingent upon congressional acquiescence or congressional inactivity. Justice Washington expressed his rule of construction in an 1814 state bankruptcy case: "But it was contended, that, if congress shall decline to exercise the power, the right to pass such laws results to the state governments. This conclusion appears to us to beg the whole question in controversy. It resigns all claim to a concurrent right in the state governments, and sets up one which is to arise on a condition, not to be found in the constitution, but which is gratuitously interpolated into it."[33] Accordingly, as the national government has its constitutional powers, so do the states. It is the responsibility of the courts to establish the parameters of those powers, not with an eye to expediency, but with the intent to uphold the constitutional separation of powers between the national and state governments. Reiterating Publius' reliance on the federal courts to maintain the balance, Justice Washington announced that "the sooner the limits which separate the two governments are marked by those authorities, which alone can define and establish them, the less danger there will be of serious, if not fatal collisions hereafter, arising respecting essential powers, to which a prescriptive right may be asserted by the one, in opposition to the chartered rights of the other."[34] (The "prescriptive right" is a right based upon practice and custom, while the "chartered rights" are based upon a written document, such as the Constitution.) For Justice Washington the prescriptive rights are not to be interpolated into constitutional law unless sanctioned by the latter. Accordingly, even though the states exercised certain powers prior to the ratification of the U.S. Constitution, once ratified the states' policies had to be measured for consistency with the rights attendant to membership in the national community. This does not rationalize a broad interpretation of national powers in the articulation of rights, rather it declares the obvious conclusion that the powers the states conferred upon the national government to some extent curtail state powers, including the power to regulate the rights of interstate citizens. When in dispute, the extent of that curtailment is to be determined by the courts and the political processes. In reference to the rules of naturalization and bankruptcies, formerly the public policy prerogatives of the states, Justice Washington concluded:

> It certainly will not be contended, that the powers to pass bankrupt and naturalization laws, are, by the amendments to the constitution [amendments nine and ten], reserved to the states in cases where they are not exercised by congress; because, this reservation is made only of such powers as are not granted to the general government; if granted, it would seem to follow, that they are not reserved to the states, or to the people. But it is not, in our opinion, correct to say, that congress, by refusing to pass laws on these subjects, has not exercised the powers confided to that body by the constitution, in relation thereto. The refusal amounts to a declaration of the public will, that such laws are unwise, and ought not to exist.[35]

The essential component of Justice Washington's rule of construction is the relationship between powers delegated to the national congress and those powers reserved to the states. If a specific public policy is not passed by the Congress, it is not to be assumed by the courts that the Congress thereby deferred to the states the option to exercise the constitutional prerogatives of the Congress. Such an assumption would disrupt the federal arrangement because "one or more states may pass laws, not only in opposition to the policy and legislative will of the general government, but to the laws of other states, enacted upon the same subjects, which, to a certain extent, they partially repeal."[36] Conversely, those powers which are, indeed, reserved to the states are not to be intruded upon by the U.S. Congress on the grounds that the states have failed to exercise those powers or because the states have exercised those powers inappropriately. The constructive basis for the courts' jurisprudence is the Constitution itself; the national government has the option to exercise the constitutionally delegated powers, with the states reserving to themselves not the powers the Congress, for whatever reason, fails to exercise, but those powers that the Congress may not exercise.[37]

Thus, if a state fails to recognize an unenumerated fundamental right, the Congress does not have constitutional authority to override the state's preference through national legislation based upon Article IV privileges and immunities. Moreover, when Justice Washington acknowledges in *Corfield* v. *Coryell* that the states have primary responsibility for fundamental rights, and that those rights are subject to state regulation, he was operating from the premise of the primacy of written constitutional law. Within the federal constitutional framework, the privileges and immunities clause was not a source of fundamental rights, but rather a constitutional mechanism through which a citizen of one state had qualified access to the privileges and immunities recognized in other states. According to Justice Washington's reasoning, inactivity on the part of a state or states to acknowledge a so-called right should not be construed by the federal courts to be acquiescence to the national government to embark on a mission to decide what is or is not a fundamental right, rather "such refusals amount to declarations of the public will" on the part of the states.

Shortly after the 1823 decision the social, political, economic, and cultural developments were thrusting upon the federal courts issues that were testing the validity and practicality of the court's interpretation of privileges and immunities in particular, and the notions of rights generally; such as, are some rights so fundamental that the states—as a consequence of their citizens' memberships in the national community—constrained from curtailing them, and if so to what extent? *Dred Scott* and *The Slaughter-house Cases* are the preeminent antebellum and postbellum test cases that address this critical question. What becomes clear is that the U.S. Supreme Court majorities in both of these cases are consistent with the court opinion in *Coryell,* even in light of the ratification of the Fourteenth Amendment.

VI

Without question *Dred Scott* v. *John F. A. Sandford* (1857) is one of the most maligned U.S. Supreme Court decisions in American history.[38] Its notoriety stems from the political and social consequences of the decision, which were disastrous; nevertheless, segments of the decision mark an important bridge between the privileges and immunities clauses of Article IV and the Fourteenth Amendment, and therefore merit our attention.

At the crux of the *Dred Scott* issues were the privileges and immunities clause of Article IV and attendant issue of fundamental rights. The privileges and immunities clause is the critical issue because it involves the relationships among the states and between national and state governments regarding the extent to which national citizenship qualifies the state prerogatives to determine what are and are not fundamental rights.

According to Chief Justice Taney, a state may confer its version of rights on anyone within its jurisdiction, but those rights can only be enjoyed within the state's territorial limits, and if the rights are conferred upon non-U.S. citizens, then those noncitizens are not entitled to privileges and immunities in other states. Justice Taney maintained that "each State may still confer them [rights and privileges] upon an alien, or any one it thinks proper, or upon any class or description of persons; yet he would not be a citizen in the sense in which that word is used in the Constitution of the United States, nor entitled to sue as such in one of its courts, nor to the privileges and immunities of a citizen in the other States. The rights which he would acquire would be restricted to the State which gave them."[39] All the states participate in determining the qualifications requisite for national citizenship through the U.S. Congress and only state citizens with U.S. citizenship are entitled to Article IV privileges and immunities guarantees. No state, through state processes such as conferring state citizenship, can unilaterally confer national citizenship on individuals unacceptable to the national community of states. Article I, section 8, clause 4 delegates to the U.S. Congress the power "to establish an uniform rule of naturalization." To allow individual states the option to exercise this power would subject other states to the constitutional requirement of extending their "privileges and immunities" to individuals who are not, in the strict sense, U.S. citizens, but merely state citizens. Thus, it is through the national congress that the states collectively determine who is entitled to national citizenship. Justice Taney deduced that when the framers of the Constitution

> gave to the citizens of each State the privileges and immunities of citizens in the several States, they at the same time took from the several States the power of naturalization, and confined that power exclusively to the Federal Government. No state (*sic*) was willing to permit another State to determine who should or should not be admitted as one of its citizens, and entitled to demand equal rights and privileges with their own people, within their own territories.[40]

Justice Taney's legal reasoning appears to run counter to the specific language of Article IV, section 2. ("*The Citizens of each State* shall be entitled to all Privileges and Immunities of Citizens in the several States.") However, implicit in his logic is the linkage of *The Citizens of each State* with dual citizenship (i.e., U.S. citizenship) in order for the privileges and immunities clause to be constitutionally extended to the former.

Approximately midway through the Court's opinion Justice Taney's argument takes a peculiar digression. The digression may be dismissed as a polemic in his attempt to make his tenuous constitutional case against the national citizenship of African Americans more politically tenable. Whatever the reason for its inclusion, this important part of his reasoning manifests the precarious balance between national constitutional guarantees and state police powers. Justice Taney unambiguously concludes that if African Americans were eligible for national citizenship and became members of the national political community, they would be entitled to all the privileges and immunities guarantees of the U.S. Constitution, with the national government being responsible for the enforcement of those privileges and immunities being abridged by a state:

> And if persons of the African race are citizens of a state, and of the United States, they would be entitled to all of these privileges and immunities in every State, and the State could not restrict them; for they would hold these privileges and immunities, under the paramount authority of the Federal Government, and its courts would be bound to maintain and enforce them, the Constitution and the laws of the State to the contrary notwithstanding. And if the State could limit or restrict them, or place the party in an inferior grade, this clause of the Constitution would be unmeaning, and could have no operation; and it would give no rights to the citizen when in another State. He would have none but what the State itself chose to allow him. This is evidently not the construction or meaning of the clause in question. It guarantees rights to the citizen, and the State cannot withhold them.[41]

Justice Taney's deference to states' rights on race relation led him to reject as unconstitutional any innovation that would have permitted the national government to extend privileges and immunities to African Americans. According to Taney, because the political and social consequences of national enforcement of rights for African Americans were not endorsed by the framers of the Constitution, one must conclude that the framers never intended to include them as citizens of the national political community, or more specifically, to confer upon them national citizenship with all the attending privileges and immunities of national citizenship. Otherwise state police powers pertaining to miscegenation, segregation of the races, and other state policies that restricted the rights of African Americans traveling interstate would not pass constitutional muster under the guarantees of privileges and immunities.[42] In a very real sense, Justice Taney realized that to concede that African Americans were eligible for U.S. citizenship, would convert the privileges and immunities clause into the mother lode of national fundamental rights for northern African Americans who chose to travel to the South and/or domicile in the territories. This, in and of itself, he feared, would have moved the nation closer toward a constitutional crisis.

Justice Taney's reasoning that state policies are qualified by the "privileges and immunities" guarantees is not contrary to case law precedent or the claim that the states are "sovereign and independent within their own limits in their internal and domestic concerns."[43] To wit, if an African American ceases to be an interstate resident, but takes up permanent residence in a state, the state may then proceed to "deny him the privileges and immunities enjoyed by its citizens."[44] Justice Taney is cognizant of a state's responsibility to be in compliance with the U.S. Constitution's privileges and immunities guarantees while simultaneously deferring to the prerogatives of a state's police powers. But because he found it to be politically and socially necessary to prevent African American citizens of the free states from having access to certain privileges and immunities in the slave states, he denied that any state could elevate Negroes to a form of citizenship from which they would be entitled to privileges and immunities in other states; he surmised that because they were neither foreigners nor members of the original political community, they were ineligible for national citizenship.[45] In short, Justice Taney manifested an unwillingness to accept certain consequences of a viable federal arrangement, even if the states through national legislation were to collectively elevate African Americans to national citizenship; Justice Taney appeared to be prepared to nullify any law conferring citizenship on African Americans, short of a constitutional amendment.

In his dissenting opinion, Justice McLean makes it clear that he is much more amenable to live with consequences of a viable federalism. Agreeing with Justice Taney that states can confer state citizenship on free African Americans, he goes on to conclude that as a consequence they are U.S. citizens with certain national constitutional rights: "Being born under our Constitution and laws, no naturalization is required, as one of foreign birth, to make him a citizen. The most general and appropriate definition of the term 'citizen' is a 'freeman.' Being a freeman, and having his domicile in a State different from that of the defendant, he is a citizen within the act of Congress, and the courts of the Union are open to him."[46] Reiterating Publius, Justice McLean places the federal courts in their proper orbit, which is respecting the sovereign prerogatives of the states without usurping them. Justice McLean's rule of construction in the *Dred Scott* case epitomizes the federal judiciary's role:

> The States of Missouri and Illinois are bounded by a common line. The one prohibits slavery, the other admits it. This has been done by the exercise of that sovereign power which appertains to each. We are bound to respect the institutions of each, as emanating from the voluntary action of the people. Have the people of either any right to disturb the relations of the other? Each State rests upon the basis of its own sovereignty, protected by the Constitution. Our Union has been the foundation of our prosperity and national glory. Shall we not cherish and maintain it? This can only be done by respecting the legal rights of each State.[47]

Implicit in Justice McLean's admonishment to the court majority are the following points: (a) the states are sovereign; (b) state policy is the voluntary action of a sovereign people; (c) in a federal system there will not necessarily be policy uniformity; (d) the U.S. Constitution protects such diversity; and (e) it is the responsibility of the U.S. Supreme Court to respect the legal (i.e., constitutional) rights of each state.

The fundamental difference between Justices McLean's and Taney's respective positions in *Dred Scott* is that Justice Taney backed away from American federalism when the consequences were intolerable to his public policy preferences, whereas Justice McLean delineated the federal model. Nevertheless, both consistently construed the privileges and immunities clause according to *Coryell,* acknowledging that the privileges and immunities clause was not a conduit for national fundamental rights to be imposed upon the states, but rather a provision designed to facilitate commercial integration between the states. This consensus was disrupted in the aftermath of the war between the states.

VII

In the aftermath of the American Civil War, the U.S. Supreme Court was called upon to determine the postbellum federal arrangement of the privileges and immunities clause of the Fourteenth Amendment. The court opinion in the *Slaughter-house Cases* reiterated the federalism of antebellum America, while the dissenting justices blazed the juridical trail toward a unitary arrangement.[48]

The facts in the *Slaughter-house Cases* involved the state of Louisiana's attempt to regulate the landing and slaughtering of livestock in the New Orleans area. State regulatory legislation, passed on 8

March 1869, created a monopoly with exclusive rights to provide facilities for the slaughtering process.[49] For our purposes, the relevant issue is: "Does the state statute abridge the Fourteenth Amendment's privileges and immunities of U.S. citizens?"[50]

In the words of the plaintiff's counsel, "The state is commanded neither to make nor enforce any law that deprives or even abridges any citizen of his enjoyment of his privileges or immunities. To limit him in the choice of a trade, to deprive him of a business he has pursued, and to give to others the sole and exclusive right to follow that trade or to prosecute that business, violates this Constitution."[51] The plaintiff's complaint dissolves the constitutional boundaries between the national and state jurisdictions in the policy areas of rights. The basis of this dissolution is the displacement of state citizenship with a national citizenship, with all the attendant national rights, privileges, and immunities that the states must not violate. These national rights are extrapolated not only from the U.S. Constitution (no mention is made of the relevance of state constitutional rights), but from the English-American legal experience under the rubric of fundamental rights. What is problematical for this type of extrapolation is the fact that the English Common Law and the post 1789 U.S. Constitution are not systematically congruous; the incongruity results from the federally based popular control basis of American law.

In the Court's majority opinion Justice Miller sets the parameters of a workable federal arrangement for the postbellum period. He accomplished this by recognizing four essential components of federalism: state citizenship, state police powers, the federal basis of privileges and immunities, and the positive origins of acknowledged rights.

Justice Miller maintained the precedent that acknowledged the dichotomy between national and state citizenship, but with a qualification attributable to the Fourteenth Amendment. By stipulating that "all persons born or naturalized in the United States and subject to the jurisdiction thereof, are citizens of the United States and of the State wherein they reside" (Fourteenth Amendment, section one), Justice Taney's jurisprudence on citizenship was constitutionally amended. Nevertheless, Justice Miller reiterated that "the distinction between citizenship of the United States and citizenship of a state is clearly recognized and established. Not only may a man be a citizen of the United States without being a citizen of a state, but an important element is necessary to convert the former into the latter. He must reside within the state to make him a citizen of it, but it is only necessary that he be born or naturalized in the United States to be a citizen of the Union."[52] In the absence of this dichotomy of citizenship, recourse to precedent in interpreting the Fourteenth Amendment's privileges and immunities clause is impossible, due to the fact that without state citizenship national citizenship would result in a uniformity of rights, thereby making privileges and immunities guarantees an absurdity because citizens going from one state to another would not experience different standards of rights.

Not only would a singular national citizenship negate privileges and immunities, but it would also significantly intrude upon the states' police powers. Citizens residing in a particular state could challenge state policies on the grounds that those policies infringe upon their rights as national citizens. Quoting Chancellor Kent, Justice Miller defines the states' police powers on the basis that "private interests must be made subservient to the general interests of the community. This is called the police power... it [state police power] is much easier to perceive and realize the existence and sources of it than to mark its boundaries, or prescribe limits to its exercise."[53] The community that Justice Miller had in mind was the state. Obviously, the general interest of the community may not be perceived by some state citizens to be compatible with their private interests; such was the case with the independent butchers of Louisiana, who challenged the state-created monopoly as a violation of their private rights. In the absence of a viable state citizenship with the attending state police powers, these disgruntled individuals would have had recourse to the national standards of rights in the attempt to have their private interests prevail over the state's general interests; moreover, if these "complainants" succeeded in persuading the Court that the general interests of the state ran counter to some abstract notion of nationally recognized fundamental rights, the state's general interests as manifested in the monopoly could then be challenged accordingly.

Reiterating the state basis of rights as expressed in *Corfield*, the court concluded that, fundamental rights "have always been held to be the class of rights which the state governments were created to establish and secure."[54] Thus, because each state may have variously defined what are fundamental rights, the privileges and immunities clauses were designed to facilitate comity among the states. Justice Miller links the privileges and immunities of the Fourteenth Amendment with Articles IV of the Articles of Confederation and the U.S. Constitution, to the extent that the construction of the clause in the Fourteenth Amendment should not alter the federal/state relationship; the purpose of its inclusion in the Fourteenth amendment is to extend the same privileges and immunities to the class of individuals who were denied those protections as a consequence of *Scott* v. *Sandford*, African Americans. He wrote, "Its sole purpose was to declare to the several states, that whatever those rights, as you grant or establish them to your own citizens, or as you limit or qualify, or impose restrictions on their exercise, the same, neither more nor less, shall be the measure of the rights of citizens of other states within your jurisdiction."[55]

The court majority forewarned that if the plaintiffs, who are citizens of the State of Louisiana, could negate this state statute designed to protect the health of the inhabitants of New Orleans on the grounds that it violated some supra-state fundamental right to pursue one's occupation, the federal courts would become perpetual censors over the state legislatures:

> [S]uch a construction followed by the reversal of the judgments of the supreme court of Louisiana in these cases would constitute this court a perpetual censor upon all legislation of the states, on the civil rights of their own citizens, with authority to nullify such as it did not approve as consistent with those rights, as they existed at the time of the adoption of this Amendment.... [T]hese consequences are so serious, so far reaching and pervading, so great a departure from the structure and spirit of our institutions; when the effect is to fetter and degrade the state governments by subjecting them to the control of Congress, in the exercise of powers heretofore universally conceded to them of the most ordinary and fundamental character; when in fact it radically changes the whole theory of the relations of the state and Federal governments to each other and of both of these governments to the people.[56]

It is significant that in 1873 a majority of the postbellum Republican U.S. Supreme Court was not prepared to support such a radical transformation of the federal system. To elevate the Fourteenth Amendment's privileges or immunities guarantees to such heights would have made Article IV's privileges and immunities guarantees, the Ninth Amendment's acknowledgment of rights retained by the people, and the Tenth Amendment's reserved state powers constitutionally incoherent.

The majority's warnings notwithstanding, in his dissent Justice Field encouraged such "radical changes." After acknowledging the "abstract justice which lies in the position of the plaintiffs in error,"[57] he delineates two types of restrictions on the police powers of the states, the constitutional prohibitions and fundamental principles. According to Justice Field, "The question presented is, therefore, one of the gravest importance, not merely to the parties here, but to the whole country. It is nothing less than the question whether the recent Amendments to the Federal Constitution protect the citizens of the United States against the deprivation of their common rights by state legislation. In my judgment the Fourteenth does afford such protection."[58] Justice Field contended that the Fourteenth Amendment placed "the common rights of the American citizens under the protection of the National government." As a consequence,

> a citizen of a state is now only a citizen of the United States residing in that state. The fundamental rights, privileges, and immunities which belong to him as a free man and free citizen, now belong to him as a citizen of the United States, and are not dependent upon his citizenship of any state.[59]

In his attempt to reverse eighty-four years of precedent, Justice Field advocates the nationalization of constitutional and unenumerated rights, the very development Justice Miller cautioned against. Furthermore, the U.S. Supreme Court was to play the prominent role in the discovery and protection of these rights.

For the *Slaughter-house* dissenters the path to discovery of unenumerated rights leads through English history. But the fallacy of the dissenters' argument is in their failure to acknowledge the differences between the political processes of England, in which popular control of the law-making process was more myth than fact, and the American political process in which popular control of the process was descriptively valid. Justice Miller was cognizant of the fallacy; his response to the dissenters' reliance on English Common Law maintains that "such references are to monopolies established by the monarch in derogation of the rights of his subjects, or arise out of transactions in which the people were unrepresented, and their interests uncared for."[60] Additionally, as important as English Common Law is for legal guidance, it is subordinate to the positive laws passed by state legislatures: "For whoever doubted the authority of Parliament to change or modify the common law?"[61] Not only do the *Slaughter-house* dissenters fail to seriously consider the prerogatives of state legislatures to modify common law, they transform common law into a form of fundamental law that in many respects is beyond the reach of legislatures. For example, when Justice Field maintained that "no one will deny the *abstract justice* which lies in the position of the plaintiffs in error,"[62] it seemed of little importance to him that a political majority of Louisiana's state legislators and judges did indeed deny the *abstract justice* of the plaintiffs' complaints.

Nevertheless, in order to obstruct the legislative will of a state legislature, the dissenters required more than the reed of abstract justice; it behooved them to promote judicial legitimacy and such promotion required that they ground their dissent in the U.S. Constitution. The constitutional grounds they set upon were expansive; expansive in the sense that the strict construction of the Fourteenth Amendment that the court majority relied upon was replaced by a construction that is latitudinal in scope and substantively ideological. Both the scope and the substance of their construction are primarily and dominantly English; conveniently, the English connection provides a politically safe juridical standard against which to measure state legislative acts. Whether the dissenters' nomenclature is *rights of man, rights of citizens in any free government, rights of Englishmen, fundamental rights, inalienable rights of humanity, natural rights, absolute rights of individuals,*[63] the intended effect was the same, to thwart the states' political processes if the results of those processes were not acceptable to the dissenting justices' concocted standards of justice. For example, as the dissenting justices proceeded to make their cases against Louisiana, they claimed that the "right to free labor" is "one of the most sacred and imprescriptible rights of man."[64] How do the dissenting justices rationalize the importance of this right? They recognize it "to be the natural right of every Englishman." This dependence on the rights of Englishmen is justified on the grounds that "the common law of England is the basis of the jurisprudence of the United States,"[65] and consequently state intrusions upon such rights are suspect, such as the monopoly established by Louisiana, which placed restrictions on the labor of butchers. However, even a cursory survey of English labor law refutes the justice's high opinion of the "right to free labor" for the English working class, not to mention that English labor law is not necessarily relevant to the *Slaughter-house* issues.

VIII

The essence of the *Slaughter-house* dissenters' rejection of American federalism was most clearly stated by Justice Bradley. What his dissenting brethren left implicit, Justice Bradley stated explicitly. According to Justice Bradley, the privileges and immunities clause of Article IV inherently incorporates the U.S. Bill of Rights, thereby making them applicable to the states; the states must not only confer these rights on citizens from other states, but also on their own citizens and noncitizens within their jurisdictions. Speciously referring to Justice Bushrod Washington's notion of fundamental rights, Justice Bradley concluded that "these, and still others, are specified in the original Constitution or in the early Amendments of it, as among the privileges and immunities of citizens of the United States, or, what is still stronger for the force of the argument, the rights of all persons whether citizens or not."[66] Furthermore, U.S. citizenship carries with it certain rights, privileges, and immunities:

> I think sufficient has been said to show that citizenship is not an empty name, but that, in this country at least, it has connected with it certain incidental rights, privileges, and immunities of the greatest importance. And to say that these rights and immunities attach only to state citizenship, and not to citizenship of the United States, appears to me to evince a very narrow and insufficient estimate of constitutional history and the rights of men, not to say the rights of the American people.[67]

According to this view, the purpose of the Fourteenth Amendment was to embody the inherent rights of U.S. citizenship into fundamental law and thereby "provide national security against violation by the states of the fundamental rights of the citizen":

> The mischief to be remedied was not merely slavery and its incidents and consequences; but that spirit of subordination and disloyalty to the national government which had troubled the country for so many years in some of the states...The Amendment was an attempt to give voice to the strong national yearning for that time and that condition of things, in which American citizenship should be a sure guaranty of safety, and in which every citizen of the United States might stand erect in every portion of its soil, in the full enjoyment of every right and privilege belonging to a freeman, without fear of violence or molestation.[68]

The burden will fall to the national courts for keeping the states in compliance with the nationally defined fundamental rights of individuals. In the event that the "business of the national courts should be increased,

Congress could easily supply the remedy by increasing their number and efficiency."[69] The intended outcome, national supremacy over the states with the national courts serving as the guardians of that supremacy, or in the vigilant words of Justice Miller, the Supreme Court would function as the "perpetual censor upon all legislation of the States."[70]

This is not to say that the dissenting justices advocated stripping the states of all their respective police powers. They acknowledged that the states had some powers within their respective jurisdictions, but the extent of those police powers were to be significantly qualified as a result of being measured by the standards of reasonableness and/or justice as established by national courts. Implementation of these nationally court-defined standards can run counter to popular control over state public policy. Anyone familiar with the nineteenth-century conditions associated with the slaughtering processes of animals realizes that some type of state regulation was justified. But to negate Louisiana's response as "onerous, unreasonable, arbitrary and unjust" is to substitute the policy preferences of the U.S. Supreme Court for that of the state's legislative process. Justice Bradley was not deterred and concluded that Louisiana's policy "has none of the qualities of a police regulation. If it were really a police regulation, it would, undoubtedly, be within the power of the legislature:[71]

> The right of a state to regulate the conduct of its citizens is undoubtedly a very broad and extensive one, and not to be lightly restricted. But there are certain fundamental rights which this right of regulation cannot infringe. It may prescribe the manner of their exercise, but it cannot subvert the rights themselves. *I speak now of the rights of citizens of any free government.*[72]

The underlying but unstated premise of the *Slaughter-house* dissenters is their lack of confidence in the state legislative processes, even though those processes are constitutionally constrained by internal and external checks. Even by nineteenth-century standards, for the members of the Butchers' Benevolent Association of New Orleans the channels of political participation were conduits for state public policy-making; such being the case, were the disgruntled butchers able to pressure the state legislature to adopt an alternative to the statute passed 8 March 1869?[73] Nevertheless, Justice Bradley implies the statute was "made in the interest of a few scheming individuals, by which some of the southern states have, within the past few years, been so deplorably oppressed and impoverished."[74] But this is neither substantiated nor convincing grounds for U.S. Supreme Court intervention, unless one accepts—on blind faith—the role of the U.S. Supreme Court in articulating and securing the universal rights of American citizens, American federalism and popular control over public policy notwithstanding.

IX

In the current political/cultural climate the privileges and immunities clauses constitute wild cards of constitutional development. Consider one possible scenario. Following the lead of Justice Scalia the U.S. Supreme Court reverses the 1973 *Roe* v. *Wade*[75] decision on the constitutional grounds that the abortion issue is nonjusticiable and therefore a political question to be resolved by the states. In the wake of the court's decision, certain states pass very restrictive antiabortion legislation. Responding to constituency pressures the Congress implements national abortion standards that approximate *Roe*. The claimed basis of the national standards is Amendment XIV, sections 1 and 5. Section one includes the privileges and immunities guarantees, and section five states that "the Congress shall have power to enforce, by appropriate legislation, the provisions of this article." It is clear that what constitutes "appropriate legislation" hinges on the interpretation of the "privileges and immunities" clause. In the event that the U.S. Supreme Court adopts the privileges and immunities model advocated by Justices Field and Bradley in the *Slaughter-house Cases,* the Congress would have constitutional authority to establish national abortion rights; conversely, if the contemporary Court upholds the precedent established by Justices Washington and Miller in the *Coryell* and *Slaughter-house Cases,* respectively, the national legislation would be declared unconstitutional. In essence, the prerogatives of the states to exercise their police powers in regard to unenumerated rights within the parameters of American federalism is at issue.

The misconstruction of privileges and immunities will significantly impact upon those state prerogatives, whereas its proper construction serves as an obstacle to the nationalization of unenumerated rights. Nevertheless, in our constitutional system of separation of powers and checks and balances, high levels of political acumen are required to move from one juridical paradigm to another; an accomplishment others have referred to as creative jurisprudence, the topic of chapter 3.

Notes

1. It should be noted that The Articles of Confederation (drafted in 1777 and ratified in 1781) sought to establish "a perpetual Union between the states," whereas the 1787 constitution aimed at "a more perfect Union," which is distinct from a "perfect Union." A perpetual union is not necessarily perfect and a perfect union is not necessarily perpetual.
2. This clause is also in the Fourteenth Amendment, section 1. The clauses are not identical; take note of the different conjunctions, "privileges *and* immunities" and "privileges *or* immunities" and the phrase *Citizens in the several States* contrasted with *citizens of the United States*. These are obviously substantive changes; for example, the substitution of *or* for *and* heightens the Fourteenth Amendment test because only one has to be abridged, whereas Article IV requires that both be infringed before a constitutional violation is committed. There are other constitutional provisions designed to promote comity between the states, or to state it conversely, to reduce hostility and enhance commercial integration between the states, including the congressional power to regulate interstate commerce (Article I, section 8), prohibiting Congress from giving preference to certain ports (Article I, section 9), prohibiting vessels going from one state to another from being charged duties (Article I, section 9), and requiring states to obtain Congress' consent before laying imposts or duties on imports or exports (Article I, section 10).
3. Robert H. Bork, *The Tempting of America: The Political Seduction of the Law* (New York: The Free Press, 1990), 37.
4. There is a pattern among commentators of equating a lack of Supreme Court activity regarding a particular constitutional provision with the insignificance of the provision. This has been the fate with the Second Amendment to the U.S. Constitution, too (see chapter 6, *infra*).
5. John Hart Ely, *Democracy and Distrust: A Theory of Judicial Review* (Cambridge, Mass.: Harvard University Press, 1980), 22, 23.
6. Implicit in the states' "constitutional prerogatives" are the limits placed upon the states by the national and their respective constitutions. It is the natures of those limits that are at issue.
7. Raoul Berger, *The Fourteenth Amendment and the Bill of Rights* (Norman, OK: University of Oklahoma Press, 1989), 31 (footnotes omitted). This research takes the contrary position, that the *Slaughter-house Cases* invigorates the clause with meaning, *infra*. What is peculiar about Berger's admission in the opening paragraph of chapter 3 is that it belies what appears to be the thrust of his argument. One must assume that this is attributable to the confusion surrounding the privileges and immunities clauses.
8. Joseph Story, *Commentaries On The Constitution Of The United States*, 3 vols. (New York: DaCapo Press, 1970), 1: 675. Story cites *Corfield* v. *Coryell* in his interpretation of the clause; as will be shown *infra*, Story's interpretation of both the clause and *Corfield* are erroneous.
9. Article IV, Articles of Confederation (emphasis added).
10. Ibid., Article II.
11. Ibid., Article IV (emphasis added).
12. Article I of the Articles of Confederation stipulates that "The style of this confederacy shall be, 'The United States Of America.'" In conjunction with Article II,

which recognizes state sovereignty, the word "united" cannot be confused with unitary nationalism.

13. Donald S. Lutz, *The Origins of American Constitutionalism* (Baton Rouge, La.: LSU Press, 1988), 63.
14. Ibid., 31.
15. Ibid., 10–11.
16. *Debates on the Adoption of the Federal Constitution, in the Convention Held at Philadelphia in 1787,* vol. V, Jonathan Elliot, ed. (New York, N.Y.: Burt Franklin, 1888), 479 (emphasis added).
17. Article I, section 9, clause 6, the U.S. Constitution.
18. Article 1, section 8, clause 3.
19. "The Judicial power of the United States shall not be construed to extend to any suit in law or equity, commenced or prosecuted against one of the United States by Citizens of another State, or by Citizens or Subjects of any Foreign State" (Eleventh Amendment, 1795).
20. *The Federalist Papers,* #80: 478; the national judiciary was given this jurisdiction in Article III, section 2. However, in the aftermath of the Chisholm v. Georgia decision the Eleventh Amendment was ratified, which protected the states from being dragged into federal court as a defendant (1 L.Ed. 440 [1793]).
21. Ibid., #3: 41.
22. Ibid., #80: 477–78.
23. 6 Fed. Cas. No. 546 (C. C. E. D. Pa.). When it comes to the privileges and immunities clauses of Article IV and the Fourteenth Amendment, all roads lead to some part of this circuit court case, as is evidenced by judicial and academic selective references to it.
24. Justice Washington, a Virginian, was appointed to the Supreme Court by President John Adams in 1798 and served until 1829.
25. Corfield v. Coryell, 548.
26. The court ruled that the plaintiff lacked constructive possession of the vessel at the time of the seizure because it was under contract to another party.
27. Ibid., 551.
28. Ibid., 551-52 (emphasis added).
29. Ibid., 552.
30. Ibid., 552.
31. Ibid., 552.
32. Ibid., 552; Article IV, section 2, clause 1 (emphasis not in original).
33. Golden v. Prince, Fed. Cas. No. 5509, Vol. 10 (1814), 542, 545.
34. Ibid., 545.
35. Ibid., 547.
36. Ibid., 547.
37. Justice Washington's reasoning was subsequently reiterated by the Supreme Court in Cooley v. Board of Wardens, 13 L.Ed. 996 (1851).
38. Ely calls it "notorious" (Ely, 1980, 16), Berger refers to it as "aberrant" (Berger, 1989, 9), and Bork claims that "the politics and morality of the Justices combined to produce the worst constitutional decision of the nineteenth century" (Bork, 1990, 28).
39. Dred Scott v. John F. A. Sandford, 15 L.Ed. 691, 701 (1857).
40. Ibid., 706. Recall Justice Washington's reasoning in *Corfield* that once a power has been granted to the U.S. Congress, the states relinquish the option to exercise the same even if Congress has refused to exercise that delegated power (*supra*).

41. Ibid., 708.
42. See ibid., 703–05.
43. Ibid., 718.
44. Ibid., 708.
45. "The question before us is, whether the class of persons described in the plea of abatement compose a portion of this people, and are constituent members of this sovereignty. We think that they are not, and that they are not included, and were not intended to be included, under the word "citizen" in the Constitution" (ibid., 700).
46. Ibid., 753.
47. Ibid., 764.
48. The official case title is The Butchers' Benevolent Association of New Orleans v. The Crescent City Live-Stock Landing and Slaughter-house Company (21 L.Ed. 394 [1873]).
49. "An Act to Protect the Health of the City of New Orleans, to Locate the Stock-landings and Slaughter-houses, and to Incorporate the Crescent City Live-Stock Landing and Slaughter-house Company" is the act's official title.
50. Other issues raised by the case involve the Thirteenth Amendment's prohibition against involuntary servitude and the Fourteenth Amendment's equal protection and due process guarantees.
51. *Slaughter-house Cases,* 396.
52. Ibid., 408.
53. Ibid., 404.
54. Ibid., 408.
55. Ibid., 409.
56. Ibid., 409.
57. Ibid., 412.
58. Ibid., 413.
59. Ibid., 414, 415.
60. Ibid., 405.
61. Ibid., 405.
62. Ibid., 412 (emphasis added).
63. In the course of the dissenting justices' opinions they resort to such wordplay.
64. Ibid., 419.
65. Ibid., 417. "All such grants [monopolies] relating to any known trade have been held by all the judges of England, whenever they have come up for consideration, to be void at common law as destroying the freedom of trade, discouraging labor and industry, restraining persons from getting an honest livelihood, and putting it in the power of the grantees to enhance the price of commodities" (ibid., 417).
66. Ibid., 422.
67. Ibid., 421.
68. Ibid., 423–24.
69. Ibid., 424.
70. Ibid., 409.
71. Ibid., 422.
72. Ibid., 421 (emphasis added).
73. This is precisely what happened; the law was changed as a result of the political process. In 1879 Louisiana adopted a new constitution that prohibited slaughter-house monopolies and provided that parish governments regulate such businesses. In light of the fact that the new constitution breached the twenty-five-year mo-

nopoly granted to the Crescent City Live-Stock Landing and Slaughter-House Company, the Supreme Court upheld the state's new policy as a proper exercise of the state's police powers. See Butchers' Union Slaughter-House and Live-Stock Landing Company v. Crescent City Live-Stock Landing and Slaughter-House Company, 111 U.S. 746 (1883).

74. Ibid., 422. Justice Bradley apparently has much more confidence in the ability of English subjects to protect their rights against government oppression than he has for American state citizens: "England has no written Constitution, it is true; but it has an unwritten one, resting in the acknowledged, and frequently declared, privileges of Parliament and the people, to violate which in any material respect would produce a revolution in an hour" (ibid., 421).

75. 410 U.S. 113; for Justice Scalia's recommendations see Webster v. Reproductive Health Services 109 S.Ct. 3040 (1989), 3064-67.

3

Roscoe Pound: Strategist for Creative Jurisprudence

I

American political culture necessitates that public policy be grounded in popular control if the policy is to be legitimate and thereby sustain the political obligation of the citizenry.[1] Popular control may be remote and indirect as a result of external and internal checks and balances, but nevertheless the relationships between citizens and their governments' policies must give credence to the image that popular control over public policy is the rule. This scheme of things is usually taken for granted and to restate the obvious seems to be somewhat verbose. However, in the public policy area of rights the historical scheme that we take for granted has not only been seriously challenged (such challenges have always been part and parcel of political debate), but effectively challenged. During the first three decades of the twentieth century an influential community of academic and legal scholars laid the theoretical groundwork for innovative rationalizations through which the official recognition and protection of rights need not be contingent upon nomocratic popular control. The alternative source for articulating rights was not the citizens through republican procedures, but experts supposedly schooled in legal science.[2] Permit me to reiterate; popular control over fundamental rights has always been subject to debate, but the watershed theoretical developments of the first few decades of the twentieth century paved the way for substantive changes. These changes are manifested not only by the nature and content of the debate, but most importantly by the legitimation of a judicially generated rights policy paradigm.

Due to the authoritativeness of its decisions, the rights policies in question are those formulated by the U.S. Supreme Court. These rights may or may not meet with the approval of or be consistent with national and/or state rights policies. What distinguishes judicially generated rights from nomocratically sanctioned rights—that is, rights policies which are the product of tradition, constitutional conventions/amendments, or legislative action—are their origins. For example, if X has been sanctioned as a right from time immemorial, it would be recognized as a traditional right. No specific legislative act designated it as such, but no legislature or court questioned the validity of X. Neither a legislature nor a court generated X as a constitutional right, but through inaction consistently affirmed X as part of the overall licit culture. Responding to popular will within the nation, the current legislature statutorily classifies Y as a constitutional right. X and Y are mutually exclusive, thus, X is statutorily (and nomocratically) repealed. On the other hand, if popular will and the legislature were content with the status quo regarding X, and the Supreme Court unilaterally declared X unconstitutional and mandated that Z be placed in its stead, then Z would constitute a judicially generated right. The caveat that Z is mandated by the constitution and therefore indirectly tied to and representative of popular will may or may not be an accurate argument. That is the issue and the reason why Roscoe Pound is key to understanding the judiciary's role. Pound calculatingly instructed justices in ways to link Z to the Constitution, an accurate reading of the Constitution notwithstanding.

The extent to which judicially generated rights policies preempt state policies is key to understanding if judicial review is compatible with the primary dictate of American political culture that public policy be grounded in popular control. For example, if the U.S. Congress conferred a title of nobility on individuals, declaring those titles as null and void is within the parameters of judicial review, based on the fact that sections 9 and 10 of Article I prohibit such titles. Even if the vast majority of Americans supported conferring those titles, a reasonably sound argument could be made that the U.S. Supreme Court was acting according to popular consent and not contrary to popular control, on the grounds that the U.S. Constitution embodies the authentic will of the people and, thus, is the controlling factor. However, when one considers the unique role of judicial review in the American political consciousness, the distinction between popular consent and popular control is paramount. The Court may exercise judicial review under the pretext that its decisions are always in accordance with the Constitution, even in those instances when it is not. The people give their consent under the false premise that they, through the Constitution, control the Court's decisions. The pretext maintains a cardinal rule of American political culture—that the U.S. Supreme Court be constrained by the U.S. Constitution, a document through which the citizenry exercises ultimate control over the Court's decisions. In those instances when the Court is truly constrained by popular control through the Constitution, its decisions are entitled to the political obligation of the citizenry even when its rulings overturn policies that have the overwhelming support of the majority and its elected representatives.

Nevertheless, presumed popular control may be at odds with political reality, because there is no guarantee that the U.S. Supreme Court's rulings are in fact tied to popular control via the Constitution, even though the citizenry consented to the ruling while under the illusion that it was the product of a legitimate constitutional process. Herein lies the dilemma; the very pretext that the U.S. Supreme Court is exercising judicial review according to the dictates of the Constitution is what provides opportunities for the Court to violate the cardinal rule of American political culture, popular control over public policy.

Early in the twentieth century juridical strategy and tactics were articulated that encouraged and instructed judges and justices on how to sever popular control when necessary for achieving unpopular or unconstitutional policy objectives, without alienating popular consent. Delineating the strategy and tactics is a difficult task. Constitutional development is a multidimensional and complex phenomenon and tracking deviations from previously established norms is difficult, especially if there is a conscious intent to obscure the actual basis of judicial policy. Explicating the dimensions involved includes not only the inner workings of the courts, but also presidential politics, legislative politics, nature of the times (such as war, threat of war, peace, condition of the economy, etc.), personalities of the justices, leadership within the court, state public policies, and other factors. However, our focus is narrowed to the juridical public policy area of unenumerated rights and discerning the twentieth-century juridical development of those rights. Accordingly, when the U. S. Supreme Court elevates an unenumerated right to constitutional status, the basis of that right should be discernible as either grounded in the Constitution or judicially generated from external sources. For example, the "right" of the people to keep and bear arms is explicitly recognized in the U.S. Constitution, whereas variations of the penumbral right to privacy may be the product of judicial creativeness.[3] Both are open to judicial interpretation, but the latter more so than the former.

In order to gain insight into the development of judicially articulated rights, especially in light of the fact that the evolution of such rights is incrementally layered with precedent, it is necessary to peel away at the surface of judicial circumlocutions and confront the central elements of judicial thinking. At the center we find the teachings of Roscoe Pound. Pound's scholarship provided his contemporaries with strategy and tactics for innovative jurisprudence, while correspondingly providing contemporary analysts with a source that discloses the intellectual ideas that fueled key aspects of twentieth-century constitutional development.

II

Tracing the Court's expanded role in public policy-making, Edward Corwin identified the 1890s as the beginning of the second generation under the Constitution.[4] His pronouncement should not be taken lightly. In the course of this formative period the impact of judicial review on American politics was accelerated as a consequence of national and state legislatures' attempts at economic regulation. This legislative activity spurred the Court's "second-generation" entry into the public policy area of rights, insofar that the right to property was the hammer used to disassemble much of the legislative economic regulation. The property question was brought to the fore by tensions between the laissez-faire theory of government and populists' attempts to regulate an increasingly monopolistic industrialized economy. This in turn raised the collateral fundamental questions about the nature of American federalism. Because the U.S. Supreme Court had the practical problem of maintaining its status in a constitutional framework that deprecates overt judicial lawmaking at the expense of popular control, national and state, the judicial rejection of the economic regulations usually involved a selectively strict interpretation of the Fifth and Fourteenth Amendments' due process clauses, selective in the sense that the Court failed in many instances to balance the right to property with the states' Tenth Amendment police powers to promote the health, safety, morals, and general welfare of their respective peoples.[5]

The Court's judicial veto of state legislation on the grounds of substantive due process hinged on a nationalistic interpretation of the Fourteenth Amendment in the attempt to substitute state diversity with national conformity. The relevant Fourteenth Amendment constraints are "No State shall make or enforce any law which shall abridge the privileges or immunities of citizens of the United States; nor shall any State deprive any person of life, liberty, or property, without due process of law; nor deny to any person within its jurisdiction the equal protection of the laws." Close textual analysis manifests that the prohibition against abridging privileges or immunities is absolute, abridging life, liberty, and property is qualified in that these rights may be abridged as a consequence of due process of law, and denying equal protection of the laws is prohibited if the denial is directed at individuals inside the state's jurisdiction. These are important qualifications. For example, if the right to control a privately owned monopoly is deemed a privilege or immunity, it would be granted greater protection than a right subject to due process or jurisdictional constraints (see chapter 2 *supra*).

At the hands of conservative chief justices—Fuller (1888-1910), White (1910-21), and Taft (1921-30)—constitutional construction was utilized to obstruct legislative responses to pressing economic and social problems.[6] As the U.S. Supreme Court Justices engaged in interpretative debates about inserting into the Fourteenth Amendment proprietarian substantive due process, influential academics engaged in dialogue with a somewhat different orientation. An important precedent had been established; the U.S. Supreme Court could either obstruct or advance public policy with virtual impunity. Although for the most part the academicians substantively disagreed with the Court's emphasis on proprietarian substantive due process, they observed with great interest how the Court had converted the Constitution into an obstacle to popular control. Conversely, the judicial system could also be effectively utilized in the advancement of policy reforms, with or without popular control. By the 1920s there was significant consensus that the debate needed to be reformulated. Instead of asking what was constitutionally permissible, much of the scholarship stressed what was socially and therefore politically imperative and how judicial review could be utilized to address what were believed to be pressing public policy challenges. There was mounting pressure for change. According to Roscoe Pound, "There are two ways in which the courts impede or thwart social legislation demanded by the industrial conditions of today. The first is narrow and illiberal construction of constitutional provisions, state and federal.... The second is a narrow and illiberal attitude toward legislation conceded to be constitutional, regarding it as out of place in the legal system, as an alien element to be held down to the strictest limits and not to be applied beyond the requirements of its expressed language."[7] Consider Louis D. Brandeis's supportive call for a "judicial awakening to the facts of life":

> Courts continued to ignore newly arisen social needs. They applied complacently 18th Century conceptions of the liberty of the individual and of the sacredness of private property.... Where statutes giving expression to the new social spirit were clearly constitutional, judges, imbued with the relentless spirit of individualism, often construed them away...law everywhere has the tendency to lag behind the facts of life. But in America the strain became dangerous; because constitutional limitations were invoked to stop the natural vent of legislation.... In the course of relatively few years hundreds of statutes which embodied attempts (often very crude) to adjust legal rights to the demands of social justice were nullified by the courts, on grounds that the statutes violated the constitutional guaranties of liberty and property.[8]

The process of ameliorating the tensions between what is constitutionally permissible as opposed to what is socially, economically, and politically necessary was descriptively characterized as creative jurisprudence. Indeed, there are differences between the various schools of thought regarding the form and extent creative jurisprudence should take; but their differences should not cloud their common ground. Concisely stated, *creative jurisprudence* combines the arts of the legislator, theologian, philosopher, and social reformer, all culminating in judges, in order to make the courts "efficient instruments of justice."[9]

III

Pound called for a new judicial creed to replace what he considered to be the obsolete and inefficient jurisprudence of the past. He categorized jurisprudence into three schools: the historical, analytical, and philosophical. The philosophical school held the keys to a brighter future: "Today we are seeing the beginning of a reaction from the juristic pessimism of the historical school and the juristic inertia of the later generations of the analytical school.... The pressure of new and unsecured interests, of new and insistent human claims, is compelling us to revise our juristic creeds."[10] This revision was to be grounded in what Pound referred to as "A Theory of Social Interests." The courts were encouraged to assume a pivotal role in the "machinery of social control or social engineering...consciously and avowedly as befits the science of today."[11]

Pound ranked the criteria for his new judicial methodology. First, general security is paramount: "In its simplest form it is an interest in the general safety, long recognized by the legal order in the maxim that the safety of the people is the highest law."[12] Second, social institutions must be protected, such as marriage, religious institutions, and political institutions.[13] Third, general morals must be secured: The "demand of society to be secured against acts or courses of conduct offensive to the moral sentiments of the general body of individuals therein for the time being."[14] Fourth, "the social interest in the conservation of social resources...in view of the infinite individual desires and limited natural means of satisfying them, the latter must be made to go as far as possible."[15] Fifth, the courts should take cognizance of the social interest in general progress and the necessity "that social engineering be increasingly and continually improved."[16] In order for judicial social engineering to successfully advance the social interest, judges must emphasize economic, political, and cultural progress, and not be obstructed by incompatible provisions of the Constitution.[17]

The sixth and last social interest recognized by Pound is, for our purposes, the most important. What was true for Pound in 1920 is even more significant for the 1990s. It is the social interest in individual life. This criterion directs the judge to balance the interest of the individual against that of society. If the individual's self-defined interests run counter to society's, and society opts to curtail the liberty of the individual, it must do so nonarbitrarily and reasonably: "If one will is to be subjected to the will of another through the force of politically organized society, it is not to be done arbitrarily but upon some rational basis which the person coerced, if reasonable, could appreciate—upon a reasoned weighing of the interests involved and a reasoned attempt to reconcile or to compromise them."[18] The preceding five criteria are all subject to the qualification that the individual has been mistreated or, to use Pound's own word, repressed. The prohibition of repression did not emanate from a commitment to natural rights, but on "what modern psychology has discovered to be the ill effects of repression."[19] Repression of the individual is unacceptable because it is in the social interest to safeguard the interest of the individual. In other words, "there is the social interest in individual life."[20] According to Pound's new judicial creed, individuals' interests are the social interest, but the former are not to be defined by society through popular control of public policy; they are to be defined—or more precisely, engineered—by the Court.

IV

Within the context of Pound's judicial creed, national and state constitutions were to be functional instruments for judges and justices as they secured social interests from the bench. Constitutional construction would be adjusted to the situation, not being locked into either a loose, strict, interpretive, or non-interpretive reading of those documents. Pound called this engineering interpretation:

> [I]nstead of these I venture an engineering interpretation. I venture to think of problems of eliminating friction and precluding waste in human enjoyment of the goods of existence and of the legal order as a system of social engineering whereby those ends are achieved. If we think of it this way we shall not fail to see that no legal institution or legal doctrine may stand fast forever as the final thing in juristic achievement any more than the products of mechanical ingenuity and engineering skill may stand for all time as the ultimate of which man is capable. New wants and new forms of old wants speedily make the best products of social engineering...and to study how the existing social and legal machinery may be improved or new machinery may be devised whereby to obviate the friction, preclude the waste, and insure the best social engineering of which in the time and place we are capable.[21]

Pound's legal positivism may appear to be countered by higher law and the English Common Law doctrines. But not according to Pound. The more interpretive models available, the greater the ease judges and justices could adjust the law to the immediate situation. All models of constitutional interpretation contributed to creative jurisprudence; they are the materials through which "engineering interpretation" constructs and reconstructs American constitutionalism.

A case in point, the leading spokesman for higher law based judicial activism was Edward S. Corwin.[22] With antiquity as his starting point, Corwin identified higher law as "one of the really great humanizing forces of history" and having a critical relationship to the American system of government.[23] Its relationship is fourfold: First, the Constitution embodies "the essential and unchanging justice" of higher law; significantly, it is the embodiment of higher law that gives legitimacy to the Constitution, and not the Constitution that gives legitimacy to higher law. According to Corwin:

> The Ninth Amendment...illustrates this theory perfectly except that the principles of transcendental justice have been here translated into terms of personal and private rights. The relation of such rights, nevertheless, to governmental power is the same as that of the principles from which they spring and which they reflect. They owe nothing to their recognition in the Constitution—such recognition was necessary if the Constitution was to be regarded as complete.... Thus the *legality* of the Constitution, its *supremacy*, and its claim to be worshipped, alike find common standing on the belief in a law superior to the will of human governors.[24]

Second, higher law's authority over human affairs is neither dependent on nor changeable by popular will. "There are, it is predicated, certain principles of right and justice which are entitled to prevail of their own intrinsic excellence."[25] Noncompliance with higher law results in injustice. Third, the principles of higher law determine what just governments may and may not do. These principles are stated only in general terms, but have a far-reaching impact. Corwin maintains that "for the history of American constitutional law and theory no part of *Magna Carta* can compare in importance with chapter twenty-nine."[26] Continuity between thirteenth-century English higher law and American constitutionalism is manifest in the fundamental propositions of American constitutional law that "*law must be general; it must afford equal protection to all; it may not validly operate retroactively; it must be enforced through the courts—legislative power does not include judicial power.*"[27] Fourth, these and attendant principles are knowable through custom and reason. Custom and reason combined result in common law. Only the courts, through the prerogative of judicial review, are competent to explicate, apply, and preserve higher law in the commotion of political affairs. In other words, Corwin was rationalizing judicial supremacy:

> The right reason which lies at the basis of the common law, on the other hand, was from the beginning *judicial* right reason. Considered as an act of knowledge or discovery, the common law was the act of experts, and increasingly so, with the ever firmer establishment of the doctrine of *stare decisis*.[28]

On the heels of the just-quoted passage Corwin, in a revealing paragraph, mentions Pound's complaint that jurisprudence constrained by higher law/common law precludes "creative activity of men as lawyers, judges, writers of books, or legislators."[29] In other words, it obstructs the social engineering Pound advocated. Corwin's response to Pound's criticism is not what one might anticipate, which is that Pound's legal positivism is the antithesis of transcendental justice. Rather, Corwin's conciliatory response is that the corpus of common law is the work of individuals spanning hundreds of years. Corwin reiterates that the "reasonableness" of a law is the most accurate measure of its justness; and the most reliable way to determine a law's reasonableness is to use the collective wisdom of judges embodied in *stare decisis*. Expounders of common law stipulate that "the Common Law is the perfect ideal of law; for it is natural reason developed and expounded by a collective wisdom of many generations.... Based on long usage and almost supernatural wisdom.... The common law is the absolute perfection of reason."[30] Considered in its totality common law is a series of creative activities, amenable to useful modification through the labors of judicial commentators and judges, as the history of common law from *Magna Carta* to Blackstone makes manifest.[31]

V

In a descriptive 1926 article Charles Warren tracks "the progress we have made from the principles of government believed in by the framers of the Constitution."[32] Identifying *Gitlow* v. *New York*[33] soon after it was decided as the watershed case for Fourteenth Amendment selective incorporation, Warren claimed that "owing to the existence of the Due Process Clause of the Fourteenth Amendment, and to the *constantly expanding interpretation* which the Court has given to the language of that Clause, the general public has now acquired the habit of assuming that practically every new State statute is to be submitted to final test before that Court."[34] The "constantly expanding interpretation" referred to by Warren is easily documented, with *Gitlow* providing an "illuminating example of the manner in which our constitutional law grows."[35] When considered objectively the constitutional law that emanates from selective incorporation has dubious origins, such as dissenting opinions, dicta, and political agendas. Warren understood the significance of the *Gitlow* decision:

> [F]or over fifty years, counsel had, time and again, attempted to get the Court to hold that rights similar to the right of freedom of speech were protected by the Fourteenth Amendment against infringement by State legislation, and that in every instance the Court had declined to so hold. Yet, in this *Gitlow* case, without even mentioning these previous cases, the Court assumes, without argument, that this right of free speech is so protected by the Fourteenth Amendment.... The history of the attempt to secure Federal guarantee and protection of rights arising simply under State Constitutions and State laws has been a long one; and this most recent development in its course may well awaken serious thought as to whether there is not danger now that the "liberty" of the States is being unduly sacrificed to this new conception of the "liberty" of the individual.[36]

According to Warren's account, *Gitlow* is exemplary of creative jurisprudence for two reasons; first, the Court was innovative in breaking down precedent that blocked the desired outcome, and second, the Court's elevation of nationally protected individual liberty at the expense of the states' police powers. Warren anticipated the subsequent diminished roles the states would have in the judicial expansion of fundamental rights, especially when rights are deemed privileges and immunities. "A State is forbidden absolutely and without limitation, to make or enforce a law abridging a privilege or immunity. It is not forbidden to deprive a person of a right of liberty or property, provided it deprives him by due process of law."[37] Hence, Warren not only realized that the privileges and immunities guarantees are potentially potent weapons in the arsenal of judicial activism, but also anticipated that this variety of activism was disrespectful of precedent and aimed at subverting traditional federalism.

VI

In a 1923 address to the New York City Bar Association Pound delivered a descriptive and prescriptive theory of jurisprudence that rationalized the expanded role of the judiciary implicit in *Gitlow*.[38] According to Pound's theory the U.S. Supreme Court (contra precedent and the concerns of contemporary commentators such as Warren) can behave rationally and responsibly when obviously contradicting previous decisions. Consider Pound's explication of standard judicial procedure for appellate courts: "Supposing the facts to have been ascertained, decision of a controversy according to law involves (1) selection of the legal material on which to ground the decision, or as we commonly say, finding the law; (2) development of the grounds of decision from the material selected, or interpretation in the stricter sense of that term; (3)

application of the abstract grounds of decision to the facts of the case."[39] These rules of procedure are carryovers from nineteenth-century juristic theory that resulted in the "mechanical application of authoritatively given precepts."[40] However, the mechanical application of precedent—what he referred to as mechanical jurisprudence—was too constraining and no longer accommodated unfolding public policy exigencies.[41] Breaking out of the mechanical mold, Pound advocated combining (1) and (2) in order to achieve the desired results, thereby permitting the judge to convert existing rules into new rules. As indicated in (2), when the judge is developing the grounds for decision, the utilization of "interpretation in the stricter sense of that term" provides the judge with flexibility to remold the law into new precedent. If a particular case does not serve as a reasonable vehicle for such transitions within the legal system (i.e., converting existing precedent into new precedent), then the judge is encouraged to go outside the legal system "in whole or in part" and use custom, comparative law, morals, and/or economics to construct new precedent.[42] To successfully construct new precedent the judge must be intuitive; and when the judge's intuitive powers are effectively implemented, thereby creating new precedent from extra-legal sources, then the judge has been creative, indeed.[43]

Pound acknowledged that judges cannot strike out on their own and create new precedent without risking a political backlash. Teachers and lawyers (collectively called jurists by Pound) must present the idealized end of law and provide the rationalization for those ends. The rationalization to be utilized by jurists includes several important items: (1) Social engineering is an important part of social control; (2) Distinctions within the legal field should be made between mechanical and intuitive application of the law; (3) Generalized social claims should be given as much effect as possible, while portraying a balance between "decision of the actual cause and the elaboration of a precedent"; and, most important; (4) Induce into the decision making of judges a consciousness of the ideal social and legal orders. In reference to (4), Pound cautions that it is important that judges' personal ideals do not deviate too far from the public's ideals, that is, the ideals of the majority. Judges must engage in "searching examination" to ensure that their social engineering does not exceed the limitations of what the public will accept. As long as they have the appearance of legitimacy and thereby maintain the support of the public, the judges can act with "assurance."[44]

VII

As important as the support of teachers and lawyers is to the legitimacy of judicial social engineering, it is the judges who must function as the vanguard, pushing society toward the ideal. Pound gave credit where credit was due:

> Our theory of judicial technique belongs to a stage of legal development that antedates the weapons of the judicial armory of today. On the whole, the judges have done their part better than the jurists and the teachers. They have pushed forward cautiously but on the whole with reasonable speed along paths worked out by judicial empiricism, while those who should have rationalized the forward movement and furnished ideal plans of the forward path have urged pseudo-scientific reasons why they should stand fast, and have preached that progress would spontaneously achieve itself.... I repeat, on the whole judges have been doing their part well.[45]

The agenda is quite clear; teachers, lawyers, and judges were encouraged to create an environment from which judicial social engineering could take root and grow.

Toward that end, it is the responsibility of the political branches to secure positions on the court for jurists with the appropriate judicial temperament, that is the willingness to engage in social engineering, because only the justices themselves are uniquely positioned to push the reforms forward.[46] According to Pound, the historical separation of powers (through which the legislature makes law, the executive enforces law, and the judiciary interprets law) has failed and by the 1920s essentially functioned as a dogmatic fiction.[47] This does not mean that the fiction of separation of powers is unimportant. To the contrary; the fiction serves "to hold down the personality of the magistrate" and to constrain the judge to act reasonably and predictably, and thereby maintain legitimacy.[48] Legitimacy is maintained if the judge functions under the guise of separation of powers and, significantly, his judicial actions are practically sound. Pound recognized the limitations "imposed upon judicial creative activity" and urged judges to be sagacious as functional agents of progress.[49]

VIII

The significance of Pound's jurisprudence cannot be fully appreciated until the content of his writings is contrasted with what it excludes.

The overriding omission is the traditional U.S. Constitution. For Pound, the issue is not strict versus loose construction, but rather strict construction versus disingenuous construction. This does not mean that for Pound the Constitution is unimportant; rather, its importance is due to its serving as the vehicle for social engineering. In other words, it provides the mechanisms of control that can result in effective social engineering, and will result in effective social engineering when judges free themselves from the obsolete constraints of the strict construction that undoubtedly obstructs their creative ambitions. This includes jettisoning federalism, a bona fide institutional separation of powers, constitutional limitations on governmental powers (national and state), and bypassing popular control when its agenda is not amenable to the policy preferences of the social engineers.

Pound also cautioned against legal realism becoming the dominant influence charting the future course of juridical development in America. He was concerned that the behaviorism that had made gains in the social sciences would detract from the creative energies of the justices: "It is conceived that observation of the phenomena of administration of justice, carried on objectively and scientifically, may give us formulas as rigidly exact and free from any personal or subjective element, either in formulation or application, as, for example, those employed by the engineer. It is argued that the only objectively valid phenomena are those discoverable by statistical investigation of the operations of judicial institutions, and the only valid method is a formulation of exact propositions on the basis thus afforded."[50] Even if it were possible, such a "science of law" was unacceptable, due to the fact that it precludes a theory of values: "Those who long for an exact science analogous to mathematics or physics or astronomy have been inclined to seek exactness by excluding this (theory of values) hard problem from jurisprudence altogether. But such a jurisprudence has only an illusion of reality. For the significant question is the one excluded."[51] Pound's rejection of a judicial behaviorism was only partial, in the sense that the behaviorists' research findings could and should be used to inform judges:

> A recognition that there are many approaches to juristic truth and that each is significant with respect to particular problems of the legal order; hence a valuing of these approaches, not absolutely or reference to some one assumed necessary psychological or philosophical basis of jurisprudence, but with reference to how far they aid law maker, or judge, or jurist in making law and the science of law

effective, the one toward the maintaining, furthering, and transmitting of civilization, the other toward organizing the materials and laying out the course of the legal order.[52]

Pound was quite determined in his attempt to steer juridical development away from the *illusion-ridden jurists of the past* and the behaviorists of the future.[53] Creative jurisprudence was the most reliable way to implement social engineering, and historical and scientific methodologies were to be used as necessary means to the judicial social engineers' extraconstitutional policy objectives. Pound's sociopolitical jurisprudence and Llewellyn's legal realism adhered to the view that law is not static and should be juristically adapted to changing economic and social conditions. In Pound's mind the primary difference between the two schools is that the legal realists dismissed values, without realizing that the very attempt at such a dismissal is value laden.[54]

IX

It is one thing to advocate social reforms from the halls of academe and quite another to exert official influence. But Pound's ideas did have consequences and there is sufficient evidence that members of the nation's highest court were in concurrence with his vision of what the appropriate role of the justices should be. With that shared vision in mind, some justices assumed the roles of social engineers, willing and able to legislate from the bench. The debate about judicial lawmaking has been ongoing and it hardly seems worth repeating here.[55] However, what does merit our attention is not so much the question "Do justices legislate from the bench?" but rather, "In what manner and to what extent do they legislate from the bench?" Addressing the second question provides us with an understanding of the Poundian creative jurisprudence behind judicial behavior, and with that understanding we can better appreciate and anticipate future developments in the area of unenumerated rights.

By the late 1930s the U.S. Supreme Court's jurisprudence was markedly redirected away from substantive due process via judicial interference with legislative regulation over commerce, and toward judicial scrutiny over legislative policy over what the court considered to be fundamental rights.[56] The public notification of the "interstitial" redirection was provided by Justice Stone in *United States* v. *Carolene Prod-*

ucts Company. The case involves the constitutionality of a congressional statute that prohibited the interstate shipment of adulterated milk. The Court upheld the statute on the grounds that "Congress is free to exclude from interstate commerce articles whose use in the states for which they are destined it may reasonably conceive to be injurious to the public health, morals or welfare."[57] The court stipulated that "regulatory legislation affecting ordinary commercial transactions is not to be pronounced unconstitutional unless in light of the facts made known or generally assumed it is of such a character as to preclude the assumption that it rests upon some rational basis within the knowledge and experience of the legislators."[58] However, the "rational basis test" for regulatory policy is not applicable to legislation challenged on the grounds of fundamental rights, thereby implying that property rights are less than fundamental. The last quotation *supra,* ends with Justice Stone's famous footnote number four:

> There may be narrower scope for operation of the presumption of constitutionality when legislation appears on its face to be within a specific prohibition of the Constitution, such as those of the first ten amendments, which are deemed equally specific when held to be embraced within the Fourteenth.... Nor need we enquire whether similar considerations enter into the review of statutes directed at particular religions, or national, or racial minorities, whether prejudice against discrete and insular minorities may be a special condition, which tends seriously to curtail the operation of those political processes ordinarily to be relied upon to protect minorities, which may call for a correspondingly more searching judicial inquiry.[59]

Abraham surmises that "Stone's Footnote Four probably evolved from the celebrated Cardozo opinion delivered a few months earlier in *Palko v. Connecticut*."[60] In *Palko* Cardozo introduced the judicial standard of "ordered liberty," which he defined as "principles so rooted in the traditions and conscience of our people as to be ranked as fundamental."[61] *Carolene* and *Palko* mark the new emphasis on what the Court deems as fundamental rights. As New Deal legislative economic regulatory policy had been given the imprimatur of the Court—the switch in time that saved nine—the Supreme Court recognized the national legislature, for all intents and purposes, as the designated branch responsible for economic public policy. Meanwhile, the Court, through its "more searching judicial inquiry," was fulfilling the Poundian ideal of creative jurisprudence in the public policy area of fundamental rights.

X

Once again, this type of creative jurisprudence had to be done with circumspection. Justice Holmes conceded that judges do legislate, but must do so interstitially in order to maintain the integrity of the judicial process.[62] To reiterate, Holmes's qualification stemmed from the political culture within which the U.S. Supreme Court operates. The Court's success in maintaining the appearance of deferring to constitutional popular control and thereby manipulating popular consent is attributable to the utilization of the spatial and temporal dimensions of precedent. For example, the spatial dimension can emanate from the *dictum* of a case; at the time the case is decided the *dictum* does not alter the current *stare decisis,* but may stand apart from the actual holding of the case with the potential to subsequently alter precedent, thereby extending outward for future utilization by later judges. Thus, the temporal dimension comes into play. In the hands of the creative judge, time is used to convert the previous *dictum* as integral to an evolving precedent, thereby facilitating the reformulation of constitutional law by linking the jurisprudence of creative judges from the past with the creative jurisprudence of contemporary judges. According to Justice Cardozo, "The emergent evolution of a formula into a precept is determined by its dimensions, spatial and temporal. To put the thought in other words: Considerations of space and time affect the capacity of the formula to shape the law thereafter.... We misread history in a most unrealistic fashion if we say that the seeds of generations of later judgments were not in Gibbons v. Ogden and McCulloch v. Maryland."[63]

Justice Cardozo realized that Chief Justice Marshall's enduring influence (and for that matter the influence of other justices who applied similar juridical skills) is due in large measure to the discretionary latitude embodied in the *dicta* he made available to his judicial progeny. This does not mean that Marshall was effective because he established binding precedent for subsequent judges. To the contrary; his effectiveness is attributable to the nonbinding nature of his precedent mixed with *dicta* and its ongoing usefulness. Cardozo revealed his version of creative jurisprudence when he cautioned that "the judicial method of the future must see to it that judicial inventiveness shall not be desiccated or stunted, that generalization shall be free and bold as in the past, perhaps freer and bolder. Unless it can accomplish this, it is headed toward disaster. What is to be changed, if anything, is the capacity of the generalized principle, the *ratio decidendi,* to reproduce in its own image, to reproduce without restraint. Its generative power must depend upon the quality of its progeny. Like the hypotheses of science it is to be judged by its results. There must be a new system of eugenics for the pullulating[64] precedents."[65]

XI

The appeal of creative jurisprudence is attributable to its usefulness in conforming constitutional law to economic, social, and political contingencies while simultaneously effecting uniformity of law within the context of a constitutional framework. Because the juridical community (members from the bench, bar, and academe) is exclusive and hierarchical, diversity of views within the community itself is formulated into uniformity by the nature of the judicial process, a process with the U.S. Supreme Court at its apex. Once again Pound is instructive.

According to Pound the social interests—in another context referred to as the general welfare—requires the advancement of civilization, without which a backward slide is not to be avoided. This is serious and difficult work, requiring the participation of philosophers, political scientists, and sociologists. Through its engagement in social engineering the judiciary is responsible for facilitating the realization of social interests. The judiciary, due to its privileged relationship with law, is in a unique position to exert effective and just control over individuals. This was not always the case. Traditional institutions such as the family and religious and private associations, but especially religion, exercised social control. But these institutions have broken down to the point where they have lost their effectiveness in securing the social interests. For example, Pound concluded that "whatever hold religion may still have, religious organizations have lost their power over the mass of mankind. Social control has been all but secularized.... Since the Sixteenth Century political organization of society has become paramount. It has, or claims to have and on the whole maintains, a monopoly of force. All other agencies of social control are held to exercise disciplinary authority subject to the law and within bounds fixed by law.... Today social control is primarily the function of the state and is exercised through law."[66] In other words, the demands on government have been heightened and if government falls short of its responsibilities, civilization will decline. Other traditional institutions, such as the family and church, are no longer available to pick up the slack.

But the laws produced by politically organized society, even those the product of popular sovereignty, are not competent to equitably address the problems of industrialized society:

> We are properly dissatisfied with the picture of the self-sufficient individual in an economically self-sufficient neighborhood and freely competing with his neighbors in an economic order based on free competitive acquisition. This ideal governed in the last century and was easily adapted to a pioneer, rural, agricultural society. We know very well that it is not a true picture of the society of today.... Hence the solution of new legal problems is very much at large. The force of politically organized society is left to itself. With no authoritative ideal to guide it, exercise of that force becomes a matter of individual wish and prejudice and predisposition—the very things law seeks to repress. A regime of force tries to do the work of a regime of law.[67]

Laws based upon force (or more specifically laws designed to promote the interests of one set of factions to the detriment of political rivals), must be substituted with laws based upon reason. The only reliable way of procuring rational laws is for the judiciary to exercise judicial review toward that end. "Civilization rests upon the putting down of arbitrary, willful self-assertion and the substitution of reason." According to Pound, history provides the evidence that the judiciary is the most qualified for the task to effectively "maintain, further, and transmit civilization." Concurring with Corwin, Pound maintains that the Ninth Amendment is instrumental in the Court's attempt to sustain progress.

Pound's most direct commentary on the Ninth Amendment is in his 1955 introduction to Patterson's *The Forgotten Ninth Amendment.*[68] In no uncertain terms, Pound identifies the ideal role for the Ninth Amendment to be a key instrument in utilizing social engineering in the promotion of social interests. The elevation of the Ninth Amendment to its proper function in American jurisprudence has five steps. First, the Ninth Amendment embodies natural law and natural rights. Second, the natural law and rights are not static, but relative to the "contemporary" conceptions of justice. Third, the contemporary conceptions of justice are derived from the ideal relations among men according to "conditions and circumstances of life in civilized society." Fourth, natural law and rights are not to be "relegated to a lumber room of outworn juristic or political ideas." Fifth, the "task" is to make natural law and rights effective "political and legal instruments in the society of today."[69] Pound was advocating what he referred to as a "natural law with a growing content."[70] The growing content facilitates natural law and natural rights adjustments to changing socioeconomic conditions, from which its instrumentality flows.

He conceded that "*if* the Ninth Amendment is to be read with the Tenth," the states may determine the content of Ninth Amendment rights, or the "people of the whole land" may make such determinations "by constitutional change, as was done, for example, by the Fourteenth Amendment."[71] Whether the national or state governments (judiciaries included) shall determine the content of Ninth Amendment unenumerated rights hinges on questions of necessity and interpretation. Are not the Ninth and Tenth Amendments challenges to the states "to undertake that work as the conditions of American life today may demand it"?[72] If the states fail to effectively meet the challenge, Ninth Amendment rights need not be violated. He approvingly cited the devolution of the Second Amendment as precedence for constitutional provisions taking on new meaning in response to changed circumstances.[73] After approvingly acknowledging the "altered significance of the right to bear arms" (Second Amendment) due to the changed conditions of military operations, Pound noted the qualified status of the Ninth Amendment:

> Shall we not say that the Ninth Amendment is the pronouncement of a solemn warning to the agencies of government that there are reasonable expectations of individual men living in civilized society which the people retain and for which recognition and security may be demanded? Though not set forth in terms in the Constitution, they *should* be borne in mind in the process of government. Where rights are defined and secured expressly by the Constitution, there is simply a question of interpretation. But where rights not declared in terms are "reserved" there is a question as to where is the power of defining them, and where is the power of securing them when defined. The Tenth Amendment *seems* to preclude definition and enforcement by the federal government except as committed to that government by the Constitution. It would *seem*, therefore, that these reserved rights *may* be defined and enforcement of them *may* be provided by the states, except as *may be precluded* by the Fourteenth Amendment, or *may* be defined and acquire secured enforcement by the people of the United States by constitutional amendment.[74]

The statement that the "Ninth Amendment is a solemn warning to the agencies of government" that the people may demand the recognition and security of rights not set forth in the Constitution indicates that the courts, through questions of interpretation, play an important role in determining the content of Ninth Amendment rights. Although the historical Tenth Amendment would preclude the nationalization of Ninth Amendment rights, creative interpretations of the Fourteenth Amendment trump the historical precedent. Criticizing jurists who too willingly deferred to the historical constitutional and political constraints of, among other provisions, the Ninth and Tenth Amendments, Pound maintained that "The world today moves too fast for such a program."[75]

XII

It would be difficult to persuasively deny that Roscoe Pound was a leading figure in American jurisprudence at such a critical juncture of its development.[76] Was he the leading light, the guru of justices who found their way onto to the Nation's highest courts? Considering the fact that American jurisprudence generated and continues to generate a corpus of constitutional law consistent with Pound's version of the proper function of judicial review, his writings, whether descriptive and/or prescriptive, provide insight into the modus operandi of the judiciary that is indispensable. As substantiated by the case analyses that follow *infra,* Poundian judicial social engineering has become a fundamental principle of the American regime.

Obviously, the linkage between Pound's scholarship and the development of American constitutional law is open to debate. Ronald Dworkin, for example, does not place much emphasis on Pound's influence, concluding that Pound's sociological jurisprudence "became the province of sociologists."[77] True enough, sociologists may have been interested in Pound's jurisprudence; however, if we are to account for the watershed developments of the early twentieth century, Pound cannot be dismissed as a curiosity for sociologists. In order to understand those developments there are three ways to read Pound: (1) Drawing from other disciplines and scholars (such as John Dewey) he applied what was then cutting-edge research methodologies from other areas to American jurisprudence, thereby articulating original ideas within his own field of study; (2) As events were unfolding, he wrote descriptively as a means to rationalize and promote developments already under way in American jurisprudence; And (3), in all probability Pound's scholarship was a combination of (1) and (2). Be that as it may, one point is quite clear; Pound's model articulated to a significant extent a merging of, among others, Corwin's natural law, Llewellyn's legal realism, and

Warren's nineteenth-century constitutionalism, and therefore goes a long way toward explaining twentieth-century constitutional development. This does not mean that the court's rationalizations for precedent-breaking decisions utilized neither natural law nor the Constitution; what it does mean is that emerging precedent was essential to judicial social engineering—a form of judicial activism that may be selectively grounded in the Constitution, but is definitely hostile to traditional popular control and utilizes the Constitution primarily as a mechanism for providing necessary legitimacy for judicial creativity. It is not coincidental that Dworkin's jurisprudence is essentially an affirmation of Pound's, while Bradford's is a repudiation of it.[78]

Notes

1. As a leading Progressive cautioned, "A clear popular understanding of the contents of the democratic principle is obviously of the upmost practical political importance to the American people. Their loyalty to the idea of democracy, as they understand it, cannot be questioned. Nothing of any considerable political importance is done or left undone in the United States, unless such action or inaction can be plausibly defended on democratic grounds" (Herbert Croly, *The Promise of American Life* [New York: The Macmillan Company, 1911], 176).
2. I use the qualification "supposedly" due to the fact that I am not convinced that legal practitioners and academics are sufficiently competent to engage in a "science" of rights, with the same level of expertise as investigators in other subject areas, such as physics and biology. See Yves R. Simon, *The Tradition of Natural Law: A Philosopher's Reflection* (New York: Fordham University Press, 1992).
3. In 1890 Louis Brandeis and Samuel Warren co-authored and article that begins with the statement: "That the individual shall have full protection in person and in property is a principle as old as the common law; but it has been found necessary from time to time to define anew the exact nature and extent of such protection. Political, social, and economic changes entail the recognition of new rights, and the common law, in its eternal youth, grows to meet the demands of society" ("The Right to Privacy," *Harvard Law Review*, vol. IV, no. 5. [15 December 1890], 193). In this article they, borrowing the phrase from Judge Cooley, endorse "the right to be let alone" (ibid., 195). Notably, the rate and extent of common law growth is the responsibility of the Courts.
4. "The fact of the matter is that judicial review as exercised by the United States Supreme Court did not become an important factor of national legislative power till about 1890, and to a lesser degree this is so even as to state legislative power. And in both instances the augmentation of the Court's role was the outgrowth of its acceptance of the *laissez-faire* theory of governmental function" (Edward S. Corwin, *Constitutional Revolution, Ltd.* [Claremont, Calif.: Claremont College, 1946], 10).
5. "The chief concern of this long era was to guard the sanctity of property. Socio-economic experimentation by the legislatures, such as minimum-wage, maximum-hour, and child-labor regulations, was regarded with almost unshakable disapproval

by a solid majority of the Court. Again and again the justices struck down, as unconstitutional violations of *substantive* due process of law, legislation that large majorities on both the state and national levels deemed wise and necessary. They reasoned that because the *substance*...of the legislation involved...such statutory experimentations deprived 'persons' (i.e., property owners, chiefly businessmen) of their liberty and property without due process of law" (Henry J. Abraham, *Freedom And The Court: Civil Liberties and Rights in the United States* [New York: Oxford University Press, 1988], 12, citations omitted).

6. Ibid., 12.
7. Roscoe Pound, "Common Law and Legislation," *Harvard Law Review*, vol. XXI, no. 6 (April 1908), 385.
8. Louis D. Brandies, "The Living Law," *Illinois Law Review*, vol. X, no. 7 (February 1916), 465, 464. Brandeis practiced what he preached. For example, in *Muller* v. *Oregon* (1908) he presented a brief on behalf of the defense, in which approximately two pages addressed legal precedent whereas over a hundred were devoted to sociological jurisprudence. See Muller v. Oregon, 208 U.S. 412.
9. Brandies, "The Living Law," 468.
10. Roscoe Pound, *Law and Morals* (Chapel Hill: The University of North Carolina Press, 1926), 82. Even among those whose jurisprudence Pound criticized, he was recognized as a leading legal authority during this critical period of juridical development. In the words of Karl N. Llewellyn, "When Dean Pound speaks on jurisprudence, men listen. The profession has too long relied on him to discover, read, digest, classify and report on jurists foreign and ancient not to rely again when he speaks of would-be jurists modern and at home" ("Some Realism About Realism-Responding to Dean Pound," *Harvard Law Review*, vol. 44, [1931], 1222, 1225); and "American jurisprudence will ever be indebted to Roscoe Pound. In the service of quickening our legal institutions and making the law effective for the task of wise social engineering, he has combined profound insight, vast legal erudition, thorough acquaintance with the work of early and contemporary legal philosophers in England and the Continent, and a wide knowledge of the social sciences" (Jerome Frank, *Law and the Modern Mind* [Garden City, N.Y.: Anchor Books, 1930, 1963 ed.], 221). For biographical accounts of Pound's career see Paul Sayre's *The Life of Roscoe Pound* (Iowa City, Iowa: State University of Iowa, 1948) and David Wigdor's *Roscoe Pound: Philosopher of the Law* (Westport, Conn.: Greenwood Press, 1974).
11. Pound, "A Theory of Social Interests." Papers and Proceedings, Fifteenth Annual Meeting, American Sociological Society, vol. XV (1920), 32–33.
12. Ibid., 33.
13. Ibid., 36–37.
14. Ibid., 37.
15. Ibid., 38.
16. Ibid., 39.
17. In Pound's juristic context, the concept "social engineering" should be taken at its face value; it is sociopolitical control through law judicially formulated and reformulated.
18. Pound, "A Theory of Social Interests," 42. Pound refers us to Stammler's fundamental principles of just law: "(1) One must not be subject to the arbitrary will of another; (2) Every legal demand can exist only in the sense that the person obliged can also exist as a fellow-creature; (3) No one is to be excluded from the common interest arbitrarily; (4) Every power of control conferred by law can be justified

only in the sense that the individual subject thereto can yet exist as a fellow-creature" (ibid., 41-41).

19. Ibid., 42.
20. Ibid., 41.
21. Ibid., 44–45.
22. As was the case with Pound and others, it is not my primary purpose to critique Corwin's ideology, but to summarize it and delineate its influence in American jurisprudence. Nevertheless, it should be noted that these theories are open to critical review; but that has been reserved for chapters 7 and 8.
23. Edward S. Corwin, *The "Higher Law" Background of American Constitutional Law* (Cornell University Press, Fourth Printing, 1961), 7. *Higher Law* was first published in the *Harvard Law Review*, 1928. Take note of the title's "Constitutional Law" as opposed to "U.S. Constitution"; Obviously the former is a product of judicial review, much more so than the latter.
24. Ibid., 5.
25. Ibid., 4.
26. Ibid., 31. Chapter 29 reads: "No free man shall be taken or imprisoned or deprived of his freehold or of his liberties or free customs, or outlawed, or exiled, or in any manner destroyed, nor shall we go upon him, nor shall we send upon him, except by a legal judgment of his peers or by the law of the land" (ibid., 32).
27. Ibid., 68; (italics in original).
28. Ibid., 26.
29. Ibid.
30. Corwin quoting Father Figgis, ibid., 34–35.
31. Ibid., 26–27.
32. Charles Warren, "The New Liberty Under The 14th Amendment," *Harvard Law Review*, vol. 39 (1925-26), 431; also consider Warren's *The Supreme Court in United States History, 1836-1918*, 2 vols. (Boston: Little, Brown, and Company, 1926).
33. 268 U.S. 652 (1925). The case called into question the constitutionality of The New York Criminal Anarchy Statute (1902); the statute's material provisions are summarized on pages 654–55 (ibid.). The court majority upheld Gitlow's conviction on the grounds that the statute is not an arbitrary or unreasonable exercise of the state's police power (ibid., 670). Nevertheless, the court concluded that for "present purposes we may and do assume that freedom of speech and of the press—which are protected by the 1st Amendment from abridgment by Congress—are among the fundamental personal rights and liberties protected by the due process clause of the 14th Amendment from impairment by the states" (ibid., 666). Justice Holmes and Brandeis agreed with the incorporation portion of the majority's opinion, but dissented on the grounds that Gitlow's activities did not pose a "clear and present danger" to society and thereby maintained that Gitlow's conviction should be overturned (ibid., 672–73).
34. Warren, "The New Liberty Under the 14th Amendment," 431 (italics not in original).
35. Ibid., 432.
36. Ibid., 433. Within the first quarter of the twentieth century the Court altered its jurisprudence on First Amendment speech rights substantially. "In 1907, the Court expressly left the question undecided; in 1920, it stated that it did not consider it or decide it, but simply conceded it for purposes of the case; in 1922, it stated that the Federal Constitution 'imposes upon the States no obligation to confer upon

those within their jurisdiction either the right of free speech or the right of silence.' Yet, in 1925, it stated that 'we may and do assume' that freedom of speech and of the press is one of the 'fundamental personal rights and liberties' protected by the Due Process Clause. And hence, in 1925, the Court adopted as the law the dissenting opinions of Judge Harlan in 1907, and Judge Brandeis in 1920" (ibid., 458).

37. Ibid., 463.
38. He stated: "We must urge upon judges that in their law-declaring function they are indeed lawmakers with the responsibilities for wise social engineering that rests upon all lawmakers" ("The Theory of Judicial Decision: A Theory of Judicial Decision for Today, *Harvard Law Review*, vol. 36 [1923], 940, 956).
39. Ibid., 945.
40. Ibid., 946.
41. Roscoe Pound, "Mechanical Jurisprudence," *Columbia Law Review*, vol. VIII, no. 8 (December 1908), 605. Keep in mind that the *Lochner* decision was in 1905, and the Supreme Court was under intense fire for adhering too closely to precedent: "Legal theory can no more stand as a sacred tradition in the *modern world* than can political theory" (ibid., 606; italics not in original). Pound was criticized for rejecting mechanical jurisprudence when human conduct is at issue, while adhering to it when property, contract, and/or business transactions were under adjudication; see Frank's *Law and the Modern Mind*, 222. However, his desire for flexibility as opposed to rigidity in the judicial process permeated his legal theory; if he was somewhat more tentative in providing judges with more discretion in the economic realm, this is attributable to his view that discretion was less necessary and could prove to be counterproductive in achieving a stable economic order.
42. Pound, "Theory of Judicial Decision," 946-47.
43. "But there is a more important form of application which is of a wholly distinct type. Frequently, application of the legal precept, *as found and interpreted*, is intuitive.... Nor need we be ashamed to confess that much that goes on in the administration of justice is intuitive" (ibid., 950-51).
44. Ibid., 958.
45. Ibid., 957-58.
46. In the heyday of conservative activism under the chief justiceships of Fuller (1888-1910), White (1910-21), and Taft (1921-30), many of the Supreme Court's critics were primarily concerned with the court's personnel, as opposed to judicial review per se. See Charles A. Beard, "The Supreme Court—Usurper Or Grantee?" *Political Science Quarterly*, vol. XXVII, no. 1 (March 1912), 1.
47. Roscoe Pound, *Law and Morals* (Chapel Hill: The University of North Carolina Press, 1926), 45-49.
48. Ibid., 49-50; "The very conception of law involves ideas of uniformity, regularity, predictability. [*sic*] Administration of justice according to law is administration by legal precepts and chiefly by rule" (ibid., 79).
49. Ibid., 50, 106.
50. Pound, "The Call For A Realist Jurisprudence," *Harvard Law Review*, vol. 44 (1931), 697, 702.
51. Ibid., 703.
52. Ibid., 711.
53. Ibid., 699.
54. See note 10, *supra*.

55. For polarized views on the subject I suggest the scholarship of Raoul Berger for the conservative perspective and Professor Tribe for the liberal perspective. In chapter 7 I present a comparative analysis of two polarized views, those of M. E. Bradford and Ronald Dworkin.
56. This period marks a theoretical thicket of major proportions. Our objective is not to clear and prune it so that the light of reason may shine through, but to enter and then quickly find our way out onto higher ground, from which we can survey where we've been and where we are going. For a discussion about the demotion of property rights, see James W. Ely's *The Guardian Of Every Other Right: A Constitutional History of Property Rights* (New York: Oxford University Press, 1992).
57. U.S. v. Carolene Products Co. 304 U.S. 144 (1938), 147.
58. Ibid., 152.
59. Ibid., 152-53 (cases and citations omitted). Henry Abraham correctly denotes that footnote four "must surely rank as one of the most significant in all legal history" (Henry J. Abraham, *The Judiciary: The Supreme Court in the Governmental Process,* 8th ed. [Dubuque, Iowa: Wm. C. Brown Publishers, 1991], 89).
60. Abraham, *Freedom and the Court,* 21.
61. Palko v. Connecticut (1937), 325. An important question that Cardozo leaves unanswered is, if these "principles" are so fundamentally rooted in the people's traditions and consciences, then why have the state legislatures transgressed them? Moreover, are people so irrational that they direct their elected representatives to transgress their communities' traditions and consciences? Or, do legislatures inadvertently or intentionally enact statutes contrary to their constituents' traditions and consciences? The fact of the matter is that Cardozo did not place much emphasis on state traditions or the consciences of state citizens. His criteria for justice are nationally based. Writing for the court majority he maintained that "we reach a different plane of social and moral values when we pass to the privileges and immunities that have been taken over from the earlier articles of the federal bill of rights and brought within the Fourteenth Amendment by a process of absorption. These in their origin were effective against the federal government alone. If the Fourteenth Amendment has absorbed them, the process of absorption has had its source in the belief that neither liberty nor justice would exist if they were sacrificed" (Palko v. Connecticut, 82 L.Ed. 288 [1937], 292).
62. Southern Pacific Co. v. Jensen, 244 U.S. 205, 221 (1917).
63. Benjamin Nathan Cardozo, "Address before the New York State Bar Association, Hotel Astor, January 22, 1932," in *Selected Writings of Benjamin Nathan Cardozo,* Margaret E. Hall and Edwin W. Patterson, eds. (New York: Fallon Publications, 1947), 21-22. Of course, the "seeds" are nurtured by the milk of judicial activism.
64. To pullulate means "germinate, sprout...to breed and produce freely" (*Webster's Ninth New Collegiate Dictionary*).
65. Cardozo, *Selected Writings,* 31.
66. Pound, *Social Control Through Law,* 23-25.
67. Ibid., 15. Pound commended natural law theorists for their attempts to resist force with reason, but concluded that their theories were too subjective (i.e., rationalizing their interests in the status quo), too divided among themselves in concurrence on fundamental tenets, and too resistant to the implementation of much needed economic, political, and/or social reforms.
68. Bennett B. Patterson, *The Forgotten Ninth Amendment: A Call For Legislative and Judicial Recognition of Rights Under Social Conditions of Today* (Indianapolis: The Bobbs-Merrill Company, Inc., 1955), iii-vii.

69. Ibid. iii–iv.
70. Ibid., iv.
71. Ibid., iv (emphasis added).
72. Ibid., vi–vii.
73. Chapter 6 *infra* analyzes the juristic fate of the Second Amendment.
74. *The Forgotten Ninth Amendment,* vi (emphasis added).
75. Ibid., v. Raoul Berger mistakenly concludes that Pound's Ninth Amendment jurisprudence was "diametrically opposed to those of Patterson's" (Raoul Berger, "The Ninth Amendment," in *The Rights Retained By the People: The History and Meaning of the Ninth Amendment,* Randy E. Barnett, ed. [Fairfax, Va.: George Mason University Press, 1989], 205–06). Pound does write that "so far as inherent rights are not committed to the federal government, defining and securing them is left to the states or to be taken over by the people of the United States by constitutional amendment" (Patterson, vi). However, in light of Pound's overall advocacy of creative jurisprudence, the qualifications in his introduction to Patterson's *The Forgotten Ninth Amendment,* and his ringing endorsement of Patterson's activist utilization of the Ninth Amendment, there can be little doubt that Pound and Patterson were closely aligned in their Ninth Amendment jurisprudence. In the passages that Berger makes references to, Pound was essentially acknowledging that the Ninth and Tenth Amendments pose a real challenge for creative jurists, but the Fourteenth Amendment ameliorates the challenge. This does not mean, however, that Pound's scholarship was on the same level of Patterson's. As Berger makes clear, Patterson's argument is plagued with inaccuracies (Barnett, 1989, 205–09).
76. Essentially the first quarter of the twentieth century and the post-World War II era.
77. Ronald Dworkin, *Taking Rights Seriously* (Harvard University Press, 1977), 3-4. The Court's reliance on social science research in Brown v. Board of Education seems to belie Dworkin's conclusion. See Brown v. The Board of Education 349 U.S. 294 (1955).
78. See chap. 8, *infra.*

4

Case Studies in Judicial Creativity

I

Griswold v. *Connecticut* marks the Ninth Amendment's "creative" entry into contemporary constitutional law. In the court opinion Justice Douglas mentioned the Ninth Amendment in conjunction with the First, Third, Fourth, and Fifth, whose "emanations" collectively form the "penumbra" that provides "life and substance" to the constitutional right of privacy.[1] Justice Goldberg agreed but was not satisfied with the court majority's uninspired remarks about the Ninth Amendment. Goldberg's concurrence rebuts the traditional Ninth Amendment jurisprudence, as represented by Justice Stewart's dissent. Justice Stewart acknowledges the high stakes: "The Court also quotes the Ninth Amendment, and my brother GOLDBERG'S concurring opinion relies heavily upon it. But to say that the Ninth Amendment has anything to do with this case is to turn somersaults with history. The Ninth Amendment, like its companion the Tenth...make clear that the adoption of the Bill of Rights did not alter the plan that the *Federal* Government was to be a government of express and limited powers.... Until today no member of this Court has ever suggested that the Ninth Amendment meant anything else."[2] Not to be deterred by the historical evidence to the contrary, Justice Goldberg maintained that "the language and history of the Ninth Amendment reveal that the Framers of the Constitution believed that there are additional fundamental rights, protected from governmental infringement, which exist alongside those fundamental rights specifically mentioned in the first eight constitutional amendments."[3]

Goldberg stated the obvious when he affirmed that there are rights other than those specifically mentioned in the Bill of Rights, but he understated the federal context of those unenumerated rights and the roles of the states in discerning the shape and form unenumerated rights should take. Neither the language nor the history of the Ninth Amendment convincingly support a nationalistic juridical process for determining the content of Ninth Amendment rights and their subsequent application to and preemption of the states. Nevertheless, Goldberg does provide evidence to the attentive reader about the rationale for his significant concurrence. His statement that "while this Court has had little occasion to interpret the Ninth Amendment, '[i]t cannot be presumed that any clause in the constitution is intended to be without effect,'" contains footnote 6, which refers readers to three studies, all of which advocate activist use of the amendment.[4] In 1936 Kelsey acknowledged the existence of rights "which have heretofore been vindicated by the ingenuity of the legal profession or the discernment of the courts," such as "the right to be let alone."[5] In 1962 Redlich advised that "the well-publicized case concerning the constitutionality of Connecticut's birth control laws may provide the opportunity for a reconsideration of basic judicial attitudes toward the individual's rights in a free society. When the well thought out formulae of the past fail to provide the answer to a case which raises issues of such fundamental importance, perhaps it is time to pause and look for fresh concepts."[6] According to Patterson, Kelsey, and Redlich, the place to "look for fresh concepts" was unambiguously within the federal judiciary, with the Ninth Amendment available as a reservoir of new judicial concepts. Goldberg's reference to them in the context of stating "while this Court has had little occasion to interpret the Ninth Amendment, it cannot be presumed that any clause in the constitution is intended to be without effect,"[7] reveals the "Poundian" origins of and the rationale behind Goldberg's Ninth Amendment jurisprudence.

The locus of those origins is neither the Constitution nor constitutional law *per se,* but rather the stream of rationalizations for creative jurisprudence that had been flowing for the past five decades. Goldberg's concurring opinion is a tributary, albeit a major one, that enhanced the flow. Consider Goldberg's key statement on the Ninth Amendment's role in the protection of fundamental rights; it is rhetorically creative and incrementally shifts significant powers from the states to the U.S. Supreme Court:

> A dissenting opinion suggests that my interpretation of the Ninth Amendment somehow "broaden[s] the powers of this Court." Post, at 1701. With all due respect, I

> believe that it misses the import of what I am saying. I do not take the position of my Brother Black...that the entire Bill of Rights is incorporated in the Fourteenth Amendment, and I do not mean to imply that the Ninth Amendment is applied against the States by the Fourteenth. Nor do I mean to state that the Ninth Amendment constitutes an independent source of rights protected from infringement by either the States or the Federal Government.[8]

Goldberg superficially maintained that his Ninth Amendment jurisprudence does not "broaden the powers" of the Supreme Court, but if what he writes immediately following his qualified denial is adopted as *ratio decidendi* for future cases, the powers of the Supreme Court would inevitably be significantly broadened in the public policy area of unenumerated rights, thereby refuting the just quoted passage *supra*:

> Rather, the Ninth Amendment shows a belief of the Constitution's authors that fundamental rights exist that are not expressly enumerated in the first eight amendments and an intent that the list of rights included there not be deemed exhaustive. As any student of this Court's opinions knows, this court has held, often unanimously, that the Fifth and Fourteenth Amendments protect certain fundamental personal liberties from abridgment by the Federal Government or the States.... The Ninth Amendment simply shows the intent of the Constitution's authors that other fundamental personal rights should not be denied such protection or disparaged in any other way simply because they are not specifically listed in the first eight constitutional amendments. I do not see how this broadens the authority of the Court; rather it serves to support what this Court has been doing in protecting fundamental rights.[9]

Goldberg's tautology that his Ninth Amendment jurisprudence does not broaden the Court's powers is inherently false. In his own words, "the Ninth Amendment simply lends strong support to the view that the *liberty* protected by the Fifth and Fourteenth Amendments from infringement by the Federal Government or the States is not restricted to rights specifically mentioned in the first eight amendments."[10] Judges are responsible for determining what these unspecified rights are; their determinations are to draw on the "traditions and [collective] conscience of our people."[11] If this does not broaden the Court's powers, then what does?

One would think that national and state statutes embody to some degree the traditions and conscience[s] of the people. But when the Court unilaterally elevates a principle to the status of being a fundamental right on the grounds that it is "rooted" in the traditions and collective conscience of the people and therefore protected under the penumbra of the Ninth and other amendments, and does so to negate a national or state statute, the Court almost always relies on juridical rhetoric, from majority and minority opinions, national as well as state opinions, to support a newly recognized right. The Court dares not unambiguously announce that the traditions and the conscience of the people are incompatible with the newly recognized right and therefore the people's traditions (their consciences are quite another thing) must capitulate to the Court-recognized right. Such bluntness on the part of the Court would run counter to a major tenet of U.S. political culture, that the people are self-governing and that the Supreme Court is constitutionally constrained from exercising legislative powers. The only politically astute alternative is for the Court to associate, however disingenuously, its newly recognized rights with the traditions and conscience of the people as implicitly embodied in the Constitution and thereby invalidate deviating statutes.

We should not loose sight of Justice Goldberg's creativity. Even the total incorporationist Justice Hugo Black found the Court's privacy jurisprudence a hard pill to swallow. He acknowledged, "I like my privacy as well as the next one, but I am nevertheless compelled to admit that government has a right to invade it unless prohibited by some specific constitutional provision."[12] Justice Black's acknowledgment that government has a right to "invade" individual privacy outlines the nature of the debate and the role of the Ninth Amendment. The Court majority took the position that individuals have spheres of autonomy (or what Justice Douglas referred to as zones of privacy) into which governmental regulation may not intrude. The acceptable boundaries of the spheres are determined by the Court, based upon what a majority of the justices deem to be rational standards. Justice Goldberg's Ninth Amendment jurisprudence, with its open-ended supply of unenumerated rights,[13] provides materials for reconstructing those boundaries on an ongoing basis. The *Griswold* dissenters take the position that there are indeed constitutional boundaries, but the states have significant discretion in defining unenumerated rights.

For the *Griswold* dissenters a constitutional curtailment of privacy rights by the community is in and of itself premised upon the right of popular control over public policy. For example, Justice Black's choice of the phrase "government has a right to invade [his privacy]" connotes that the issue under litigation involves the collective rights of state citizens to override the claimed right of an individual, using the government as an agent of the community to achieve the former; in this case governmental invasion of Griswold's privacy is not a violation of a constitutional right. Justice Black acknowledged that the rights of the people of Connecticut to be self-governing supersede the interest—or for that matter penumbral right—of Griswold to distribute contraceptives.

II

An instructive sequel to *Griswold* is *Eisenstadt* v. *Baird* (1972).[14] Analysis of the juridical ties between *Griswold* and *Eisenstadt* manifests the "interstitial" nature of the U.S. Supreme Court's creativity. The Supreme Court's recognition of an unenumerated right is crucial to both cases, but without *Griswold* setting the precedent, *Eisenstadt* could not have been decided as it was. We take that for granted, but logic cautions against such inductions. Consider, if X equals Y and Y equals Z, then Z must equal X. It would be illogical to maintain that Z does not equal X. However, if X is the Ninth Amendment, Y is *Griswold,* and Z is *Eisenstadt,* then X equals Y and Y equals Z, but Z does not necessarily equal X. The Court concedes as much in its *Eisenstadt* opinion.

In *Eisenstadt* the primary issue stems from a Massachusetts law that made it a felony to distribute to unmarried persons "a drug, medicine, instrument, or article for the prevention of contraception."[15] There can be little doubt that with the *Griswold* precedent the state statute was constitutionally problematical. Nevertheless, the approximately seven years that transpired between *Griswold* and *Eisenstadt* was sufficient for an embryonic constitutional concept to emerge upright on the stage of juridical drama, to such an extent that even the *Griswold* dissenter Justice Stewart is to be found applauding its performance.[16]

Eisenstadt is an extension of *Griswold*'s penumbral range. What was a fundamental right of privacy for married couples was extended to include unmarried persons. Writing for the *Eisenstadt* majority, Justice Brennan maintained that "if the right of privacy means anything, it is the right of the *individual,* married or single, to be free from unwarranted governmental intrusion into matters so fundamentally affecting a person as the decision whether to bear or beget a child."[17] The suspect classification of married and unmarried persons is unacceptable. Justice Brennan makes a subtle distinction in order to extend *Griswold* from married to unmarried persons. He does so by atomizing the marital relationship. He wrote that "it is true that in *Griswold* the right of privacy in question inhered in the marital relationship. Yet the marital couple is not an independent entity with a mind and heart of its own, but an association of two individuals each with a separate intellectual and emotional makeup."[18] This view of the marital relationship is indistinguishable from that of unmarried persons. No one doubts that a husband and wife is an association of "two individuals each with a separate intellectual and emotional makeup." However, one would also have to concede that it is more than that. But by simplifying the nature of the marital relationship and making it indistinguishable from that of unmarried persons, Justice Brennan is able to extend the *Griswold* precedent beyond its 1965 limits. Moreover, the constitutional soundness of his contention that individuals, married or single, are to be free from "unwarranted" governmental intrusion regarding the decision whether to "beget or bear a child," hinges on the process that determines what is unwarranted. This was not problematical for judicial activists in this case, due to the fact that the Constitution was kept in lockstep with the policy outcomes that the Court preferred. Recall that *Griswold* prohibited Connecticut from barring contraceptives to married couples. In response to the *Griswold* decision Massachusetts enacted legislation that sanctioned the distribution of contraceptives to married persons by healthcare professionals, but not to unmarried persons. By concluding that access to contraceptives was a fundamental right, and that the state's statutory distinction between married and unmarried couples was constitutionally untenable, it was only a short leap in logic to the penumbral coverage provided by the Fourteenth Amendment's equal protection clause. The statute fails the equal protection test due, according to Justice Brennan, to its invidious under inclusion of unmarried persons.

Not challenging *Griswold*'s "tenuous moorings to the text of the Constitution,"[19] Chief Justice Burger, the lone *Eisenstadt* dissenter, maintained that *Eisenstadt* seriously invades "the constitutional prerogatives of the States and regrettably hark[s] back to the heyday of substantive due process."[20] Just one year prior to *Roe* v. *Wade,* Chief Justice Burger confessed that he "cannot believe that unanimity of expert opinion is a prerequisite to a State's exercise of its police power, *no matter what the subject matter of the regulation....* The commands of the Constitution cannot fluctuate with the shifting tides of scientific opinion."[21] The chief justice had a change of heart by 1973 when he supported Justice Blackmun's utilization of expert opinions (e.g., The

American Medical Association, The American Public Health Association, and The American Bar Association) in *Roe*.[22]

III

Since 1973 constitutionally protected access to an abortion is attributable to the personal privacy guarantees of the First, Fourth, Fifth, Ninth, and Fourteenth Amendments; or shall we say that the collective emanations from these amendments culminate in a constitutional right to personal privacy, which includes a woman's right to procreative autonomy, which in turn includes the constitutional right to terminate a pregnancy up to the point where a state has a compelling interest in the health of the mother and/or the potentiality of human life in the fetus. The Ninth Amendment's role in this schema is revealing. The appellant's challenge to the Texas statute found Justice Goldberg's *Griswold* Ninth Amendment jurisprudence integral to success, as did the court majority.

Justice Blackmun's expansion of *Griswold*'s right to privacy in order to confirm the constitutional right to an abortion is also subtle. The District Court preferred the Ninth Amendment via incorporation into the Fourteenth as the basis for setting aside state prohibitions of abortions, whereas Justice Blackmun preferred the Fourteenth Amendment's equal protection/due process. However, Justice Blackmun's preference for the Fourteenth Amendment has in tow the Ninth. He reasoned that "this right of privacy, whether it be founded in the Fourteenth Amendment's concept of ordered liberty and restrictions upon state action, as we feel it is, or, as the District Court determined, in the Ninth Amendment's reservation of rights to the people, is broad enough to encompass a woman's decision whether or not to terminate her pregnancy."[23] Note the rhetorical structure of the preceding sentence. It can be restated to read:

> The constitutional right to privacy has an existence that is not necessarily dependent on both the Fourteenth and Ninth Amendments simultaneously, but, if need be, has an existence that can maintain sustenance from either one or both; we (a majority of Supreme Court justices) prefer the Fourteenth Amendment as our constitutional support for personal privacy, however, the Ninth Amendment is an alternative source for constitutional support in the utilization of personal privacy to negate state laws that infringe thereon.

This is not unintended circumlocution. To the contrary, it is a rational means, consistent with theoretical practice, to elevate dictum to the status of constitutional authority, which in this case means taking several steps forward in elevating the concurring opinion of Justice Goldberg's *Griswold* Ninth Amendment jurisprudence to controlling authority. An understanding of Justice Blackmun's utilization of *Griswold* makes this evident.

First and foremost, Justice Blackmun concedes that the fundamental issue of *Roe* is whether the predominate "theory of life" in Texas (i.e., that life begins at conception) should prevail over a pregnant woman's personal right to privacy. The Court's response is a qualified no and yes. The continuum between no and yes parallels the development of the fetus. The more developed the fetus the more compelling a state's case that it has a "legitimate interest in protecting the potentiality of human life." Conversely, the closer a decision to terminate the pregnancy is to conception, the less compelling is a state's interest in prohibiting abortion.[24] The Court's use of the phrase "the potentiality of human life" belies its claim that it "need not resolve the question of when life begins."[25] Post-conception categorization as "potentiality of human life" is an acknowledgment by the Court that its modus operandi is that life does not begin at conception, due to the obvious fact that "potential human life" is distinct from "actual human life." Justice Blackmun wrote that

> Texas urges that, apart from the Fourteenth Amendment, life begins at conception and is present throughout pregnancy, and that, therefore, the State has a compelling interest in protecting that life from and after conception. *We need not resolve the difficult question of when life begins.* When those trained in the respective disciplines of medicine, philosophy, and theology are unable to arrive at any consensus, the judiciary, at this point in the development of man's knowledge, is not in a position to speculate as to the answer.[26]

Such disclaimers notwithstanding, Justice Blackmun invests a significant portion of his reasoning in refuting the belief that human life begins at conception, as is evidenced by his references to authorities from antiquity to modernity.[27] The intellectual attempt to articulate a reasonable theory of when human life begins is not sufficient constitutional grounds for overturning the Texas statute, as maintained by Chief Justice Burger's 1972 contention that expert opinion should not be allowed to displace a State exercising its legitimate police powers.[28] Justice Blackmun needed more and found it in federal and state courts, which in turn relied upon *Griswold*'s fundamental right to personal privacy.

His strategy was to present the *Roe* majority opinion as being in line with and supportive of national and state jurisprudence. He wrote:

> We, therefore, conclude that the right of personal privacy includes the abortion decision, but that this right is not unqualified and must be considered against important state interests in regulation. We note that those federal and state courts that have recently considered abortion law challenges have reached the same conclusion. A majority, in addition to the District Court in the present case [which was grounded in the Ninth Amendment], have held state laws unconstitutional, at least in part, because of vagueness or because of overbreadth and abridgment of rights.[29]

What Justice Blackmun fails to mention is that the federal and state courts were following *Griswold* precedent. He does list the federal and state cases that support *Roe*'s conclusions, and these citations do give his opinion the air of authority. However, one must ask if there was no *Griswold,* not to mention selective incorporation, how extensive would Blackmun's supporting list be. Even so, if forty-nine states recognized the right to privacy as articulated in *Roe,* within the context of constitutional federalism, is the U.S. Supreme Court thereby constitutionally authorized to impose those same standards on the people of Texas?

IV

A case that goes a long way in disclosing the extent to which post-*Griswold* Ninth Amendment jurisprudence qualifies state participation in the articulation of unenumerated rights involves the constitutionality of Georgia's anti-sodomy statute.[30] As *Bowers* v. *Hardwick* demonstrates, U.S. Supreme Court rationalizations for and parameters of unenumerated rights have been substantially advanced.

Bowers revolves around a disused Georgia statute that criminalizes sodomy. It stipulates that: "(a) A person commits the offense of sodomy when he performs or submits to any sexual act involving the sex organs of one person and the mouth or anus of another. And (b) a person convicted of the offense of sodomy shall be punished by imprisonment for not less than one nor more than twenty years."[31] Relying on *Griswold* the Court of Appeals for the Eleventh Circuit held the Georgian statute to be unconstitutional on the grounds that it violates the fundamental rights of personal privacy and due process as protected by the Ninth and Fourteenth Amendments. In light of the emanations from *Griswold, Eisenstadt,* and *Roe,* one would think that the anti-sodomy statute must fall on the grounds that it is vague, overbroad, and a violation of fundamental rights of personal privacy. The Court, however, backed down, and in a five to four decision narrowly[32] reversed the Eleventh Circuit's decision on interpretative grounds, that is, the unenumerated rights embodied in the Ninth Amendment do not sanction sodomy.

Writing for the majority, Justice White acknowledged the wanderings of the Court into the political thicket and cautioned that "the Court is most vulnerable and comes nearest to illegitimacy when it deals with judge-made constitutional law having little or no cognizable roots in the language or design of the Constitution.... Otherwise, the judiciary necessarily takes to itself further authority to govern the country without express constitutional authority. The claimed right pressed on us today falls far short of overcoming this resistance."[33] What does Justice White mean by "most vulnerable" and "comes nearest to illegitimacy"? Most vulnerable to what, a political backlash because the public has recognized particular "judge-made constitutional laws" as "having little or no cognizable roots in the language or design of the Constitution"? Moreover, a Supreme Court that takes to itself *further* authority to govern the country without express constitutional authority would in fact be illegitimate, and not simply nearest to illegitimacy." The phrase "further authority" is an admission by Justice White that the Court has in fact governed some areas of public policy without constitutional authority—such as the articulation and implementation of personal privacy as a constitutionally protected fundamental right—and still avoided the illegitimate label. From this perspective it becomes clear why the Court has balked at recognizing sodomy as a constitutional right of personal privacy; such a decision was simply too *avant garde* for the times.

The avowed reason the claimed right falls far short, according to Justice White, is not necessarily because of anything a majority of Georgians may or may not have expressed through their state's constitutional/political processes. Rather, the reason the claimed right falls far short is because it is not sanctioned by English Common Law and is not "deeply rooted in this Nation's history and tradition."[34] Because there is no linkage to the past—English and American common laws do not sanction homosexual conduct—the states may regulate and even prohibit such conduct. Common Law is the admitted controlling factor of Justice White's opinion, but toward the end of his opinion he concedes that his real concern is the emergence of an unenumerated rights jurisprudence that would prove to be functionally very problematical for the Court. He cautioned that to strike down the Georgian statute would place the Court on an unenumerated rights slippery slope, with many undesirable consequences:

> And if respondent's submission is limited to the voluntary sexual conduct between consenting adults, it would be difficult, except by fiat, to limit the claimed right to homosexual conduct while leaving exposed to prosecution adultery, incest, and other sexual crimes even though they are committed in the home. We are unwilling to start down that road.[35]

As Justice White must have known, the Court traveled down that slippery road on *Griswold, Eisenstadt,* and *Roe*. The dissenters correctly admonished the court majority for failing to acknowledge the logical juridical link from *Griswold* to *Bowers* and staying the course.

Justice Blackmun's *Griswold* dissent relies on the Ninth Amendment and its presumed guaranteed right of privacy, or what he refers to as "the right to be let alone."[36] His dissent did not challenge the majority's reliance on common law per se, but rather an interpretation of common law that was informed by Judeo-Christian values, that is a common law that proscribed homosexual conduct. It was Justice Blackmun's position that "the right to be let alone" should not be subordinated to "a blind imitation of the past" or "traditional Judeo-Christian values,"[37] no matter that such values were the preference of most Georgians:

> The assertion that traditional Judeo-Christian values proscribe the conduct involved, Brief for the Petitioner 20, cannot provide an adequate justification for 16-6-2. That certain, but by no means all, religious groups condemn the behavior at issue gives the State no license to impose their judgments on the entire citizenry. The legitimacy of secular legislation depends instead on whether the State can advance some justification for its law beyond its conformity to religious doctrine.[38]

Justice Blackmun's legitimacy test is certainly in line with the Court's reasoning regarding state regulations of contraceptives and the countervailing fundamental right to personal privacy. However, Justice Blackmun has walked onto a slippery slope of his own making. Suppose the people of Georgia, the majority that is, base their proscription of homosexual conduct on, among other grounds, Judeo-Christian values. The same might be said about public policy involving indigents, the terminally ill, the insane, capital punishment, the environment, and the like. It is one thing for laws to fly through a state legislature on the wings of "fundamentalist religious fervor" (which is unlikely due to the fact that radical fundamentalists constitute only a small minority of the population), and quite another for religious values to have played an important part in the formation of the people's cultural and political consciousness.

Nevertheless, not to be deterred, Justice Blackmun is unequivocal in his determination to subordinate the religiously based values of the majority to judicially defined unenumerated rights of individuals. The Georgia statute presumably violates no other provision of the Constitution; there are neither equal protection nor due process exceptions. Nevertheless, the secular test advocated by Justice Blackmun would prevent the states from legislating in those areas in which Judeo-Christian values were instrumental in the formation of the public policy and subsequently found to be inconsistent with Supreme Court articulated fundamental rights.[39] Justice Blackmun concludes with his notion of a fundamental right, nonconformity, the very thing feared by Justice White because of the unintended consequences for the Court:

> I can only hope that here, too, the Court will soon reconsider its analysis and conclude that depriving individuals of the right to choose for themselves how to conduct their intimate relationships poses a far greater threat to the values most deeply rooted in our Nation's history than tolerance of nonconformity could ever do. Because I think the Court today betrays those values, I dissent.[40]

Taken to this extreme, Blackmun's fundamental right of personal privacy is the constitutional semantical equivalent to nonconformity. Essentially, what is at issue is the prerogative of an individual to constitutionally evade state-based popular control over the area of public policy as it pertains to public morality.

Justice Blackmun assumes that his judicially mandated tolerance of sexual nonconformity should prevail over Georgians' right to popular control, and that the Ninth Amendment provides him cover (through its incorporation into the Fourteenth Amendment) to make the former prevail over the latter. Justice Blackmun failed to balance his contrived right of personal privacy with the fundamental right of the people to be self-governing within the context of federalism. The dissent's unsubstantiated axiom that *Bowers* v. *Hardwick* "is about the most comprehensive of rights and the right most valued by civilized men, namely, the right to be let alone,"[41] dismissed without serious discussion another fundamental right, the right of the community to be self-governing. It is important to note that, based upon their traditional state police powers to promote the health, safety, and morals of their citizens, twenty-four states and the District of Columbia in 1986 had criminal penalties for homosexual conduct between consenting adults.[42] It is through institutionalized popular control at the state level, particularly the respective state constitutions and legislative processes, that the values communities hold most dear are consensually determined.[43] Justice White dared not follow this fundamental right to its logical conclusion, because *Roe, Eisenstadt,* and *Griswold* (to name three) blocked his way and he would have had to relinquish the bulk of the Court's power to engage in social engineering through creative jurisprudence if *Bowers* were to be placed upon constitutional *terra firma.*

V

In the wake of *Griswold* what methods have been developed by the Court to determine when the government's curtailment of individual privacy is constitutionally sanctioned? Ninth Amendment jurisprudence is critical to the resolution of this question, as is evidenced by Justice Goldberg's 1965 insertion of Ninth Amendment unenumerated rights into the lexicon of national fundamental rights. However, it is not the amendment itself that is of primary importance, but rather the tools of construction that are utilized in an effort to build a system of creative jurisprudence, using unenumerated rights as important building blocks supporting judicial policy objectives. The Ninth Amendment has emerged as the conduit through which unenumerated rights can be channeled into constitutional law,[44] court-generated rights that do not recognize meaningful national and state jurisdictional boundaries. Even a case such as *Bowers,* which was hailed as a victory for federalism, manifests the extent to which the Court has dismissed the state police powers as qualifying national prerogatives. Neither the court majority nor the dissenting minority indicated a willingness to defer to Georgia's attempt to maintain state statutes considered to be in their citizens' best interests, that is, promoting their health, safety, morals, and general welfare. The state's exercise of its police powers is contingent upon state statutes that are products of the fundamental right of self-government. These procedural processes do not preclude "discrete and insular" minorities from engagement in the political process; Hardwick and like-minded advocates were and are at liberty to participate in an attempt to have their policy preferences prevail at the state level.

This sort of political participation fuels the nomocratic federal arrangement. It is a process through which factions can in a deliberative manner seek to have their interests prevail and converted into official public policy.[45] But it is essential for the representative decisionmakers to be tied to the citizenry through an electoral process; to the extent that it is not, popular control over the process has been compromised. Of course, the least representative branch is the federal judiciary. It is for this reason that "the Framers carefully and with deliberate forethought refused to enthrone the judiciary. In this situation [malapportionment], as in others of a like nature, appeal for relief does not belong here. Appeal must be to an informed, civically minded electorate. In a democratic society like ours, relief must come through an aroused popular conscience that sears the conscience of the people's representatives."[46] Justice Frankfurter correctly maintained that the U.S. Supreme Court has a constitutional responsibility to defer political questions to the state and national legislatures. As factions engage in the deliberative process in order to prevail over their political rivals, the public is socialized about issues and the political rationale behind public policy. According to Justice Frankfurter, making the political branches deal with political questions enhances the prospect of public policy being placed on public opinion *terra firma*.[47]

Post-*Griswold* Ninth Amendment jurisprudence has run counter to nomocratic federalism.[48] Whether the nomenclature is natural rights, higher law, fundamental rights, natural law, the law of nature, common law, or the unwritten constitution, U.S. Supreme Court utilization of open-ended Ninth Amendment unenumerated rights is problematical for American federalism. To reject the *carte blanche* version of the Ninth Amendment is not meant to imply that the Ninth Amendment is without effect, as Justice Goldberg would have us believe:

> To hold that a right so basic and fundamental and so deep-rooted in our society as the right to privacy in marriage may be infringed because that right is not guaranteed in so many words by the first eight amendments to the Constitution is to ignore the Ninth Amendment and to give it no effect.... The Ninth Amendment shows a belief of the Constitution's authors that fundamental rights exist that are not expressly enumerated in the first eight amendments and an intent that the list of rights included there not be deemed exhaustive.[49]

Justice Goldberg is correct in maintaining that the first eight amendments are not an exhaustive list of fundamental rights, but he is incorrect in assuming that the U.S. Supreme Court is thereby authorized by the Ninth Amendment to fill in the blanks. That responsibility was the prerogative of the respective states in the absence of national interference (see chapter 1, *supra*). Echoing Justice Iredell, Justice Frankfurter forewarned that if the Supreme Court uses its elevated status to inform and admonish the political branches to adhere to fundamental principles, then the Court serves the federal nomocratic process well. However, since the watershed Warren Court, the evidence indicates that the Court is more inclined to substitute its definition of unenumerated rights for that of the states. This, in the course of time, will convert the people into subjects progressively less capable of self-government, as they become increasingly dependent on the Court to resolve intractable and tractable political issues. This in turn will move the Court deeper into the political thicket and further away from their constitutional role of interpreters of the law and closer to the dreaded Platonic formulators of the same.

VI

In light of the centralizing tendencies of national standards for unenumerated rights, the expectation that the U.S. Supreme Court's ideological pendulum is swinging back toward a renewed judicial federalism is untenable.[50] To reiterate, having been descriptively denoted as the *new judicial federalism,* the concept is mostly form with little content. In order to determine whether this development constitutes the emergence of a *bona fide* judicial federalism it is necessary to analyze the *federal* component of judicial federalism. Because federalism is the *sine qua non* of the constitutional arrangement between U.S. and state judiciaries, such an analysis facilitates addressing three essential questions: (a) Is the new judicial federalism primarily the consequence of the federal courts attempting to alleviate their own docket overloads by deferring to state courts, while reserving for itself the opportunity to overturn straying state decisions on appeal? (b) Is the new judicial federalism the consequence of legal practitioners (judges and lawyers) looking to state courts for adjudicative results unlikely to come from the U.S. Supreme Court, but in the final analysis the latter having the final word? Or (c) is the new judicial federalism primarily the consequence of an ideological commitment to federalism in general and judicial federalism in particular on the part of a majority of the justices on the U.S. Supreme Court? Neither (a) nor (b) are sufficient for a viable judicial federalism, while (c) is essential for it.

As is the case with federalism in general (the problematical *imperium in imperio*), judicial federalism is difficult to conceptualize.[51] (This explains why scholarship on the subject fails to define it.) American federalism involves two distinct levels of government, national and state. Each level has its institutional separation of powers between the legislative, executive, and judicial branches. Because the Tenth Amendment to the U.S. Constitution stipulates that certain powers are reserved to the "States respectively, or to the people," a revived "judicial federalism" must involve a resuscitation of state judiciaries' reserved powers' functions in relation to the U.S. government (and the U.S. Supreme Court specifically), and not simply state judicial supremacy over their respective state legislative and executive branches. The latter is not precluded, but neither is it in and of itself sufficient for a revived judicial federalism. Nevertheless, the *mutatis mutandis* of a new judicial federalism would have to include a revived federalism based upon the prerogative powers of the states under the Tenth Amendment, because state judiciaries are integral parts of state governments in contradistinction to subordinate administrative extensions of the national judiciary. In the absence of a meaningful shift of power from the nation to the states the new judicial federalism is merely administrative procedural changes, (a) and (b) *supra,* lacking substantive adjustments to the balance of power between national and state judiciaries;[52] furthermore, (a) constitutes cooptation of state judiciaries by the national judiciary, as opposed to a revived judicial federalism.

On the other hand, an affirmative answer to (c) would reinvigorate not only state judiciaries, but also the role of the states vis-à-vis the U.S. Government, due to the augmented state public policy autonomy that would accompany a meaningful judicial federalism. The evidence that the Supreme Court is ideologically committed to federalism is inconclusive; to the contrary, neither the role of the states nor that of the state courts in the federal system have substantively changed. In the final analysis claims about a *new judicial federalism* are, at best, premature, due to the fact that the power relationship between the U.S. and state supreme courts has not significantly changed. There is consensus that the state courts have been the focus of renewed interest and adjudicative activity, but the increased adjudication has been quantitative and not qualitative. And there is insufficient evidence that a meaningful shift of power from the national to the state courts has or will occur. The standard model of national supremacy over the American judicial process is still intact. This does not mean that there have not been attempts to modify the model, but these modifications have been administrative and trivial when their impact on the federal balance of power is considered. There has been a failure to distinguish between a slight modification of the prevailing model and significant modifications that actually return requisite amounts of judicial discretionary power to the state courts, thereby reviving judicial federalism.

Moreover, attempts to revitalize state courts at the expense of the national courts is not a new phenomenon; recall the reaction of progressives to the "proprietarian notions" of the Fuller, White, and Taft Courts (1888-1930)[53] and the conservative response to the Warren Court in their attempts to revitalize state supreme courts in the federal system.[54] During the Warren era state courts were viewed as bulwarks against the liberal agenda of the U.S. Supreme Court, whereas during the Reagan years they were viewed by liberals as opportunities to thwart the conservative orientation of the Rehnquist Court or by conservatives to unravel U.S. Supreme Court liberal precedent. According to Steve Pressman, "A quiet legal revolution now under way has lawyers and judges reading the fine print in their state constitutions. As a result, there has been a dramatic increase in the number of cases decided on state rather than on federal grounds. This new judicial federalism began as a reaction to an increasingly conservative U.S. Supreme Court, but it has since won plaudits from some conservatives who favor handing decisions over to the states."[55] But such increases are not synonymous with a viable judicial federalism.

VII

The fact that jurisdictions between the U.S. Supreme Court and state supreme courts are open to such political agenda setting is a *problem of demarcation.*[56] This ongoing problem is collateral with U.S. constitutional development. Constitutionally, the jurisdictional lines between federal and state courts were to be determined by constitutional federalism and the constitutional prerogatives of the U.S. Congress to establish tribunals inferior to and regulate the appellate jurisdiction of the U.S. Supreme Court.[57] But jurisdictional boundaries between the state and federal courts has primarily been established by the U.S. Supreme Court through constitutional law.[58] Therefore, it is to the U.S. Supreme Court's formulation of constitutional law (which includes questions of justiciability over federal issues) that we must look for any modifications to judicial federalism. In other words, the state courts cannot, in the face of two hundred years of evolving Supreme Court precedent, strike out on their own; in the absence of new national legislation, groundbreaking constitutional law, and/or constitutional amendment, increased state court autonomy cannot—has not—occurred.

According to one commentator's analysis of the Supreme Court's role, "enduring decision rules and representative structures must be established to protect fundamental values—such as federalism, the separation of powers and individual rights."[59] The importance of establishing "enduring rules and representative structures" is critical, especially in the area of unenumerated Ninth Amendment rights. From a historical view the U.S. Supreme Court has not fulfilled this role, but emerges as the loose cannon on the deck of American federalism. The fact that jurisdictional fluidity is endemic to the American judicial process does not mitigate its impact on federalism, which was designed to facilitate popular control over public policy. Unlike national statutes that are tied to the electoral processes, the U.S. Supreme Court's jurisdictional public policy lacks meaningful accountability to state popular control.[60] Consequently, if there is a new judicial federalism, it is a creature of the U.S. Supreme Court and serves at its pleasure. This is a far cry from the principles of federalism inherent in the reserved powers of the Tenth Amendment. A case study of recent Louisiana abortion cases, vortical federalism, and the U.S. Supreme Court's standing policy toward judicial federalism manifest the nature and scope of the so-called *new* judicial federalism.

Notes

1. Griswold v. Connecticut, 85 S. Ct. 1678, 1681 (1965).
2. Ibid., 1706.
3. Ibid., 1684.
4. Ibid., 1685. They are Bennett B. Patterson's *The Forgotten Ninth Amendment* (Indianapolis: Bobbs-Merrill, 1955), Norman Redlich's "Are There *Certain*

Rights...Retained by the People?" 37 N.Y.L.U. Rev. 787 (1962), and Knowlton H. Kelsey's "The Ninth Amendment of the Federal Constitution," 11 Indiana Law Journal, 309 (1936).

5. Kelsey, "The Ninth Amendment," 320–21.
6. Redlich, "Are There *Certain Rights,*" 795. Redlich was not advocating that the place to look was the states. In his own words, "The issue may be simply stated: were the states to be raised to the standards emblematized by the Bill of Rights or was the Bill of Rights to be watered down to conform to the lower standards of state governments. The adoption of the Fourteenth and Fifteenth Amendments, containing specific restrictions on state power, transferred to the federal judiciary the ultimate power to resolve the question" (ibid., 790).
7. Griswold v. Connecticut, 1685.
8. Ibid., 1686.
9. Ibid.
10. Ibid.
11. Ibid. The phrase "our people" certainly has a condescending ring to it. Also take note of the distinction between the plural "traditions" and the singular "[collective] conscience." As discussed in chap. 3 (*supra*), unanimity is the goal and converting "traditions" into a "conscience" is a major step toward realizing that goal.
12. Ibid., 1695–96.
13. Just how open-ended is the supply of unenumerated rights? Consider the Ninth Amendment jurisprudence of one of the authorities Goldberg relied upon: "Natural rights, such as are declared to be inalienable and which, as such, are personal to every individual as a citizen of a free community, include: the right to personal liberty, to personal security, to acquire and enjoy property, to religious liberty, to freedom of conscience, to freedom of contract, to freedom of press, speech, assemblage, petition, to freedom to engage in profession, trade, business, or calling, and the right to privacy.... Those rights which are innate, and which come from the very laws of nature, such as life, liberty, pursuit of happiness, and self-preservation. Natural rights, arising, if they do arise, from the nature of man and from the laws of nature, may be as indefinite as the law of nature which Bentham says is but a phrase to justify some individuals in their personal classification of what is right and what is wrong" (Kelsey, 313).
14. 405 U.S. 438.
15. Ibid., 440–41.
16. In *Eisenstadt* there is no trace of Justice Stewart's stinging *Griswold* dissent. Justice Black, the other *Griswold* dissenter, joined Justice White's concurring opinion that the state failed to demonstrate that the distribution of certain contraceptives posed health risks (ibid., 463–65).
17. Eisenstadt v. Baird 405 U.S. 438 (1972).
18. Ibid., 453.
19. Ibid., 472.
20. Ibid., 467.
21. Ibid., 470 (emphasis not in original).
22. Roe v. Wade 93 S.Ct. 705 (1973) 721–24.
23. Ibid., 727; the federal district court maintained that "the fundamental right of single women and married persons to choose whether to have children is protected through the Ninth Amendment, through the Fourteenth Amendment, and that the Texas criminal abortion statutes were void on their face because they

were both constitutionally vague and constituted an overbroad infringement of the plaintiffs' Ninth Amendment rights" (ibid., 711).

24. Ibid., 731.
25. Ibid., 730.
26. Ibid.
27. See notes 9, 10, 20, 21, 22, 23, 38, 39, 40, 43, and 44" (ibid., 715-25).
28. Eisenstadt v. Baird, 407.
29. Roe v. Wade, 727.
30. Bowers v. Hardwick 106 S.Ct. 2841 (1986).
31. Ibid., 2842.
32. To say that the circuit court's ruling was narrowly overturned is an understatement. To wit, subsequent to his retirement Justice Powell stated that he erroneously sided with the majority and upon reflection thinks that the dissent had the better argument. He confessed that "when I had the opportunity to reread the opinions a few months later, I thought that the dissent had the better of the arguments" (Anand Agneshwar, "Ex-Justice Says He May Have Been Wrong," *National Law Journal,* vol. 13 [5 November 1990], 1). I suspect that it was not rereading the opinions that swayed his mind, but the commentaries on the heels of the decision.
33. Bowers v. Hardwick, 2846.
34. Ibid., 2844.
35. Ibid., 2846.
36. Ibid., 2848. As mentioned in chapter 1, the phrase "the right to be let alone" can be traced to an economic commentary by Judge Cooley; see Samuel D. Warren and Louis D. Brandeis, "The Right to Privacy," *Harvard Law Review,* vol. IV, no. 5 (1890), 195. Obviously, the right to be let alone with one's property is now passé.
37. Bowers v. Hardwick, 2848, 2854.
38. Ibid., 2854-55.
39. See Justice Scalia's dissenting opinion in Edwards v. Aguillard 107 S.Ct. 2573, 2591 (1987); Justice Scalia adroitly considers the role of religious values in formulating public policy.
40. Bowers v. Hardwick, 2856.
41. Ibid., 2848.
42. Ibid., 2845, 2846.
43. For a contemporary discussion about the limits of democratic rule see Robert A. Dahl, *Democracy and Its Critics* (New Haven: Yale University Press, 1989), especially 135-231.
44. John Hart Ely acknowledged as much when he admitted, "[i]ts true that read for what it says the Ninth Amendment seems open-textured enough to support almost anything one might wish to argue, and that thought can get pretty scary" (John Hart Ely, *Democracy and Distrust: A Theory of Judicial Review* [Cambridge, Mass: Harvard University Press, 1980], 34). Being an opponent of strict construction, or at least the possibility of strict construction, Ely was not adverse to an open-ended Ninth Amendment to be filled in by the Court.
45. We must be circumspect, however, in assuming too much. The U.S. Supreme Court's rights policy has been so pervasive that state initiatives—state constitutional amendments included—must be tested in the crucible of fundamental rights. For example, Amendment 2 was approved by voters in Colorado by 53.4 percent to 46.6 percent margin in November, 1993. It provides that "neither the State of

Colorado, through any of its branches or departments, nor any of its agencies, political subdivisions, municipalities or school districts, shall enact, adopt or enforce any statute, regulation, ordinance or policy whereby homosexual, lesbian or bisexual orientation, conduct, practices or relationships shall constitute or otherwise be the basis of or entitle any person or class of persons to have or claim any minority status quota preferences, protected status or claim of discrimination. This section of the constitution shall be in all respects self-executing." The state supreme court of Colorado declared Amendment 2 unconstitutional; relying on U.S. Supreme Court precedent, the state court decided that Amendment 2 was repugnant to the equal protection clause of the Fourteenth Amendment to the U.S. Constitution. See Justice Rovira's opinion in Evans v. Romer, 854 P. 2d 1270 (Colo. 1993); the U.S. Supreme has placed Romer v. Evans on its docket.

46. Baker v. Carr 369 U.S. 186, 270 (1962). Justice Frankfurter was not convinced that malapportionment in the Tennessee legislature was justiciable on either the guaranty or equal protection clauses, whereas Justice Brennan, the opinion's author, concluded that "the claim pleaded here neither rests upon nor implicates the Guaranty Clause," but that "the appellants' claim that they are being denied equal protection is justiciable" (ibid., 209-10). Justice Frankfurter was cognizant of the Court's responsibility to defer political questions to the state and national legislatures. Such deference serves as a means of socializing the public about public policy issues through the political process.
47. It is not my intention to address the important public socialization function of having legislatures debate and attempt to resolve high conflict and high salient issues. Nevertheless, the theoretical commitment to popular control over public policy notwithstanding, I am convinced that the concomitant public socialization will help to place public policy on *terra firma,* as opposed to having "fundamental rights" policies imposed upon the public without the benefit of extensive legislative debate. See Robert Booth Fowler, *The Dance With Community: The Contemporary Debate In American Political Thought* (Lawrence, Kans.: University Press of Kansas, 1991); of particular relevance is chap. 4, "Participatory Community," 42-63.
48. More recent cases include Planned Parenthood v. Casey, in which Justices O'Connor, Kennedy, Souter, Blackmun, and Stevens reaffirmed through *stare decisis* the national standards of rights (112 S.Ct. 2791 [1992]). Conservative justices also have such proclivities; see David H. Lucas v. South Carolina Coastal Council, in which the "taking clause" of the Fifth Amendment is applied to South Carolina as a fundamental right (112 S.Ct. 2886 [1992]).
49. Griswold, 1685-86.
50. For a sampling of the literature, see John Kincaid, "The New Judicial Federalism," *Journal of State Government,* vol. 61, no. 5 (1988); Michael E. Solimine, "State Court Protection of Federal Constitutional Rights," *Harvard Journal of Law & Public Policy,* vol. 12, no. 1 (Winter, 1989), 127; Phylis Bamberger, "Beware of the Dark Side of Constitutional Law," *Human Rights,* vol. 19, no. 1 (Winter, 1992), 22; Shirley Abrahamson, "Reincarnation & Reawakening: Long Forgotten By Civil Libertarians, State Courts Are Now Getting The Respect They Deserve," *Human Rights,* vol. 19, no. 1 (Winter, 1992), 26; Vicki Quade, "State Courts: The Next Frontier For Civil Liberties," *Human Rights,* vol. 19, no. 1 (Winter), 14; Steven Pressman, "Protecting Rights In State Courts," *Editorial Research Reports,* vol. 1, no. 20 (27 May 1988), 27; Priscilla Painton, "One Nation, Very Divisible," *Time* (8 October 1990), 76; Steven A. Hllmes, "Frustrated

By Change In Federal Courts, A.C.L.U. To Concentrate On States," *The New York Times*, vol. 141 (30 September 1991), 12 and 14; Ted Gest, "The Swing to the Left in State Courts," *U.S. News & World Report*, vol. 107, no. 16 (23 October 1989), 32; and "The States' Turn," *National Law Journal*, vol. 12, no. 7 (23 October 1989), 12. However, the 1992 election of President Clinton will cause many to reassess their predictions that the Republicans will control the direction of the Supreme Court for the foreseeable future.

51. For example, the supremacy clause of Article VI, which stipulates that "this Constitution, and the laws of the United States which shall be made in Pursuance thereof; and all Treaties made, or which shall be made, under the authority of the United States, shall be the supreme Law of the Land; *and the Judges in every State shall be bound thereby, any Thing in the Constitution or Laws of any State to the Contrary notwithstanding*" (emphasis added), does not necessarily imply national judicial supremacy. The language of the clause can reasonably be interpreted as a rule of construction for state judges in the event of a conflict between U.S. and state laws, in contradistinction to national judicial supremacy, Chief Justice John Marshall's opinion in McCulloch v. Maryland notwithstanding (4 L.Ed. 579 [1819]).
52. Publius stated the obvious when he observed: "Is the administration of justice between the citizens of the same State the proper department of the local government? These must possess all the authorities which are connected with this object, and with every other that may be allotted to their particular cognizance and direction. Not to confer in each case a degree of power commensurate to the end would be to violate the most obvious rules of prudence and propriety" (Hamilton, Madison, and Jay, *The Federalist Papers*, #23, Clinton Rossiter, ed., [New York: New American Library, 1961], 155). Of course, the judicial theories of selective and total incorporation have for all intents and purposes nationalized rights and placed the U.S. Supreme Court at the pinnacle of rights adjudication. As will be discussed *infra*, there is no evidence that the Rehnquist Court questions this pillar of national judicial dominance over the states, and correspondingly a significant obstacle to judicial federalism.
53. See Henry J. Abraham, *Freedom and the Court: Civil Rights and Liberties in the United States*, 5th ed. (New York: Oxford University Press, 1988), 12.
54. "The extent to which the Supreme Court assumes the functions of policy-maker is also of concern to us in the conduct of our judicial business.... We believe that in the fields with which we are entitled to speak, the Supreme Court too often has tended to adopt the role of policy-maker without proper judicial restraint" ("The Conference of Chief Justices." Report of the Committee on Federal-State Relations as Affected by Judicial Decisions, adopted August, 1958 [Pasadena, California, 1958], 34). Also see "Amending the Constitution to Strengthen the States in the Federal System," *State Government* (Winter, 1963), 10-15.
55. Steve Pressman, "Protecting Rights In State Courts," *Editorial Research Reports* (27 May 1988), 274). According to commentators, "federal attempts, legislative and judicial, to contract rights have acted as a rights-enforcing federalism catalyst. If nothing else, the occasional conservatism of the Burger Court has had the salutary effect of reminding the states that the protection of rights is not confined to judicial interpretations of the Fourteenth Amendment" (Ronald K. L. Collins and Peter J. Galie, "Models of Post-Incorporation Judicial Review: 1985 Survey of State Constitutional Individual Rights Decisions," *Publius: The Journal of Federalism*, vol. 16, 111 [Summer 1986], 139).

56. Karl R. Popper, *Conjectures and Refutations: The Growth of Scientific Knowledge* (New York: Basic Books, 1962), 33-59; obviously this is a different application of Popper's phrase, but its descriptive qualities merit such use.
57. See Article III, sections one and two.
58. This policy was established early in the Court's history; see Martin v. Hunter's Lessee, 4 L.Ed. 97 (1816) and Cohens V. Virginia, 5 L.Ed. 257 (1821).
59. John Kincaid, "A Proposal to Strengthen Federalism," *The Journal of State Government,* vol. 62, no. 1 (1989), 36,
60. Of course there is some measure of accountability, but it is remote and for all intents and purposes ineffectual. See William Lasser, *The Limits of Judicial Powers* (Chapel Hill: The University of North Carolina, 1988).

5

A Case Study of Judicial Federalism

I

Preceding the 1991 Louisiana statute criminalizing abortion in most instances, U.S. Supreme Court qualifications on *Roe* v. *Wade* reformulated the debate about the constitutional right to procure an abortion.[1] Anticipating that *Roe* was about to be overruled, in 1991 the State of Louisiana passed a statute criminalizing abortion in most instances, hoping to provoke the Rehnquist Court to act, that is, reverse the status quo established by *Roe* and move toward a federal approach to the issue. The statute was passed over the governor's veto, which is sufficient evidence of overwhelming public support for the law in Louisiana and it is reasonable to conclude that the traditions and consciences of Louisianians are opposed to abortion from conception to and beyond the point of fetal viability. Act 26, section 1, of the 1991 statute stipulates:

> It is declared to be the public policy of the state of Louisiana that it has a legitimate compelling interest in protecting, to the greatest extent possible, the life of the unborn from the time of conception until birth. We also affirm our belief that life begins at conception and that life thereafter is a continuum until the time of death.
>
> In furtherance of this compelling interest we declare it to be a reasonable and proper exercise of the police power of the state to prohibit and otherwise reasonably regulate, through the imposition of criminal penalties, the performance of abortions.[2]

The statute makes exceptions for preserving the health of the fetus, saving the life of the mother, and for pregnancies resulting from incest and rape. The criminal sanctions are limited to physicians performing unlawful abortions. Obviously, the statute raises several constitutional questions not yet ripe for judicial review, such as exempting the female who has an abortion from criminal penalties and the legislature's definition of "unborn" and "conception," which technically includes fertilized eggs for *in vitro* procedures. These issues were raised in the various court briefs, but what is of primary concern is not how the particular constitutional questions are answered, but the larger question of who, within the context of judicial federalism, is authorized to adjudicate this constitutional dispute.

II

Two separate suits were simultaneously filed in state and U.S. courts; the first, *Planned Parenthood of Louisiana, Inc., et al.* v. *State of Louisiana,* was filed in Louisiana's Nineteenth Judicial District Court, and the second, *Sojourner T., et al.* v. *Buddy Roemer, etc., et al,* was filed in the U.S. District Court for the Eastern District of Louisiana. The state district court scheduled trial on the merits for 29 August 1991; however, due to the pending federal trial the state district court continued trial without date. The primary rationale behind the continuance was that in the event a federal court declared the statute unconstitutional, the suit in the state court would have been dismissed as moot. On the other hand, if the federal courts declared the statute constitutional, trial in the state courts would have commenced within thirty days.[3] According to the state, "the continuance is a reasonable effort to avoid wasting judicial resources on duplicative litigation."[4] The U.S. District Court declared the statute to be unconstitutional on the grounds that the Louisiana statute is "in all Pertinent respects identical" to the Texas statute overturned in *Roe*; and only the U.S. Supreme Court is authorized to reverse *Roe*.[5] U.S. District Court Judge Duplantier enjoined the State from enforcing Act 26.

As *Sojourner* worked its way through the U.S. appellate process, the plaintiffs in *Planned Parenthood* were dissatisfied with the state district court's order and appealed to the Louisiana Supreme Court for writs to review the state district court's continuance order. The writs were denied. Subsequent to these denials, Planned Parenthood and the American Civil Liberties Union (respectively the primary plaintiffs in the state and federal cases) filed motions in the U.S. Fifth Circuit to certify questions to the Louisiana Supreme Court, that is, to direct the state courts to end the continuance. The motion of most significance for judicial federalism was filed by the Plaintiffs-Appellees. It requested that the U.S. Fifth Circuit "certify the following legal issue to the Supreme Court of Louisiana: Whether the Louisiana anti-abortion statute...violates Art.

I, Sec. 5 of the *Louisiana Constitution of 1974*, as amended, which guarantees that '*Every person shall be secure in his person... against... invasions of privacy.*'"[6] The plaintiffs maintained that "the proper course would have been, and remains, for the federal courts to abstain in order to allow the state courts to interpret the Act and resolve its validity under the state constitution."[7] Counsel for Louisiana responded to the rationale of the plaintiffs' counsel:

> The known facts more than suggest that the American Civil Liberties Union and Planned Parenthood sought first to invoke the protection of the federal courts on the basis of *Roe* v. *Wade*, but then to frustrate the normal procedure of appellate review within the federal system by shifting the case to the state court in order to avoid further review of *Roe*. Such manipulation of the federal jurisdiction perverts the very purpose of the certification process cited by appellees, namely the promotion of conservation of time, energy and resources and the promotion of cooperative federalism.[8]

The immediate cause of this jurisdictional dilemma was the perception at the time that the U.S. Supreme Court's *Roe* restrictions on state regulation of abortion had become increasingly tenuous,[9] while a more plausible case could be made about Louisiana's constitutional sanctions of abortion.[10] Consequently, the litigants were jockeying to place the issue in the most favorable judicial forum. This judicial jurisdictional muddle results in *vortical* federalism, by which I mean a situation in which the U.S. and state supreme courts are utilized in ad hoc fashion, in contradistinction to established rules of procedure with the requisite lines of demarcation between federal and state courts. The crux of this jurisdictional dilemma is the vagueness of the U.S. Supreme Court-devised abstention doctrine, through which the federal courts retain their dominance over state courts by converting the latter into administrative functionaries of the former. At the apex of this extended judiciary is the U.S. Supreme Court, intolerant of substantive deviations from its nationalized jurisprudence, especially in the policy area of unenumerated rights.

III

The abstention doctrine may be exercised at the discretion of a federal court when it defers a case to a state court, even though the federal court also has jurisdiction over the case. According to one commentator,

> A policy of abstaining for state adjudication of federal constitutional challenges to state action would be grounded in a concern both to relieve federal courts of congestion and to "steer around head-on collisions with the States by avoiding unnecessary constitutional decisions." It would rest on the propositions that state courts are as capable of deciding these controversies as are federal courts, and that Supreme Court review would adequately protect federal rights.[11]

The doctrine can be invoked for four distinguishable but overlapping reasons: "(1) to avoid decision of a federal constitutional question where the case may be disposed of on questions of state law; (2) to avoid needless conflict with the administration by a state of its own affairs; (3) to leave to the states the resolution of unsettled questions of state law; and (4) to ease the congestion of the federal court docket."[12] As stated, the abstention doctrine appears to be an important component of judicial federalism. However, because implementation by federal judges is discretionary, as opposed to statutory rules of procedures, its contribution to judicial federalism is minimal. From civil and criminal cases it is evident that the rules of procedure dividing U.S. and state courts' jurisdictions are, at best, ambiguous. In the words of Justice Rehnquist, "[A]s our cases abundantly illustrate, this area of law is in constant litigation, and it is an area through which our decisions have traced a path that may accurately be described as sinuous."[13]

The overlapping boundaries between *Planned Parenthood* v. *Louisiana* and *Sojourner* v. *Roemer* manifest the uncertainty surrounding jurisdiction in judicial federalism. Dissatisfied with the state district court's decision to continue proceedings until the U.S. Supreme Court decides the case, the plaintiffs in *Planned Parenthood* v. *Louisiana* appealed to the Louisiana Supreme Court to reconsider the continuance, thereby directing the trial court to proceed with the trial in spite of Louisiana's Code of Civil Procedure which, according to the state's counsel, sanctions the continuance; thus, the Louisiana Supreme Court sanctioned continuance could contravene the U.S. Supreme Court's abstention doctrine.[14]

Forum shopping for the most favorable court to litigate, the plaintiffs relied on a twofold procedural argument that epitomizes the new judicial federalism. First, the states are the front line of defense for the rights of the people. Plaintiffs argued:

> The state constitutions were the original guarantors of the rights of the people. The federal bill of rights was modeled on them, not the reverse. For the first century of the nation's history the federal constitution protected individuals only against in-

> cursions on liberty by the federal government, while state constitutions protected the liberty of the people against abuse by state authorities. Indeed, only the last thirty years have seen the Bill of Rights extended to state action through the Fourteenth Amendment. Nevertheless, while the federal Bill of Rights provides "ultimate" protection to the people's liberty the states, in our federal system, "remain the primary guardian of the people."[15]

Relying on the federal courts' abstention doctrine, state controversies must be first adjudicated in the state courts, in order to make most efficient use of the federal courts, that is, avoid "unnecessary federal constitutional litigation."[16] Quoting portions of the Pullman doctrine (1941), an often cited case for articulating the abstention doctrine, the plaintiffs maintained:

> [W]hen the state court's interpretation of the statute or evaluation of its validity under the state constitution may obviate any need to consider its validity under the Federal Constitution, the federal court should hold its hand, lest it render a constitutional decision unnecessarily.[17]

The plaintiffs, in short, maintained that if a constitutional issue can be resolved at the state level, the federal courts should abstain from preempting the state processes. Thus, in an ironic twist of judicial politics, the state of Louisiana was advocating judicial nationalism, while civil libertarians such as Planned Parenthood and the American Civil Liberties Union were supporting judicial states' rights. Obviously, their preferences for one or the other levels is not motivated by a disinterested view of the rules for civil procedure or constitutional federalism, but rather lodging the case in a judicial forum most favorable to their policy objectives. This type of forum shopping, that is jurisdictional opportunism, is made possible by the ambiguous and manipulative linkages between the federal and state courts. But as pointed out, "Supreme Court review would adequately (meaning ultimately) protect federal rights."

IV

The most important bridge linking the national and state courts is Section 25 of the First Judiciary Act; it provides the U.S. Supreme Court with appellate jurisdiction over state high courts.[18] Section 25 became increasingly controversial as writs began to issue from the U.S. Supreme Court to state courts. In response to a writ of error directed to the Virginian Court of Appeals in 1813, the state responded that "the court is unanimously of opinion that the appellate power of the Supreme Court of the

United States does not extend to this court under a sound construction of the constitution of the United States; that so much of the 25th section of the act of Congress, to establish the judicial courts of the United States, as extends the appellate jurisdiction of the Supreme Court to this court, is not in pursuance of the constitution of the United States."[19] Virginia and like-minded states advocated a judicial federalism in which state high courts were not placed in inferior appellate positions to the U.S. Supreme Court. If a case commenced in the state court system, it was to be terminated within that system; whereas if a case commenced within the federal system, the U.S. Supreme Court was the court of last resort. In 1821 Virginia made a similar claim that the appellate jurisdiction of the federal courts cannot be exercised over the judgment of a state supreme court.[20] Chief Justice Marshall upheld the constitutionality of Section 25, rejecting Virginia's claims on constitutional and practical grounds.[21] He advocated that "the necessity of uniformity, as well as correctness in expounding the constitution and laws of the United States, *would itself* suggest the propriety of vesting in some single tribunal the power of deciding, in the last resort, all cases in which they are involved."[22]

The U.S. Supreme Court's tendency toward judicial "correctness and uniformity" has animated its jurisprudence, and will continue to do so, talk about a new judicial federalism notwithstanding. The statutory limitations on the U.S. Supreme Court's jurisdiction are for all intents and purposes open-ended, due to the fact that the court has jurisdiction whenever there is a federal question involved, and in this post-incorporation era most, if not all, disputes involving unenumerated rights raise federal questions.[23] According to Justice Holmes, "[W]hatever springes [sic] the State may set for those who are endeavoring to assert rights that the State confers, the assertion of Federal rights, when plainly and reasonably made, is not to be defeated under the name of local practice."[24] In other words, the U.S. Supreme Court is the court of last resort on the adjudication of unenumerated rights.

V

A recent case manifests the actual, as opposed to the surmised, role of the U.S. Supreme Court in the new judicial federalism.[25] On the heels of *Planned Parenthood* v. *Casey* the U.S. Court of Appeals for the Fifth

Circuit trumped the prospects for judicial federalism in the Louisiana controversy. Judge Jolly concluded, "we hold that the Louisiana statute, on its face, is plainly unconstitutional under *Casey* because the statute imposes an undue burden on women seeking an abortion before viability."[26] What becomes clear is that in spite of some state judicial independence on the periphery, the mainstay of constitutional law in the area of unenumerated rights continues to be the U.S. Supreme Court. In fact the *dicta* of *Casey*[27] is symptomatic of the Court attempting to hold the center of power against the centrifugal tendencies of a viable judicial federalism, tendencies which would inevitably reduce the influence of the U.S. Supreme Court in national politics.

The issues in *Casey* involve five state provisions to regulate abortion; unlike the Louisiana statute (Act 26), Pennsylvania did not seek to prohibit most abortions outright.[28] What is of interest is not so much the results of the case, which facially deferred to the people of Pennsylvania on four of five issues, but rather the U.S. Supreme Court's nationalistic jurisprudence truncating federalism in general, and judicial federalism in particular. That jurisprudence has two pillars of support, institutional integrity and nationalized rights.[29]

First, the Court's qualified commitment to *stare decisis* marks an unwillingness to change its *modus operandi* toward the states. More than any other issue *Roe* was the litmus test for judicial federalism. It has been the central issue in the nominating and confirmation processes for Supreme Court justices for the Reagan, Bush, and Clinton administrations; it has been the subject of national and state legislative wrangling; it has been the subject of political campaigns from the presidency to local elections; and it has been the driving force behind peaceful and violent civil protests. In short, it has been if not the most important issue confronting the political process, certainly among the most important.[30] Within this political and social context the Supreme Court resolved to reaffirm the basic holding of *Roe* that there is a fundamental right for a woman to terminate a pregnancy up to the point of fetal viability outside the womb, thereby prohibiting the state to place "undue burdens" on a woman's option to exercise that right. In the words of the Court:

> After considering the fundamental constitutional questions resolved by *Roe*, principles of institutional integrity and the role of *stare decisis*, we are led to conclude this: the essential holding of *Roe* v. *Wade* should be retained and once again reaffirmed.[31]

Notice the language of the Court; "the *principles* of institutional integrity" and "the *role* of *stare decisis.*" The former is the objective by which the latter is a means to maintaining the prestige of the Supreme Court. The Court's majority opinion makes it quite clear that invoking *stare decisis* protects the Court from the perception that it has caved in to political pressures. Moreover, the Court majority reasoned that the threshold for overruling previous cases wrongly decided is higher in a charged political environment, because in those instances the rule of law is commingled with that segment of public opinion that gives the Court legitimacy and supports its "institutional integrity."[32] According to the Court,

> In the present case, however, as our analysis to this point makes clear, the terrible price would be paid for overruling.... To understand why this would be so it is necessary to understand the source of this Court's authority, the conditions necessary for its preservation, and its relationship to the country's understanding of itself as a constitutional republic.... The Court's power lies, rather, in its legitimacy, a product of substance and perception that shows itself in the people's acceptance of the Judiciary as fit to determine what the Nation's law means and to declare what it demands.... The Court must take care to speak and act in ways that allow people to accept its decisions on the terms the Court claims for them, as grounded truly in principle, not as compromises with social and political pressures having, as such, no bearing on the principled choices that the Court is obliged to make. Thus, the Court's legitimacy depends on making legally principled decisions under circumstances in which their principled character is sufficiently plausible to be accepted by the Nation.... So to overrule under fire in the absence of the most compelling reason to reexamine a watershed decision would subvert the Court's legitimacy beyond any serious question.[33]

Adhering to the first lesson of creative jurisprudence,[34] the U.S. Supreme Court's commitment to its institutional integrity should not be confused with its "constitutional institutional integrity"; the two are not necessarily synonymous. This is not to say that the Court has abandoned its constitutional function, but the Court does make it quite clear that it is willing to sustain constitutionally questionable precedent through *stare decisis* in order to protect it's legitimacy, that is, "the people's acceptance of the Judiciary as fit to determine what the Nation's law means and to declare what it demands."[35] This jurisprudential attitude does not appear to be receptive to a form of judicial federalism through which state courts could effectively question the omnipotence and omniscience of the nation's highest court.

Second, the Court has reaffirmed the expansively extensive limits of nationally sanctioned rights, rights that would qualify all inconsistent state policies. After stating that "neither the Bill of Rights nor specific practices of States at the time of the adoption of the Fourteenth Amendment marks the outer limits of the substantive sphere of liberty which the Fourteenth Amendment protects," the Court, almost cryptically, cites "See U.S. Const., Amend. 9."[36] In other words, the U.S. Supreme Court does not intend to narrowly read the Constitution in the articulation of rights, but will extend protection well beyond the document's plain language, in effect constituting *an ongoing constitutional convention* in the definition of unenumerated rights; thus, the significance of "See U.S. Const., Amend. 9."

Significantly, the Court approvingly quotes segments of Justice Harlan's dissenting opinion in *Poe* v. *Ullman,*[37] in which the Justice criticizes the majority for its dismissal of the case for want of jurisdiction:

> "[L]iberty" is not a series of isolated points pricked out in terms of the taking of property; the freedom of speech, press, and religion; the right to keep and bear arms; the freedom from unreasonable searches and seizures; and so on. It is a rational continuum which, broadly speaking, includes a freedom from all substantial arbitrary impositions and purposeless restraints...and which also recognizes, what a reasonable and sensitive judgment must, that certain interests require particularly careful scrutiny of the state needs asserted to justify their abridgment.[38]

The criteria for determining what constitutes "substantial arbitrary impositions" and "purposeless restraints" will be produced by the U.S. Supreme Court. In the words of the dissenting Chief Justice Rehnquist, even though "the decision to abort necessarily involves the destruction of a fetus" and, as posed by Justice Scalia, "The whole argument of abortion opponents is that what the Court calls the fetus and what others call the unborn child *is a human life,*" the Court preempts popular control by constitutionally classifying views of rights that are inconsistent with its own as "arbitrary and purposeless."[39]

The notable difference between *Casey*'s court majority and minority is the latter's willingness to defer to the states to resolve questions of unenumerated rights *which* are not delineated in the U.S. Constitution, thereby, in the words of Justice Scalia, "allowing for regional differences" and dethroning the "Imperial Judiciary."[40] Only *Casey*'s dissenters come close to challenging the very engines of national judicial activism—uniformity and correctness—and only in the remote event that *Casey*'s dissenters' jurisprudence should pervade the Court, could judicial federalism perchance take root and maybe blossom.[41]

VI

Within the context of U.S. Supreme Court judicial review over unenumerated rights there is little room for the states to deviate from the national rights standards. However, the extent to which the states may deviate is contingent upon the parameters established by the U.S. Supreme Court, and should a state overstep those parameters they are certain to be reeled back by the U.S. Supreme Court. To appreciate the magnitude of the Court's power in the area of unenumerated rights it is necessary to keep in mind that the definition of rights in general is two-directional, and that the Court is more or less receptive to state deviations depending upon whether the state is expanding or retracting U.S. Supreme Court defined rights. A state retraction challenges the role of the U.S. Supreme Court as the leader in the definition of rights, whereas a state expansion accepts the major premise of the Court's definition of rights and builds upon national standards. Thus, the U.S. Supreme Court is more likely to tolerate the latter and reject the former; but failing to tolerate both is an implicit rejection of a viable federalism in general, and a rejection of judicial federalism in particular.[42] Accordingly, all the commotion in the Fifth Circuit surrounding Louisiana's Act 26 was for naught, because the bottom line is that the U.S. Supreme Court reaffirmed in *Casey* the fundamental right to an abortion.[43]

The abortion issue is not unique. There is a litany of cases that can be brought forward to substantiate the Supreme Court's proclivities toward a vortical judicial federalism; whereas cases that significantly bolster a viable judicial federalism are few and in the larger scheme of things inconsequential. An increase in state court litigation in the area of rights should not be confused with a viable judicial federalism. The increase could be the result of the U.S. Supreme Court's willingness to permit state courts to adjudicate "rights" disputes, but with the qualification that such adjudication be done in accordance with national standards, making the state courts *de facto* extensions of the federal court bureaucracy.[44] In other words, it is a practical concession to reduce the case load of the federal courts, which has increased significantly.[45] Moreover, the fact of the matter is that the U.S. Supreme Court has not tolerated substantive state deviations from its vision of fundamental rights and the application of that vision through the Fourteenth Amendment.[46]

Creative jurisprudence has not only permeated the adjudication of unenumerated rights, but also an enumerated right. In his introduction to Patterson's *The Forgotten Ninth Amendment,* Pound advised practitioners of creative jurisprudence to use Second Amendment jurisprudence as a model,[47] to which our attention now turns.

Notes

1. 93 S.Ct. 705 (1973). See Webster v. Reproductive Health Services, et al. 109 S.Ct. (1989) for the watershed case in this development. As stated by counsel for Louisiana, "If *Roe* is still good law, then the Louisiana Abortion Statute is unconstitutional" (Brief filed on 16 October 1991, No. 91-3677, 1).
2. Act No. 26, section 1, 1991, *State of Louisiana, Acts of the Legislature,* vol. 1, Regular Session (1991), 229.
3. 19th Judicial District Court, Civil No. 370,917, Div. "A"; filed 14 August.
4. Brief of Respondent (15 May 1992), no. 92-CC-0431, 4.
5. U.S. District Court, Eastern District of Louisiana, *Reasons for Judgment* (7 August 1991), Case no. 91-2422, 2-3.
6. Motion filed by Appellee, D. Ifeanyi Charles Okpalobi (4 October 1991), no. 91-3677, 1. Summarily, Planned Parenthood claimed in the state court that the "Act violates the following provisions of the Louisiana Constitution's Declaration of Rights (Article I): The right to privacy and medical self-determination (Section 5); the right to equal protection of the laws and freedom from discrimination on the basis of sex (Section 5); the right not to be subjected to involuntary servitude (Section 3); the right not to be discriminated against on the basis of religious beliefs (Section 3); the right to free speech (Section 7); the right to due process of law (Section 2); and the protection against the State establishing a religion or prohibiting the free exercise of religion (Section 8)" (Brief Amicus Curiae of Planned Parenthood, U.S. Fifth Circuit [17 October 1991], no. 91-3677, 1).
7. Ibid., ii.
8. Brief for Appellant Harry F. Connick, no. 91-3677, 6 (footnotes and citations omitted).
9. See Harris v. McRae 448 U.S. 297 (1980), Webster v. Reproductive Health Services 492 U.S. 490 (1989), Hodgson v. Minnesota 497 U.S. 417 (1990), Rust v. Sullivan 111 S. Ct. 1759 (1991), and Planned Parenthood v. Casey (1992).
10. See John Devlin, "Privacy and Abortion Rights Under the Louisiana State Constitution: Could *Roe* v. *Wade* be Alive and Well in the Bayou State?" *Louisiana Law Review,* vol. 51 (1991), 685–732.
11. Martha A. Field, "Abstention In Constitutional Cases: The Scope of the Pullman Abstention Doctrine," *University of Pennsylvania Law Review,* vol. 122, no. 5, 1071 (1974), 1079 (notes omitted). Field raises the "hypotheses that federal judges are more capable of deciding questions of federal law and are more sympathetic to federal constitutional claims than are state court judges. Federal judges are primarily responsible for mastering federal law, while state judges concentrate on state law" (ibid., 1083; notes omitted). One could conceptually maintain that there is "parity" between the U.S. and state courts, but practically the U.S. courts are presumed to be superior: "Parity does not have the unanimous support of either

the judicial or academic community. Most of the critics of parity posit an overt hostility on the part of state courts to the vindication of federal constitutional rights. Bereft of modern evidence of the purported hostility, critics also contend that federal courts are more competent and comfortable with federal law than state courts because they deal with it more often. They claim it is simply unwise to route federal litigation to state courts" [Michael E. Solimine and James L. Walker, "State Court Protection Of Federal Constitutional Rights," *Harvard Journal of Law & Public Policy,* vol. 12, no. 1, 127, 130 (1989); notes omitted].

12. Charles Alan Wright, *The Law Of Federal Courts* (St. Paul, Minn.: West Publishing Co., 1983), 303.
13. Ibid., note 44, 326; see 302–30 for an account of the Supreme Court's attempt to articulate and apply the rules involved.
14. Article 532 reads: "When a suit is brought in a Louisiana Court when another is pending in a court in another state or of the United States on the same transaction or occurrence, between the same parties, in the same capacities, a motion of the defendant or on its own motion; the court may stay all proceedings in the second suit until the first has been discontinued or final judgment has been rendered" (Louisiana Code of Civil Procedure, Article 532); see Defendant-Respondent's Exhibit B-1, 6-9.
15. Brief for Plaintiff, Planned Parenthood, for Supervisory Writs (14 February 1992), 12 (notes omitted).
16. Ibid., 12.
17. Ibid., 13 (notes omitted); quoting from Railroad Commission of Texas v. Pullman Co., 85 L.Ed. 971 (1941).
18. See Act of 24 September 1789, section 25, 1 Stat. 73, 85, 736.
19. Martin v. Hunter's Lessee, 4 L.Ed. 97 (1816).
20. See Cohens v. Virginia, 5 L.Ed. 257 (1821) 258–76. In reference to section 25 of the 1789 Judiciary Act, counsel for the state maintained that "Congress cannot authorize the Supreme Court to exercise appellate jurisdiction over decisions of the state courts, unless they have legislative power over those courts. Can Congress give an appeal from a federal district court to a state court of appeal? I presume it will be admitted that they cannot. And why can they not? Because they have no power over the state court. And if they cannot give an appeal to that court, they cannot give an appeal from that court" (ibid., 272). As stated by Wright, "Criticism over the appellate jurisdiction continued over the years—indeed even today it is not entirely stilled—and famous opinions by Chief Justices Marshall and Taney were required to restate the principles of Martin v. Hunter's Lessee" (Wright, 737, notes omitted).
21. "We are not restrained, then, by the political relations between the general and state governments, from construing the words of the constitution, defining the judicial power, in their true sense. We are not bound to construe them more restrictively than they naturally import. They give to the supreme court [*sic*] appellate jurisdiction in all cases arising under the constitution, laws, and treaties of the United States. The words are broad enough to comprehend all cases of this description, in whatever court they may be decided" (Cohens v. Virginia, 294).
22. Ibid., 294 (italics not in original). Quoting from Hamilton's *The Federalist Papers* #80, Chief Justice Marshall: "Thirteen independent courts... of final jurisdiction over the same causes, arising upon the same laws, is a hydra in government, from which nothing but contradiction and confusion can proceed" (ibid., 294).

23. The acts of 24 September 1789, 25, 1 Stat. 73; 23 December 1914, c. 2, 38 Stat. 790; and 13 February 1925, c. 229, 1, 43 Stat. 937 mark the major legislative attempts to delineate the scope of Supreme Court review of state court decisions; (see Wright, 736-54.)
24. Davis v. Wechsler, 68 L.Ed. 143 (1923); cited in Wright, 749.
25. For overly optimistic, premature conclusions about judicial federalism, see Vincent Martin Bonventre, "Beyond The Reemergence—'Inverse Incorporation' And Other Prospects For State Constitutional Law," *Albany Law Review*, vol. 53 (Winter 1989), 403-18; Collins and Galie, "Models of Post-Incorporation Judicial Review: 1985 Survey of State Constitutional Individual Rights Decisions," *Publius: The Journal of Federalism* 16 (Summer 1986), 111-39; Collins, Galie, and Kincaid, "State High Courts, State Constitutions, and Individual Rights Litigation Since 1980: A Judicial Survey," ibid., 141-61; and Stanley H. Friedelbaum, "Reactive Responses: The Complementary Role of Federal and State Courts," *Publius* (Winter 1987), 33-50. In a more revealing discussion of the subject, Professors Solimine and Walker maintain that state courts do not deserve parity with the federal courts until the former become more like the latter, administratively and ideologically (see Michael E. Solomine and James L. Walker, "State Court Protection Of Federal Constitutional Rights," *Harvard Journal of Law & Public Policy*, vol. 12 [Winter 1989], 127-62, especially 162).
26. Sojourner T., et al., v. Edwards, et al., (Fifth Circuit), no. 91-3677, 8, filed 22 September 1992 (footnote omitted).
27. Planned Parenthood of Southeastern Pennsylvania, et al., v. Robert Casey, et al., 60 LW 4795 (1992).
28. See syllabus, on 4795, ibid. Of the five provisions (married women were required to notify husbands; informed consent prior to the abortion and a minimum twenty-four hour waiting period; parental consent for minors with a judicial bypass, exceptions for medical emergencies; and certain reporting requirements for abortion providers) only the first was declared to be unconstitutional.
29. Of course, Justices Rehnquist, Scalia, White, and Thomas dissented in the case, and consequently do not fit the mold of the majority; see *infra*.
30. See David M. O'Brien, *Storm Center: The Supreme Court in American Politics* (New York: W.W. Norton & Company, 1990), 23-61.
31. Planned Parenthood v. Casey, 4798.
32. Ibid., 4803-04; "Where, in the performance of its judicial duties, the Court decides a case in such a way as to resolve the sort of intensely divisive controversy reflected in *Roe* and those rare, comparable cases, its decision has a dimension that the resolution of the normal case does not carry" (ibid., 4804).
33. Ibid., 4804.
34. See chap. 3, *supra*.
35. Ibid., 4804.
36. Ibid., 4799.
37. Poe v. Ullman, 367 U.S. 497 (1961); take note of the creativeness of citing dissenting opinions as authoritative and the "interstitial" nature of displacing the precedent of *Poe* almost inadvertently (see chap. 3, *infra*).
38. Planned Parenthood v. Casey, 4799.
39. Ibid., 4828, 4836.
40. Ibid., 4842, 4840.
41. It is not my purpose to discern the etiology of the Court's jurisprudence toward federalism; nevertheless, the love of power and political ambition are plausible

motivations (see *The Federalist,* nos. 6 & 10), as opposed to constitutional exegesis (see Raoul Berger, *Federalism: The Founders' Design* [Norman, Okla.: University of Oklahoma Press, 1989]).

42. Some commentators understate the obvious. They acknowledge the dominance of the Supreme Court while at the same time overstating the impact of increased state activism.
43. In the wake of *Casey,* the Fifth Circuit overturned the state law; Louisiana appealed to the U.S. Supreme Court, with certiorari being denied (see 61 LW 3620, 92-1066).
44. Obviously, U.S. Supreme Court precedent has an incalculable chilling effect on state supreme courts. Once again, see Evans v. Romer, 854 P. 2d. 1270 (Colo. 1993). In this Colorado case, a state constitutional amendment, passed by a margin of 813,966 to 710,151 (53.4 percent to 46.6 percent) on 3 November 1992 was declared unconstituional by the supreme court of Colorado. Amendment 2 was titled, "No Protected Status Based on Homosexual, Lesbian, or Bisexual Orientation" (ibid., 1272). Relying on U.S. Supreme Court precedent, the state supreme court concluded that "in short, Amendment 2, to a reasonable probability, infringes on a fundamental right protected by the Equal Protection Clause of the United States Constitution" (ibid., 1286).
45. See Harold W. Stanley and Richard G. Niemi, *Vital Statistics On American Politics,* 4th ed. (Washington, D.C.: CQ Press, 1994), 301-306.
46. The Supreme Court's jurisprudence on federalism cannot be neatly classified as liberal, moderate, or conservative. As evidenced by a case decided the same day as Casey, even the most staunch advocate of state prerogatives on one issue can take the nationalistic view on another (see Justice Scalia's court opinion in *David H. Lucas* v. *South Carolina Coastal Council,* where regarding the issue of property rights he discusses the Court's "taking jurisprudence," the South Carolina's power over the "bundle of rights," its "legitimate exercise of its police powers," and "the Takings Clause that has become part of our constitutional culture" (60 LW 4842 [1992], 4848-49).
47. See chap. 3, *infra.*

6

The Second Amendment and Creative Jurisprudence: A View from the States

A well regulated Militia, being necessary to the security of a free State, the right of the people to keep and bear Arms, shall not be infringed (Second Amendment to the United States Constitution).

I

In contemporary political discourse few issues are as salient and divisive as governmental regulation of the right to bear arms. The escalating demands for regulation (resulting in local, state, and national legislative assemblies proposing, formulating, and implementing gun-control laws) is in response to increasing homicide rates, drug trafficking, paramilitary organizations, and other real and imagined transgressions against the public order. Notably, I have not preoccupied myself with the effectiveness of gun-control legislation on protecting society from such antisocial behavior, the alleged public policy concern of gun-control interlocutors. This is not meant to imply that the public order implications of gun control are trivial. To the contrary; such implications are obviously of great importance, but for our purposes secondary to the issue of creative jurisprudence.

Obviously the federal arrangement has been and will continue to be transformed as national public policymakers attempt to remedy what they consider to be the deficiencies of state public policies. One needs only to consider the public policy areas of commerce, education, health, and civil rights to appreciate the magnitude of the transformation. Concerns about popular control and the relevance of federalism is, at best, an afterthought as the public policy prerogatives of the states are shifted to the national government. Gun-control legislation is no exception. However, and this is exceptional, the status of the states in the American federal system is especially compromised by national gun-control legislation. Whereas most of the national government's policy discretion over the states hinges on various U.S. Supreme Court decisions and congressional intergovernmental transfers, such as categorical and block grants,[1] they are subject to constitutional and political alterations, whereas national gun control strikes at a much more significant pillar of American federalism, a pillar that is in a constitutional class unique to the American system of popular control. This important but not so obvious fact has been overlooked by the participants in the ongoing gun-control debate.

National gun-control policies undermine American federalism by incrementally removing a significant check of the states on the national government and preempting, with U.S. Supreme Court sanction, the states' rights of self-defense. This national preemption (or more precisely usurpation, as will be argued) is not limited to who has the final say over "the right to bear arms," the national or state governments; more importantly the right to bear arms is itself a main line of defense against the most contentious forms of national government aggrandizement of the public policy prerogatives of the people within their respective states.[2] As is the case with separation of powers, the electoral process, and amending the Constitution (Article V), the Second Amendment was intended to provide security for the lives, liberties, and properties of the American people within their respective states vis-à-vis—among other immediate and remote threats—an overbearing national government. A fundamental tenet of early American political culture is that all governments have an inherent tendency to exceed their legitimate ends and oppress the governed. Hence, the framers' insistence upon a system of governing with limited powers and constrained within those limits by specified internal and external checks, with a recourse to arms being of the latter category.

In order to explicate the nature of Second Amendment creative jurisprudence, the intent of the framers, Second Amendment case law, and contemporary congressional initiatives will be analyzed. This analysis provides valuable insight into the processes of creative jurisprudence.

II

The framers[3] (both Antifederalists and Federalists) anticipated that the federal arrangement would not be static, but fluctuating and occasionally confrontational. Federalism, it must be remembered, was originally the distribution of political power between communities of individuals within the political jurisdictions of their respective states and a national organization of states. The people, living in their distinct state communities, created the national government in contradistinction to the national government being the product of a national community of individuals the states notwithstanding. Put otherwise, there is no hard evidence that the U.S. Constitution authorizes the U.S. Congress and/or the U.S. Supreme Court to gradually divest the states of their place in the federal arrangement to the extent that American federalism has been displaced by a unitary national government. Toward that end the framers included in the Constitution provisions that secure the status of the states vis-à-vis the national government.

Because American federalism embodies two levels of republican government, each with their corresponding constitutional powers, the system is doubly confronted with the perennial problem "that power is of an encroaching nature and that it ought to be effectually restrained from passing the limits assigned to it."[4] Effectively restraining power is no easy task, especially when the restraint is directed toward governments.[5] Publius maintained that "this tendency is not difficult to be accounted for. It has its origin in the love of power. Power controlled or abridged is almost always the rival and enemy of that power by which it is controlled or abridged."[6] Accordingly, because the national and state governments attempt to constrain each other, they inherently compete for power and influence within the federal framework. Therefore, there is the necessity for effective means to keep the respective governments within their assigned constitutional spheres. The peaceful means of institutional separation of powers (judicial review included), elections, and the amendment process were augmented by the presence of armed state citizens.[7]

The check and balance function of an armed citizenry on government is significant, especially in light of the framers' operational assumptions of human nature and their conviction that governments are inclined to illegitimately expand their powers at the expense of the peoples' liberties. To forbid citizens to possess firearms, or to concede that such possession was not a fundamental right, would have been inconsistent with their distrust of government, particularly a distant and unknown national government. Thus, including an armed citizenry in the federal formula was consistent with the Antifederalists' concerns about the centralizing and potentially oppressive tendencies of the national government.

The objective of American federalism was to promote collective interests of the states. Elections, the legislative process, and the amendment process were the procedural means to be used to discern the collective interests while simultaneously grounding the national government's policies in popular control. Should these mechanisms fail, arms are the constitutional means at the peoples' disposal to secure their interests against an oppressive national government. Consistent with the framers' view of human nature, posterity is cautioned that men are "ambitious, vindictive, and rapacious,"[8] and because people are much more disposed to "vex and oppress each other than to co-operate for their common good,"[9] effective means are necessary to protect the governed from the government. If such were not the case, then the internal and external checks on government—state and national—would be superfluous.[10] A state armed citizenry is one of the essential checks on a national government that has gone too far in the exercise of its powers, to the point where a state or states are compelled to resort to armed resistance.

Obviously, the framers wanted political compromise and not armed confrontation as the means to resolve trivial or transient political differences. Nevertheless, the citizens of a state or states, acting through their agents in state government, have the option of resorting to armed conflict to resist oppression.[11] Publius acknowledged as much in his attempt to allay the fears of opponents to the proposed Constitution. He claimed that the armed citizens of the respective states would outnumber the national forces twenty-five to one in the event of a constitutional crisis that deteriorated into military confrontation between the national and state governments. Furthermore, he anticipated that the states would prevail in such a contest:

> Let a regular army, fully equal to the resources of the country, be formed; and let it be entirely at the devotion of the federal government: still it would not be going too far to say that the State governments with the people on their side would be able to repel the danger. The highest number to which, according to the best computation,

> a standing army can be carried in any country does not exceed one hundredth part of the whole number of souls; or one twenty-fifth part of the number able to bear arms. This proportion would not yield, in the United States, an army of more than twenty-five or thirty thousand men. To these would be opposed a militia amounting to near half a million of citizens with arms in their hands, officered by men chosen from among themselves, fighting for their common liberties and united and conducted by governments possessing their affections and confidence.[12]

The states' armed citizens would be animated with a spirit to defend their rights and liberties: "Let us not insult the free and gallant citizens of America with the suspicion that they would be less able to defend the rights of which they would be in actual possession than the debased subjects of arbitrary power would be to rescue theirs from the hands of their oppressors."[13]

Such acknowledgments on the part of the nationalistic Publius are significant because they reveal underlying assumptions on the part of the framers that: (1) the citizens in the states will be armed; and (2) those same citizens could and would use their arms to protect their liberties in the event of an armed contest between them and the national government.

The Second Amendment protected through fundamental law the means of such state resistance to an usurping national government. There is no provision of the U.S. Constitution that contradicts this method of protection. The U.S. Congress does have the power to protect the states against invasion and, if requested by the state legislature or executive, domestic violence.[14] Furthermore, the Congress has the power "to provide for calling forth the Militia to execute the Laws of the Union, suppress Insurrections and repel Invasions."[15] Under such circumstances the state and national governments would be on amiable terms acting cooperatively to maintain public order. These national powers were designed to protect the states, in contradistinction to subjecting the states to unwanted national policies. For example, the power to suppress insurrections was directed toward rebellion against the U.S. Government by private individuals and not by a state. An insurrection by definition is an act of revolting against civil authority, whereas military confrontation between the national and state governments is a state of war. This distinction was a major concern for the Federalists and the basis of their rationale to extend the authority of the national government to individuals, unlike the Articles of Confederation where national authority was limited to the states: "In an association where the general authority is confined to the collective bodies of the communities that compose it, every breach of the laws must involve a state of war."[16] To be sure, such states of war were to be avoided at all costs, but the possibility of such wars, never mind how remote, constitutionally precluded national disarmament of the states.

This attitude toward potential conflict and the right of the states to be armed as a measure toward self-defense was more than the consequence of philosophical deliberations among the delegates at the Philadelphia Convention. The agreement to adopt amendments after ratification, the right to bear arms included, was for the most part inevitable. Its inevitability was a consequence of the fact that the commitment to self-defense was an integral part of the American political culture. This is evidenced by the state constitutions, most of which included as part of their fundamental law declarations of rights that included self-defense. A brief overview of fundamental law along the continuum of post-1776 independence, the ratification period circa 1787 to 1789, and the early period of admission of territories into the Union make unmistakably clear the determination of the states to provide for their defense by incorporating into their fundamental laws the right to bear arms.[17]

Five of the original thirteen states' post-1776 constitutions made no specific declaration maintaining the right to keep and bear arms for either the state or the individual. This is not to say that such a right was not ensured by custom; the citizens in those same states were armed. Both Connecticut and Rhode Island are special cases, insofar that their organic laws, until 1818 and 1842, respectively, were carryovers from their colonial days. They are *The Fundamental Orders of Connecticut 1638* and *The Charter of Rhode Island and Providence Plantations 1663.* In those constitutions Connecticut fundamental law stipulated "Every citizen has the right to bear arms in defence of himself and the State"[18] and Rhode Island's that "the right of the people to keep and bear arms shall not be infringed."[19]

The constitutions of Pennsylvania (1776 and 1790), Vermont (1786 and 1793), Kentucky (1792 and 1799), and Ohio (1802) each included provisions that stipulated "that the people have the right to bear arms for the defence of themselves and the State."[20] The North Carolina Constitution of 1776 stipulated "that the people have a right to bear arms, for the defence of the State."[21] The Massachusetts Constitution of 1780 protected "the right of the people to keep and bear arms for the common defence."[22] The constitutions of Virginia (1776 and 1830),

New Hampshire (1784 and 1792), and Maryland (1776), respectively, stipulated "that a well-regulated militia, composed of the body of the people, trained to arms, is the proper, natural, and safe defence of a free State," "A well-regulated militia is the proper, natural, and sure defence of a State," and "that a well-regulated militia is the proper and natural defence of a free government."[23]

Thus, the fundamental laws of a majority of the states affirmed not merely the right of the citizens of the states to possess arms in the defense of themselves and their state, but also the necessity. This was a constitutional prerogative of the states and the Second Amendment to the U.S. Constitution essentially reaffirmed that prerogative. Moreover, without evidence to the contrary one must assume that the ratifying conventions of the states (which approved both the U.S. Constitution and the subsequent Bill of Rights) and the Congresses that admitted the various territories into the Union during this period were in the possession of rational men. Such being the case, it is obvious that the Second Amendment to the U.S. Constitution emanated from the determination of the U.S. Constitution's drafters and ratifiers to provide the constitutional means whereby individuals and the states could protect their lives, liberties, and properties, not only through the political mechanisms of elections and separation of powers, but also through the right to resort to force when necessitated by circumstances, as stipulated in the organic laws of their states. Otherwise most of the states would have ratified a national constitution obtrusively inconsistent with a basic tenet of their own state constitutions.

Publius's acknowledgment of the states' military superiority was not merely reassurance for the states who were concerned about national oppression, but a political imperative; he had no other politically viable alternative. The Second Amendment was the constitutional means to maintain this military imbalance of power between the two levels of government. This is not to imply that the U.S. Constitution is devoid of restrictions that limit a state from an impulsive recourse to arms, or that such a recourse was desirable. First, the entire scheme of federalism diverts political discontent through conflict resolution channels, such as the electoral process, the legislative process, judicial review, and the amendment process of Article V, all of which are designed to resolve conflict peaceably. Second, Article I, section 10, specifically prohibits states from keeping troops and ships of war in time of peace without the consent of the Congress. This limitation was designed to forestall the natural rivalry among the states themselves and between the states and the national government from degenerating into armed confrontation.[24] Significantly, however, should the people of a state decide to exercise their natural right of revolution,[25] the armed citizenry would be at the state's disposal to organize and place in the field, congressional objections notwithstanding. Hence, the U.S. Constitution's qualification (to be found in the same clause of Article I, section 10) that congressional consent to engage in war may be bypassed if a state is "actually invaded, or in such imminent danger as will not admit of delay," emanates from the state's responsibility to defend its interests against belligerents, whomever they may be.

In extreme circumstances states were expected to defend their interests, with the right to bear arms being a means toward that end.[26] Thus, state constitutional provisions that protected the right of the people to bear arms for the defense of themselves and their states were consistent with the Second Amendment; the latter simply reaffirmed the former.

III

Contrary to some commentaries, American jurisprudence has not bypassed the Second Amendment.[27] It is neither a "relic" nor a "fossil of a lost tradition," but an aspect of American political culture that permeates the politics of millions of Americans. Minimal overt Second Amendment U.S. Supreme Court cases should not be misconstrued as evidence of the Amendment's irrelevance; to the contrary, there have been significant changes *sub rosa* regarding the amendment's place in constitutional law. It should be kept in mind that U.S. Supreme Court decisions not to grant certiorari, in the midst of significant national gun-control legislation, substantially impact Second Amendment jurisprudence by upholding innovative decisions by U.S. courts of appeal.

Although they may be numerically minimal, the jurisprudence of the Second Amendment is represented by several cases that make manifest the development of case law, which has substantially altered the meaning of the Second Amendment. The four cases are *United States* v. *Cruikshank et al.* (1876), *Presser* v. *Illinois* (1886), *United States* v. *Miller* (1939), and *United States* v. *Warin* (Sixth Circuit 1976).

IV

The facts of *United States* v. *Cruikshank* involve the denial of the rights of assembly, bearing arms, and the voting rights of two African American citizens of Louisiana. In this post-Fourteenth Amendment and preselective incorporation decision the U.S. Supreme Court concluded that the issue of the "right to bear arms" is beyond the scope of national legislation, the U.S. Enforcement Act of 1870 notwithstanding. Even though the Fourteenth Amendment provides Congress with the mandate to protect African Americans in the exercise of their basic rights from state infringements, "the duty of a government to afford protection is limited always by the power it possesses for that purpose" and the United States government possessed no power to regulate the right to bear arms.[28] The right to bear arms is a state issue in the federal system and congressional intervention on behalf of African Americans via the Fourteenth Amendment cannot, the Court concluded, constitutionally supplant this state prerogative:

> We have in our political system a government of the United States and a government of each of the several States. Each one of these governments is distinct from the others, and each has citizens of its own who owe it allegiance, and whose rights, within its jurisdiction, it must protect. The same person may be at the same time a citizen of the United States and a citizen of a State, but his rights of citizenship under one of these governments will be different from those he has under the other.[29]

Accordingly, to claim the right to bear arms under the U.S. Constitution is a misnomer: "This is not a right granted by the Constitution. Neither is it in any manner dependent upon that instrument for its existence. The second amendment declares that it shall not be infringed; but this, as has been seen, means no more than that it shall not be infringed by Congress."[30] Moreover, the U.S. Bill of Rights, including the Second Amendment, "left the authority of the States just where they found it, and added nothing to the already existing power of the United States."[31]

The Court's ruling in *Cruikshank* is a straightforward affirmation of federalism. The Second Amendment restricts the national government from intruding upon the prerogatives of the states to regulate their respective inhabitants' access to and possession of firearms, an important qualification.

Cruikshank involved the issue of private relations within a state, which involved private citizens disarming other citizens. Ten years later the

U.S. Supreme Court specifically addressed the issue of state gun control. In *Presser* v. *Illinois* (1886) the Court did acknowledge some limits to the states' regulatory power over the right to bear arms.[32] Those limits stem from the Congress' delegated power to raise and support armies and to provide for calling forth the militia to execute the laws of the Union.[33] A state may not disarm its inhabitants to the point where it obstructs Congress' ability to utilize the state militia for national objectives. According to *Presser,*

> It is undoubtedly true that all citizens capable of bearing arms constitute the reserved military force or reserve militia of the United States as well as of the states, and, in view of this prerogative of the general government, as well as of its general powers, the states cannot, even laying the constitutional provision in question out of view, prohibit the people from keeping and bearing arms, so as to deprive the United States of their rightful resource for maintaining the public security, and disable the people from performing their duty to the general government.[34]

Presser qualified the parameters of the Second Amendment to the extent that a state could not interfere with the right to bear arms within its jurisdiction insofar as such interference impaired the ability of the Congress to utilize armed people within the state for national objectives. The Court reasoned that the Second Amendment does not prohibit the national government from enhancing the right to bear arms within a state if such national policy is designed to maintain "public security," but it does prohibit the states from restricting that right to the point of disarming their respective citizens where the national government's responsibility to maintain an army is impaired. The Court was essentially balancing two constitutional mandates, the congressional task of arming the national military[35] and the state prerogative to regulate the right to "keep and bear arms within its jurisdiction." This balancing was designed to minimize unwarranted state interference into national foreign policy.

From this qualification in *Presser* the Court moved to the more intrusive infringement of Second Amendment rights in *United States* v. *Miller* (1939). In *Miller* the Court extended the rationale of *Presser* to the point where Second Amendment rights are subservient to the Congress' delegated powers to regulate interstate commerce, raise and support armies, and execute the laws of the Union.[36] The Court conceded that the Second Amendment protects state prerogatives to maintain well-regulated militias:

> The Militia which the States were expected to maintain and train is set in contrast with Troops which they were forbidden to keep without the consent of Congress.... the Militia comprised all males physically capable of acting in concert for the common defense.[37]

However, the Court also concluded that it is the responsibility of the national government, specifically the Congress, to decide what weapons are appropriate for the state militias:

> The Constitution as originally adopted granted to the Congress power—"To provide for calling forth the Militia to execute the Laws of the Union, suppress Insurrections and repel Invasion; To provide for organizing, arming, and disciplining, the Militia, and for governing such Part of them as may be employed in the Service of the United States, reserving to the States respectively, the Appointment of the Officers, and the Authority of training the Militia according to the discipline prescribed by Congress." With the obvious purpose to assure the continuation and render possible the effectiveness of such forces the declaration and guarantee of the Second Amendment were made. It must be interpreted and applied with that end in view.[38]

With such an "end in view" the Court concluded that a shotgun having a barrel of less than eighteen inches in length does not "have a reasonable relationship to the preservation or efficiency of a well regulated militia" and that the Second Amendment does not protect one in the possession of such a weapon: "Certainly it is not within judicial notice that this weapon is any part of the ordinary military equipment or that its use could contribute to the common defense,"[39] the common defense being national in scope, in contradistinction to a state's defense against a potentially oppressive national government.

The Court's reasoning flies in the face of common sense construction of the Second Amendment as delineated in *Cruikshank*'s conclusion that "the right to bear arms is not granted by the Constitution; neither is it in any manner dependent upon that instrument for its existence. The Second Amendment means no more than that it shall not be infringed by Congress, and has no other effect than to restrict the powers of the national government."[40] But what the Court initiated in *Presser* (i.e., applying other constitutional provisions to the Second Amendment thereby permitting the national government to override state policy preferences regarding the right to bear arms) it established as precedent in *Miller*. But that precedent is not on constitutional *terra firma*.

In *Miller* the Court relied upon the arming policies of a colony and a few states[41] to make the claim that the right to bear arms was from the very beginning a very much qualified and regulated right. A case in point,

> The New York Legislature directed: "That every abled body Male person be enrolled in the Company of such Beat.... That every Citizen so enrolled, shall within three Months thereafter, provide himself, at his own Expense, with a good Musket or Firelock, a sufficient Bayonet and Belt, a Pouch with a Box therein to contain not less than twenty-four Cartridges suited to the Bore of his Musket or Firelock."[42]

The Court concluded that the National Firearms Act of 1934 was consistent with the precedents of early state regulation on the right to bear arms. Remarkably, (or shall we say "creatively") the Court failed to make the important and elementary distinction between state regulation and Congressional regulation on the right to bear arms. Once such a legislative power is conceded to and acted upon by the U.S. Congress, the right of the people to bear arms within their respective states has been infringed.

As delineated in *Cruikshank* the Second Amendment was intended to restrict the Congress, not the states.[43] If *Cruikshank* were still the controlling precedent, state gun-control laws would be consistent with the Second Amendment, whereas Congressional gun control—exercised as a national police power to address domestic crime—would be voided on Second Amendment grounds. Nevertheless, the *Miller* decision essentially overturned *Cruikshank* by subordinating the Second Amendment to national policy objectives, specifically as those objectives pertain to national politics, and not states' rights. Because a sawed-off shotgun is not a part of the national arsenal, and therefore not necessary to national security, citizens within their respective states can be denied the "right" to possess such weapons by national legislation. The U.S. Congress will determine what is and is not appropriate weaponry, the Second Amendment notwithstanding.

From a structural perspective it is untenable to maintain that Congressional regulatory power over commerce and national defense neutralizes what would otherwise be Second Amendment infringements. The Second Amendment, as is the case with the Bill of Rights in general, was added to the Constitution to clarify and qualify the limits of the delegated national powers, especially those in Article I, section 8. In this instance the delegated powers to regulate interstate commerce and raise armies should defer to the Second Amendment limitations, just as the necessary and proper clause of Article I, section 8, defers to First Amendment limitations. For example, judicially it would be difficult to maintain that Congress' regulatory power over interstate commerce would constitutionally legitimatize a law "establishing a religion" on the grounds that a national religion is more conducive to economic growth or national security.[44] The same holds true for the Second Amendment. As the First Amendment qualifies and restricts the power of the Congress, so too should the Second.

Furthermore, to interpret the *Miller* decision as conducive toward the maintenance of Second Amendment rights is attributable to a failure to put the issue within the context of federalism. Consider one commentator on the subject who applauds *Miller* on the grounds that it "stands for the proposition that the people, in their capacity as individuals, could keep and bear arms appropriate for militia use,"[45] the sawed-off shotgun simply is not such a weapon. But the primary constitutional issue is not which weapons are and are not appropriate for the militia; the constitutional issue is where are such determinations to be made, within the national or state political processes? The evidence indicates that the intent of the Second Amendment's framers was to leave these public policy determinations to the states.

Not to be deterred, the pro-gun advocates also disingenuously attempt to circumvent the Second Amendment. In their zeal to remove actual and potential obstacles to their assumed minimally regulated right to bear arms, including state regulation,[46] recourse to the selective theory of incorporation has provided cover. One such advocate contends that "the United States Supreme Court would seem logically and historically compelled by the fourteenth amendment to recognize that the fundamental right to keep and bear arms is protected from states' infringement, just as this right is protected from national infringement by the second amendment."[47] This contention is premised upon a misreading of the Fourteenth Amendment. It assumes "that the framers of the fourteenth amendment agreed that the second amendment was, indeed, incorporated."[48] This position is untenable and borders on the absurd. There is not credible evidence—especially in light of *Cruikshank*, which was decided only eight years after the Fourteenth Amendment was ratified—to support the claim that the Second Amendment was incorporated into the Fourteenth by the framers in 1868, thereby making the former applicable to the states.[49]

Nevertheless, the issue has become so highly politicized that the status of Second Amendment constitutional law has radically deviated from the original intent of its framers, to the point where the states have been divested of a fundamental right essential to the federal arrangement. The capstone of this constitutional law development is manifested in the U.S. Court of Appeals, Sixth Circuit *United States* v. *Warin* (1976) decision.[50]

The primary issue as defined by Judge Lively in *Warin* is the determination "of whether certain provisions of the National Firearms Act as amended by the Gun Control Act of 1968 are invalid infringements on the right to keep and bear arms guaranteed by the Second Amendment."[51] The significant conclusions of the Court are as follows: (a) The Second Amendment does not protect the individual's right to bear arms; (b) The Second Amendment is a collective right; (c) This collective right is only applicable to those members of the state militia; (d) There is a distinction between the "sedentary militia" and the "active militia"; (e) Members of the sedentary militia (i.e., adult males eligible to be called into the militia but presently inactive) do not have private rights to keep and bear arms under the Second Amendment; and (f) Members of the active militia who have the collective right to keep and bear arms under the Second Amendment are not exempt from Congressional regulations.[52]

Using *Miller* as precedent, the Sixth Circuit shifted to Congress the prerogative to regulate the right to keep and bear arms nationwide. The justification for this shift from the states (*Cruikshank*) to the Congress (*Miller*) was principally political, rather than constitutional. Judge Lively conceded as much when he wrote:

> As the legislative history of the Act under consideration clearly shows, Congress was dealing with problems which threaten the maintenance of public order. There can be no question that an organized society which fails to regulate the importation, manufacture and transfer of the highly sophisticated lethal weapons in existence today does so at its peril. The requirement that no one may possess a submachine gun which is not registered to him in the National Firearms Registration and Transfer Record is a reasonable regulation for the maintenance of public order.[53]

Another major flaw of Judge Lively's political justification is not only his misconstruction of the Second Amendment, but also the Tenth Amendment and the corresponding police powers of the states. The "maintenance of public order" is a state responsibility and the United States is constitutionally prohibited from interfering until the state's legislature or the executive ("when the Legislature cannot be convened") applies for assistance from the United States Government.[54] In light of the Second and Tenth Amendment guarantees the policy objectives of a well-intentioned Congress should have been negated by the courts, on the grounds that those policies are inconsistent with the fundamental law of the land. To conclude the contrary is to reveal one's lack of confidence in the popular control, the federal system, and the constitutions (state and national) which were designed to maintain them.

V

Given this virtual carte blanche by the U.S. Supreme Court to the Congress for legislating more restrictive gun-control policies, the primary obstacle to disarming the American people is political in contradistinction to constitutional, meaning that a state's constitutional right of self-defense is now placed at the discretion of national electoral politics.[55] The support in the congressional and executive branches to enhance or repeal national gun-control legislation waxes and wanes with the political tides, in contradistinction with constraints grounded in the constitutional rule of law.

For example, congressional initiatives directed toward restricting citizens' access to firearms focus on handguns at one end of the firearm spectrum and assault rifles at the other.[56] Recent Congressional activity, ranging from waiting periods prior to purchasing firearms to outright bans on certain types of weaponry, make clear that the Congress is at the Second Amendment's door with a battering ram. With rare exception[57] the Congress has discarded the constitutional constraints of the Second Amendment and, correlatively, the integrity of American federalism, as Congressional public policy initiatives incrementally advance in their quest to disarm the American public. From a realistic viewpoint a government that (a) requires registration could with much greater ease disarm the people of a state defending their freedoms, and (b) people within the states deprived of assault weapons and other state-of-the art weaponry would prove to be no match for a well-armed national force. In short, the *raison d'être* of the Second Amendment (to tolerate the presence of armed citizens within the states for defensive purposes) is not the *modus operandi* of the Congress.

The Antidrug, Assault Weapons Limitation Act of 1989 is instructive. This legislation was designed to control and limit the availability of assault weapons,[58] in order to limit the "number of deaths and injuries attributable" to them.[59] This is to be effected by prohibiting the importation of specified weapons[60] and attaching stiff penalties for unlawful possession and use in the commission of a crime with the specified weapons.

Detractors of Second Amendment guarantees contend that only constitutional iconoclasts would question the congressional option to approve such legislation, because the Congress' regulatory power over commerce provides legitimacy for the much-needed ban on imported assault weapons. This regulatory power is broad, indeed, but it is not absolute, and in this instance it should be balanced against the guaranteed right of the Second Amendment. Otherwise, the congressional preoccupation with crime could be used as a guise to curtail the constitutional right to bear any and all firearms. Even if such curtailment is in the public interest, procedurally it would condone a precedent that would make shambles of the constitutional limitations on the legislative branch. The comments of Senator Kennedy's additional views in reference to the 1989 Act reveal the disposition of congressional gun-control advocates toward the Second Amendment:

> I support S. 747, but we should do more.... S. 747 is a weak compromise that covers only a small portion of the domestic assault weapon problem. Instead, we should direct the Bureau of Alcohol, Tobacco and Firearms to apply the same exacting standards to domestic weapons that it applied in determining which imports to ban. We should authorize the Treasury Secretary to ban domestic assault weapons that are found to be dangerous and that serve no sporting purpose. It makes no sense to ban 43 types of imported weapons under this standard, but permit similarly menacing weapons, manufactured here, to continue to be sold. Fear of the National Rifle Association is no excuse for the perpetuation of this deadly double standard.[61]

Senator Kennedy's position underscores the Clinton Administration's support for stricter gun-control legislation, support given impetus by politicians who have negligible regard for the role of the states in the federal system, a role mandated by the U.S. and state constitutions.

VI

Emphasizing the need to rid American society of menacing weapons either incrementally or in one national swoop, pro-gun-control advocates dismiss the thought of armed confrontation between the people and their national government, relying on the ideal that the national government—or more precisely, the union over which it governs—is perpetual and indissoluble.[62] However, this dismissal is an oversimplification of the relationship between governments and the governed. The fundamental principle underlying American constitutionalism is that all governments are inherently oppressive and must be controlled by internal and external checks if the people are to be secure in their lives, liberties, and properties. One such check is the embodiment in fundamental law of the people's right to keep and bear arms. For the U.S. Supreme Court to sanction congressional curtailment of the states' Second Amendment rights—thereby placing them at the mercy of a potentially omnipotent and oppressive national government—not only removes an important external "federal" check on the national government, but condones the deprivation of a fundamental and enumerated constitutional right. It is one thing for the respective states to decide to limit access to weapons deemed to be detrimental to public order; such is their constitutional public policy prerogative. It is quite another for the national government to do the same. Notably, most of the recent gun-control legislation has been the product of state legislatures responding to public pressure within the state.

The beauty of the American federal design is that policies conducive to the public order in Massachusetts are not necessarily imposed upon the people of Montana, and vice versa. The framers would caution that if the states are to be secure in their own long-term political destinies, the Second Amendment must be restored to its original constitutional status. Such a restoration is not inherently inconsistent with gun-control legislation per se. Rather, it is inconsistent with deferring to the national government the option to arm or disarm the people within the respective states. If gutting the Second Amendment is rationalized on the grounds that a patchwork of gun-control laws, varying from state to state, is neither practical nor effective, then a significant pillar of American federalism has collapsed under the weight of political expediency and shortsightedness. Just as the Ninth Amendment was designed to preclude a national cultural tyranny over the states, the Second Amendment was included in the Bill of Rights to serve as a barrier to national tyranny, a contingency not dismissed by the framers in their quest to "*secure* the Blessings of Liberty to ourselves and our Posterity,"[63] but obviously dismissed by the "creative" justices on the U.S. Supreme Court.

Notes

1. See Raoul Berger's *Government by Judiciary: The Transformation of the Fourteenth Amendment* (Cambridge: University of Harvard Press, 1977) for an exposition of the U.S. Supreme Court's role in the development of national supremacy. Insofar as intergovernmental transfers are concerned, Professor Dye notes that "the date 1913 marked the end of traditional federalism in the United States. The states, by ratifying the Sixteenth Amendment to the Constitution and granting the national government the power to tax incomes directly, unwittingly set in motion the institutional forces that would shift the balance of power from the states to Washington. The income tax gave the federal government the power to raise large sums of money, which it proceeded to spend for the general welfare as well as for defense. Congress did not restrict its spending to its enumerated functions in Article I, section 8 of the Constitution. Instead it chose to spend money for functions previously thought to be reserved to the states. It is no coincidence that the first major cash grant-in-aid programs (agricultural extension in 1914, highways in 1916, vocational education in 1917, and public health in 1918) came shortly after the inauguration of the federal income tax" (Thomas R. Dye, *American Federalism: Competition Among Governments* [Massachusetts: Lexington Books, 1990], 99).
2. This is not to say that the national government has necessarily usurped the public policy prerogatives of the states. The position of this paper is prospective, as was the case with the framers; prospective in the sense that, like all governments, the national government is inclined to pursue policies oppressive to the peoples' rights; thus, the necessity of separation of powers and checks and balances.
3. It is important to keep in mind that the designation "framers" is not limited to the men who in 1787 met in Philadelphia; the framers also include the participants in the various States who ratified not only the Constitution, but also the Bill of Rights, the Second Amendment included (see Professor M. E. Bradford, "The Authoritative Constitution: A Reading of the Ratification Debates," *Texas Tech Law Review*, vol. 21, no. 4 [1990], 2349–74).
4. Alexander Hamilton, et. al, *The Federalist Papers*, #48, Clinton Rossiter, ed. (New York: New American Library, 1961), 308.
5. Publius consistently maintained that "regard to reputation has a less active influence when the infamy of a bad action is to be divided among a number than when it is to fall singly upon one. A spirit of faction, which is apt to mingle its poison in the deliberations of all bodies of men, will often hurry the persons of whom they are composed into improprieties and excesses for which they would blush in a private capacity" (ibid., #15, 111).
6. Ibid.
7. Although the Constitution makes no mention of judicial review, Publius was convinced that judicial review was an integral part of limited government, contending that the federal courts "were designed to be an intermediate body between the people and the legislature in order, among other things, to keep the latter within limits assigned to their authority" (*The Federalist Papers*, #78, 467).
8. Ibid., #6, 54.
9. Ibid., #10, 79.
10. "It may be a reflection on human nature that such devices are necessary to control the abuses of government. But what is government itself but the greatest of all reflections on human nature? If men were angels, no government would be neces-

sary. If angels were to govern men, neither external nor internal controls on government would be necessary. In framing a government which is to be administered by men over men, the great difficulty lies in this: you must first enable the government to control the governed; and in the next place oblige it to control itself" (ibid., #51, 322).

11. The rights of resistance and revolution are embodied in the Declaration of 1776; these rights are certainly an integral part of the American political culture. Also see Justice Chase's postbellum opinion in Texas v. White, 74 U.S. 700 (1869), in which he confirms the right to revolution.
12. *The Federalist Papers,* #46, 299.
13. Ibid., #46, 300.
14. Article IV, section 4.
15. Article I, section 8, clause 15.
16. *The Federalist Papers,* #15, 110.
17. The origin of this right in the state constitutions is complex. To maintain that the origin "is the English tradition the colonists inherited, and the English Bill of Rights from which much of the American Bill of Rights was drawn" (Joyce Lee Malcolm, "The Right of the People to Keep and Bear Arms: The Common Law Tradition," *Hastings Constitutional Law Quarterly,* vol. 10: 285 [Winter, 1983], 287), is an oversimplification. For example, while the English upper classes viewed the possession of arms in the working classes as menacing and a means toward rebellion and insurrection, Americans viewed them as a means of defense and sustenance for their families. To deny the early Americans of their firearms was to deny them important means of survival. Unlike the European gentry, which was theorizing about the right to bear arms for sport and status while simultaneously disarming the majority of their people in order to fend off rebellion, Americans were using their arms for practical purposes, such as hunting and defense. See Lawrence Delbert Cress, "An Armed Community: The Origins and Meanings of the Right to Bear Arms," *The Journal of American History,* vol. 71, no. 1, June 1984.
18. Francis Newton Thorpe, *The Federal and State Constitutions: Colonial Charters, and Other Organic Laws of the States,* vol. I (Washington: Government Printing Office, 1909), 1: 538.
19. Ibid., vol. VI, 3224.
20. Ibid., vol. V, 3083 and 3101; vol. VI, 3753 and 3794; vol. III, 1275 and 1290; and vol. V, 2911.
21. Ibid., vol. V, 2788.
22. Ibid., vol. III, 1892.
23. Ibid., vol. VII, 3813 and 3820; vol. V, 2456 and 2474; and vol. III, 1688.
24. See *The Federalist Papers,* #25, 163-65. According to Publius, "Reasons have already been given to induce a supposition that the State governments will too naturally be prone to rivalship with that of the Union, the foundation of which will be the love of power" (ibid., 163).
25. One needs only to turn to paragraph four of The Declaration of Independence to reaffirm the importance of this natural right. In part, it reads: "Prudence, indeed, will dictate that government long established should not be changed for light and transient causes; and accordingly all experience hath shown that mankind are more disposed to suffer while evils are sufferable, than to right themselves by abolishing the forms to which they are accustomed. But when a long train of abuses and usurpations, pursuing invariably the same object, evinces a design to

reduce them under absolute despotism, it is their right, it is their duty, to throw off such government, and to provide new guards for their future security."

26. The mere possibility of armed conflict would in and of itself have a psychological impact on the parties to negotiate an equitable settlement in order to avoid armed confrontation; the fate of President Jackson's "Force Bill" comes to mind. The element of armed conflict between the national and state governments gives rise to a federal version of mutual assured destruction, that is, it is in the interests of the parties to resolve the conflict through negotiations in order to avoid a potential zero sum contest.
27. For example, "Every generation suffers to some degree from historical amnesia. However, when the history of a major political tradition, along with the assumptions and passions that it forged, are forgotten, it becomes extraordinarily difficult to understand and evaluate its legacy. This is particularly unfortunate when that legacy has been written into the enduring fabric of government. The Second Amendment to the United States Constitution is such a relic, a fossil of a lost tradition" (Malcolm, "The Right of the People," 285).
28. United States v. Cruikshank, 92 U.S. 549.
29. Ibid., 549
30. Ibid., 553.
31. Ibid., 552.
32. The facts in this case revolve around Presser's private army (Lehr und Wehr Verein) of about four hundred members who "did unlawfully belong to, and did parade and drill in the City of Chicago with an unauthorized body of men with arms, who had associated themselves together as a military company and organization, without having a license from the governor, and not being a part of, or belonging to, 'the regular organized militia' of the State of Illinois, or the troops of the United States" (Presser v. Illinois, 6 S. Ct. 581 [1886]).
33. See Article I, section 8.
34. Presser, 584.
35. The pertinent clauses of Article I, section 8, are "to raise and support armies" and "to provide for organizing, arming, and disciplining the Militia."
36. The pertinent issue in this case is whether the 1934 National Firearms Act "offends the inhibition of the Second Amendment" [United States v. Miller, 307 U.S. 174 (1939)]. The Act required, among other stipulations, the affixing of federal stamps on all rifles and shotguns having barrels less than eighteen inches in length when such weapons are transferred through interstate commerce (see Act of June 26, 1934, National Firearms Act, 48 stat. 1236-1240, 26 U.S. C.). The Court in *Miller* concluded that such weapons lack Second Amendment protection because they are not the weaponry of the state Militias (Miller, 178).
37. Ibid., 178–79.
38. Ibid., 178.
39. Ibid.
40. Cruikshank, 542.
41. The examples are Massachusetts 1632 and 1784, New York 1784, and Virginia 1785 (Miller, 179–82).
42. Ibid., 180–81.
43. Cruikshank, 542.
44. One should not be too optimistic, however. For example, Justices Breyer, Stevens, Souter, and Ginsberg recently revealed their preferences for a very broad reading of Congress's commerce powers in their opinions to uphold the constitutionality

of the Gun-Free School Zones Act of 1990 (Pub. L. 101-647, 104 Stat. 4844). Justice Souter maintained that "the only question is whether the legislative judgment is within the realm of reason" (U.S. v. Lopez, 63 LW 4343, [1995] 4362). Justice Breyer writes that "in sum, a holding that the particular statute before us falls within the commerce power would not expand the scope of that Clause. Rather, is simply would apply preexisting law to changing economic circumstances" (ibid., 4365). In his concurring opinion, Justice Thomas makes clear where such expansive interpretations of the rational basis test inevitably leads (see ibid., 4353–59).

45. Stephen P. Halbrook, "The Jurisprudence of the Second and Fourteenth Amendments," *George Mason University Law Review*, vol. 4: 1 (1981), 50.
46. For example, in response to the 1989 Stockton, California, school-yard massacre in which five children were murdered and seventeen wounded, the State recently imposed a fifteen-day waiting period before certain types of weapons can be purchased. Some NRA types questioned the State's authority to impose such restrictions.
47. Halbrook, "The Jurisprudence of the Second and Fourteenth Amendments," 65.
48. Ibid., 59.
49. Once again, see Berger, *Government by Judiciary*, particularly chap. 8, for a convincing argument against the theory of incorporation.
50. Certiorari was denied on 21 June 1976; see 96 S. Ct. 3168.
51. United States v. Warin 530 F. 2d 104 (1976); the facts center on Warin's failure to register his 9mm prototype submachine gun, a weapon made by the defendant who was a designer of firearms and the employee of a weapons developer for the Government (ibid., 105).
52. Ibid., passim.
53. Ibid., 107–08.
54. See Article IV, section 4, of the U.S. Constitution.
55. One commentator approvingly acknowledges as much. Regarding his recently published book, he approvingly wrote: "To return to the primary policy questions guiding this book, the Second Amendment poses no obstacle to gun control as it is debated in modern America. Consistent with social regulatory policy theory, the courts have indeed provided a key avenue for defining the issue") Robert J. Spitzer, *The Politics Of Gun Control* [Chatham, N.J.: Chatham House Publishers, Inc., 1995], 49). Chapter 2 of this book, "The Second Amendment: Meaning, Intent, Interpretation, and Consequences," is obviously the work of a gun-control zealot who gives little credence to the constitutional rule of law.
56. Assault rifles are weapons with detachable magazines capable of automatic fire with a capacity of twenty or more cartridges. While assault rifles have become the weapons of choice for organized crime (e.g., drug traffickers), handguns are overwhelmingly the weapons used in homicides. For example, in 1987 out of 10,556 slayings, handguns were used in 7,807 (see U.S. Department of Justice, Federal Bureau of Investigations, *Crime In the United States*, Uniform Crime Reports, 1987. Cited in "Testimony To Be Delivered To The Constitution Subcommittee On The Judiciary, 10 May 1989" by Edward C. Ezell, Ph.D.
57. One such exception is Rep. Crane's H. Con. Res. 27, which "Expresses the sense of the Congress that the Constitution provides that all citizens have the right to keep and bear arms and that such right supersedes the power and authority of any government" (LEGISLATIVE INFORMATION, 101ST CONGRESS, 1). However, even Rep. Crane's resolution is contrary to the Second Amendment because it fails to defer to the states' regulatory authority.

58. The original bill was cited as "Assault Weapon Control Act of 1989" (see S. 386, 101st Congress, 1st Session, 1). Obviously, adding "Antidrug" to the title makes the bill much more palatable.
59. "The Antidrug, Assault Weapons Limitation Act of 1989" (S. 747, 101st Congress, 1st Session, 1). The minority report of Senators Thurmond, Hatch, Simpson, Grassley, and Humphrey takes issue with the intent and effectiveness of the Act (see ibid., 16-21).
60. See Sections 3 and 4, ibid., 6.
61. Ibid., 14.
62. The idea of the "perpetuity and indissolubility of the Union" was elevated to the status of constitutional law in Texas v. White (19 L.Ed. 227 [1869]) but, as previously mentioned, even in this case Chief Justice Chase acknowledged the right of revolution, not to mention the role of revolution in American political culture. No reasonable American would deny the existence of such a right and the resort to arms, if necessitated by circumstances, in exercising that right.
63. The Preamble to the U.S. Constitution (emphasis not in original).

7

Contrasting Theories on the Articulation of Unenumerated Rights, *Bradford* v. *Dworkin*

As U.S. Supreme Court unenumerated rights jurisprudence unfolds, the significance of academic and political discourse among jurists, scholars, politicians, and journalists looms ever larger in charting the future developments of American constitutional rights. Because the articulation and monitoring of unenumerated rights has become primarily the responsibility of the U.S. Supreme Court, academic debate now has a more direct conduit to the halls of power, in contradistinction to a republican process in which the intuitive political sense of the people gave form and content to unenumerated rights. In other words, judicial supremacy was not always the norm, as is evidenced by the nature of the American regime before and after the twentieth-century phenomenon of selective incorporation and the nationalization of rights. As happened in the first quarter of the twentieth century (see chapter 3 *supra*), paradigm shifting juridical ideas are first tested in the crucible of academic debate, later to be countenanced by justices who have been socialized through education and politics.[1] The unique prerogatives of judicial review can elevate the unenumerated rights policy objectives of the intelligentsia to the status of constitutional law, the policy preferences of average Americans notwithstanding. Accordingly, by contrasting the theories of Bradford and Dworkin we are presented with polarized academic views about the Supreme Court's legitimate role in articulating unenumerated rights policy.[2] Due to the polarization of their respective jurisprudence, they are uniquely useful in manifesting the essence of current jurisprudential developments regarding unenumerated rights.

What I hope to make clear is that the prognosis for American constitutional law is essentially Dworkian, and that there will be significant consequences for American constitutionalism and the popular control it traditionally embodied, as is evidenced by Bradford's scholarship. If my assessment is accurate, then perhaps it is time to follow the example of the American framers and devise a republican remedy to the ongoing concentration of power in one branch of the national government, and in this instance a factious judiciary. On the other hand, if we embrace the Dworkian model of rights jurisprudence, thereby rejecting that of Bradford's, then for all intents and purposes U.S. Supreme Court justices are the central planners of unenumerated rights, thereby displacing constitutional federalism. If such is the case, then regarding unenumerated rights policy we should be prepared to justify an exception to Publius's political maxim that "the accumulation of all powers, legislative, executive, and judiciary, in the same hands, whether of one, a few, or many, and whether hereditary, self-appointed, or elective, may justly be pronounced the very definition of tyranny."[3]

I
M. E. Bradford: A Southern Conservative's Affirmation Unenumerated Rights

M. E. Bradford's constitutional theory is firmly grounded in the original intent of the framers. His scholarly links to that model are twofold; first, original intent is the only way to legitimately apply the U.S. Constitution to contemporary politics and, second, it is better than any alternative at procuring good government. Due to the emphasis placed on original intent as the appropriate standard for constitutional interpretation and the rejection of public policies that deviate from it, his scholarship has an inherently reactionary thrust, to the extent that Bradford's constitutionalism is reactive against U.S. Supreme Court sanctioned comprehensive national supremacy.[4] Turning the clock back to a viable federal paradigm would reestablish the states as sovereigns regarding many of the currently nationalized high-conflict and high-salient issues, such as school prayer, abortion, criminal justice, and commerce policies, and others including issues under the rubric of unenumerated rights; in short, the status of the states would be restored to its pre-Fourteenth Amendment incorporation paradigm, thereby negating the substantive due process activism of the *Lochner*[5] variety. This does not mean that Bradford's scholarship is by design a vehicle for advocating specific policy outcomes on these and other issues. He certainly had his policy preferences, but his scholarship focuses on the constitutionality of the processes utilized in the formation of past, present, and future public policies, inevitably leading him to confront the constitutional legitimacy of pervasive national public policy supremacy.

Obviously, this makes Bradford controversial and provocative, especially in light of his southern roots and the extension of those roots to the southern states' nineteenth-century unsuccessful resistance to national supremacy. For some academicians the southerness of Bradford's scholarship is, indeed, problematical, as is evidenced by the academic ostracism imposed on him due to his southern states' rights brand of conservatism. Garry Wills's recent reference to Bradford as a "suicidally frank" conservative is an accurate observation that reveals as much about the ideologically charged academic climate as it does about Bradford.[6] Such biases notwithstanding, M. E. Bradford's scholarship does merit the attention of constitutional scholars, not merely as a curiosity, but as a significant resource to critique constitutional theorists who rationalize a model of national supremacy not only inconsistent with an original intent model of American federalism, but with the rule of law itself.

The facts that the U.S. Constitution was contentiously drafted, barely ratified, and occasionally the subject of divisive interpretations, make evident that instituting and maintaining the constitutional government was and is serious work. The framers realized the seriousness and complexity of their undertakings as they crafted a constitutional system respectful of securing the public good, private rights, and the spirit and form of popular government. Bradford's appreciation of the framers' constitutional craftsmanship sustained his interest in the "original" constitutional federal arrangement, through which the states had meaningful public policy roles vis-à-vis the national government. Because he was convinced that the original U.S. Constitution has been substantively altered via judicial activism, Bradford contrasted the *original* from the judicially concocted Constitution. The concocted Constitution was incrementally constructed to legitimize ideological agendas that in its original form the U.S. Constitution would not sanction. By explicating the framers' intentions, Bradford distinguishes the constitutional federalism through which the states had exceptionally meaningful functions, from contemporary national supremacy through which a national elite essentially governs the nation (what in earlier times was known as oligarchy or plutocracy), with the states functioning as not much more than the administrative agents of the national government. Reinstating the constitutional federalism would require undoing a good portion of twentieth-century constitutional law, especially as it gives life and sustenance to national supremacy over unenumerated rights. Nevertheless, Bradford was hopeful, claiming that "hidden from us in our day by the inventions and concoctions of judicial distortion [the original constitution is] subject to recovery even now."[7] Whether or not a recovery occurs depends upon the uncertainties of political circumstance, such as electoral results, legislators' policy preferences and, most importantly, U.S. Supreme Court justices with the inclination and opportunities to undo six decades of precedent-setting policies. Elucidating the "inventions and concoctions of judicial distortion" for what they are (an important first step) is the responsibility of scholarship, one taken seriously by Bradford.

II

As we initially discussed in chapter one, the core of Bradford's constitutional theory is a nomocratic, in contradistinction to teleocratic, national constitution. To reiterate, the distinction between nomocratic and teleocratic constitutions is concisely explained by Forrest McDonald in the forward to Bradford's posthumously published book: The nomocratic view

> is that the Constitution was designed to bring government under the rule of law, as opposed to achieving any specific purposes.... [T]he Constitution is primarily a structural and procedural document, specifying who is to exercise what powers and how. It is a body of law, designed to govern, not the people, but government itself; and it is written in language intelligible to all, that all might know whether it is being obeyed. The alternative, teleocratic view, is one that has come into fashion the last few decades and has all but destroyed the original Constitution. This is the notion that the design of the Constitution was to achieve a certain kind of society, one based upon abstract principles of natural rights or justice or equality or democracy or all of the above. It holds that the specific provisions of the document are of secondary importance or none at all; what counts are the "principles" it supposedly embodies, usually principles based upon the Declaration of Independence or Lincoln's Gettysburg Address, neither of which has any standing in law.[8]

Indeed, the nomocratic Constitution has been significantly altered by teleocratic perspectives;[9] the seeds of the alterations were sown by

Abraham Lincoln, to be subsequently nurtured and harvested by latter-day teleocratic reformers. But we are getting ahead of ourselves. Why is the issue of nomocratic versus teleocratic significant and what evidence does Bradford present to support his claim that the original Constitution was nomocratic?

Whether the Constitution is predominantly nomocratic or teleocratic is a significant question because the two forms are not necessarily equally conducive to traditional American constitutionalism and the rule of law embodied therein. If the Constitution is essentially nomocratic, then the federal courts would be restricted to the enforcement of constitutionally established procedures through which participants in the political process compete against one another in the attempt to have their respective interests prevail in the public policy-making process, whether those interests are economic, social, cultural, religious, regional, and/or political. Judicial review would be invoked when the procedures are allegedly breached, with the courts being responsible for upholding the constitutional integrity of the political process. Under this model political questions are nonjusticiable. This does not mean that the Constitution fails to place limits on nomocratic procedures for making public policy. It certainly does (see Art. I, sections nine and ten and the Bill of Rights), but these limits were nomocratically produced through the drafting and ratifying of constitutional provisions.[10]

Furthermore, the nomocratic constitution is not immune to alterations; through the amendment process (Article V) states may nomocratically alter the procedures by expanding or contracting what is constitutionally permissible political behavior. Thus, the nomocratic U.S. Constitution does not preclude teleocratic principles from the political process. Teleocratic principles may be embodied in state constitutions, state statutes, national statutes, and even in the U.S. Constitution itself, which is built upon the teleocratic commitment to "a Republican Form of Government" (Article IV, 4). But for the U.S. Supreme Court to utilize judicial review as a vehicle to implement their teleocratic preferences over the objections of a state or states, on the basis that there are laws higher than the Constitution and they, the Justices, decide what those laws are, is inconsistent with the nomocratic basis of the Constitution; this type of judicial activism inevitably raises questions of constitutional legitimacy and political obligation. Nevertheless, if the U.S. Constitution is construed to be a teleocratic *a priori* embodiment of truth, justice, and righteousness, with U.S. Supreme Court justices serving as its privileged interpreters, then popular control over important areas of public policy becomes precarious and subject to the domination of exclusive interests—usually ideological in nature—which at any particular period of constitutional development may exercise control over the policy-making process through the institutional Supreme Court. Such ideological influence over judicial review is inconsistent with the constitutional rule of law, which would be putty in the hands of the dominating interest groups. It was for this reason that the framers emerged from Philadelphia with nomocratic institutional separation of powers, electoral processes, and a federal as opposed to a unitary system of public policy-making. Under the framers' federal model, factious domination over the broad apparatus of national policy-making is much less probable, than is the case under a unitary alternative that provides shelter to an activist Supreme Court.

Bradford provides us with ample evidence to support the Constitution's overriding nomocratic nature and the framers' rationale for it. In *Original Intentions On The Making And Ratification Of The United States Constitution,* Bradford explicates the plurality of intentions implicit in the U.S. Constitution, including the variable intentions of the participants attending the Philadelphia Convention and the variable intentions of state voters (as represented by their delegates) at the respective state ratifying conventions. This obvious but too often neglected historical fact is important. When discerning the "intent of the framers" it is important to factor in the states, not only their intentions during the ratification process, but also their respective state constitutions. The U.S. Constitution cannot stand alone; state constitutions are integral parts of American constitutionalism. In this sense the U.S. Constitution is, indeed, a living document, alive with actively viable states pursuing their distinct public policy preferences within the context of constitutionally recognized collective national interests. This was certainly the political landscape with which the framers were familiar and it is critical to our contemporary understanding of the American version of the rule of law.[11]

The American rule of law has a continuity that predates the drafting of the Constitution and can be traced to colonial America. It is also important to remember that the Philadelphia Convention was a political event and that the delegates were politicians, not philosophers acting independently of political realities. This self-evident fact merits reinforcement, particularly due to the misunderstanding that the convention was the next logical step in the implementation of 1776 declaratory principles. Bradford considered this to be an "important impediment to our understanding of the original American politics. There is a myth industriously cultivated by statist, sentimental egalitarians, high-ranking Washington bureaucrats, and latter-day radicals of the New Left variety that the fifty members of the Great Convention in Philadelphia were Framers who 'invented' the polity we now struggle to preserve; not public men, lawyers and rhetoricians, but philosophers who wrote the Constitution to embody a paradigm derived *a priori* from the modern 'science of politics'.... Only those with special training in history are likely to know better."[12]

What history reveals is an American Revolution that was not a radical transformation of the existing political system (as the French Revolution was); furthermore, the U.S. Constitution was produced by delegates determined to complement their respective state governments, not to obliterate them. Even if a few delegates were determined to play the role of philosopher-kings, necessitating the forthright establishment of an unitary system of government the sovereignty of the states notwithstanding, their efforts would have been politically rejected. There are examples. Bradford describes as "comic" the behavior of a few leading delegates, who in the excitement of the moment occasionally deviated too far from the constraints of practical politics. One such delegate was James Madison, the reputed father of the Constitution. Madison was not politically naive; he realized the political nature of the process and acted accordingly, as is evidenced by his manipulation of the agenda and strategically appointing capable and politically acceptable delegates (such as Edmund Randolph) to present his resolutions to the Convention. But by focusing attention on someone as politically capable and influential as Madison, Bradford makes evident the extent to which a nomocratic process dominated the drafting process, as opposed to teleocratic philosophizing about "self-evident" truths. According to Bradford,

> there is no place in a healthy political atmosphere for domination by the *idée fixe*—a warning against system, ideology, and abstraction, even of the modest sort. The making of the Constitution was a limited, political, non-philosophical act, reflecting a consensus about the nation's future hopes and present character, performed by men whose agreements with one another grew in the process of hammering out

> certain differences of opinion about the common good in relation to the particular good of their own communities.[13]

Bradford characterized apolitical behavior as comical,[14] because it ran counter to the political realities, was ineffective and/or risked wrecking the Convention. This was the case during the debates on state representation in the Senate and Madison's apolitical attachment to the Virginia Plan. What motivated Madison to risk success for abstraction? "[H]e was either self-deceived or else cared less for union than for the abstract purity of his plan, which is the attitude of the doctrinaire and the ideologue, not the statesman."[15] In the words of John Dickinson of Delaware, on this issue Madison simply "pushed things too far."[16]

It was not Bradford's contention that the Philadelphia Convention was devoid of doctrinaire nationalists, but that their influences were politically kept in check, the most important check being the continued integrity of the thirteen states. Each state had distinct identities in pursuit of distinct interests that more or less converged whenever the Convention collectively reached agreement:

> Because they had for raw material subject to their shaping hands a going, functional, social, economic, and political order instead of some philosophical *tabula rasa,* the eventually successful Framers worked outward from that given reality. They assumed responsibility for the preservation of that order: a structure in which the states were the most important ingredients of continuity, elements that defined what kind of polity Americans would accept as a legitimate consequence of their Revolution.[17]

As his analyses of the ratification processes in Massachusetts, South Carolina, and North Carolina[18] make clear, the states viewed the proposed Constitution "according to their own needs and purposes—out of their distinctive histories and political dispositions,"[19] and when those political dispositions coincided (such as interstate commerce, national security, raising national revenue, the importation of Africans, and a stable currency) consensus was reached and constitutional provisions agreed to. What initially tied the states together was not an ideological commitment to an abstract Union, but the "natural fellow-feeling" generated by fighting and defeating a common enemy,[20] which explains why General Washington's mere presence at the Convention was crucial to holding it together.[21] It was the states' common experiences, in contradistinction to abstractions about nationhood, that made the Union possible in the first place. There were ample opportunities for ideological politics within each state, especially during elections, while at the national constitutional convention the political realities of the drafting and ratification processes significantly curtailed ideological impulses. This is consistent with Madison's rationale for an extended republic model of federalism. Because of the multiplicity of interests and their natural distrust of one another, the impact of ideology is diminished at the national level, whereas at the state and local levels dominant interest groups, whether religious, ideological, economic, or political, have freer reign.[22] Madison was voicing a truism that his own political experiences confirmed.

Emphasizing nomocratic processes in contradistinction to teleocratic idealism, Bradford confirms that "[t]he purpose of our [national] form of government is embodied in the procedures for dealing with one another politically that are its primary regulations." He dismisses the notion that the Constitution mandates that the national courts secure *a priori* rights or establish the just society.[23] Americans' *national* rights and the best possible *national* society would result from the political equivalent of Adam Smith's invisible hand. From 1787 to 1791 the states would have it no other way; they would not relinquish their own police powers to what was a distant, unknown, and potentially liberty-threatening national government. Implicit in the states retaining their respective police powers is mutual recognition among the states of their respective corporate rights, that is, their public policy prerogatives to maintain their respective social, economic, and political orderings in the absence of teleologically driven national interference. The Constitution "is not an instrumental, substantive document drawn up to foster the favorite capital-letter abstractions of the millenarians. It is more concerned with what government will not do for each of us than with the positive description of acceptable conduct, which is left to local and idiosyncratic definition—to society, local custom, and tested ways. Most important, it is not about enforcing the abstract rights of man or some theory of perfect justice and aboriginal equality, not even with the Bill of Rights added to it."[24]

The terms corporate rights and state rights are closely related, with the former lacking the negative anti-civil rights connotations. But whether the nomenclature is corporate rights or state rights the constitutional principle is the same: Unless precluded by some specific constitutional provision, the states were responsible for their respective citizens' health, safety, morals, and welfare, which included the prerogative of continued state membership in the Union. For those who consider the states to be the backwaters of democratic government, and others who correctly see the states as obstacles to their self-interested national public policy objectives, Bradford's commitment to the states is a frightening prospect. Nevertheless, it must be admitted on all sides that, as both Federalists and Antifederalists agreed, popular control over public policy is more viable at the state than at the national level, provided the channels of participation are consistent with a "Republican Form of Government" (Article IV, sec. 4).

The rationale behind and the effect of this model of state/corporate rights is exemplified by the rule of law as it pertains to free exercise and nonestablishment of religion, a model applicable to unenumerated rights policy.

III

Few areas are as susceptible to and instructive about national teleocratic politics than the application of popular control in the policy area of religion. Religion, as a system of beliefs and behavior, could be either instrumental or problematical in achieving national teleocratic policy goals. If placed within the domain of national public policy prerogatives religion could promote national standards, contrarily, if part of the states' police power prerogatives to promote the *morals* of the respective state populations, religion could clash with national policy objectives. Suppose that the dominant religious beliefs of a state resulted in public policy that recognized only monogamous heterosexual marriages, whereas the U.S. Supreme Court supported teleocratic interpretations of privacy, due process, and equal protection of the law that sanction all consensual conjugal unions, whether they be of the same gender, same family, whatever. In the final analysis, the only way around the state's policy preference for a Christian model of marriage would be to displace the role of religion at the state level with national standards. This is exactly what a teleocratic U.S. Constitution facilitates, substituting state laws or customs grounded in the policy preferences of state citizens, with national standards based upon the values of dominant national elites.

Bradford presents solid evidence to support his position that a teleocratic Constitution that trumps the role of religion in formulating state public policy is, in most instances, the illegitimate product of judicial concoctions and inventions. From the vantage point of original intent, the biographical evidence reveals that approximately 95 percent of the framers were "members in good standing of the various Christian communions found in early America."[25] About 5 percent were deists and secularists.[26] Which influence dominated the drafting and ratification processes, the Christian, deists, or secularists? According to Bradford, "the assumption that this majority was likely to agree to totally secular institutional arrangements in the very structure of American politics contradicts almost everything we know about human nature, as well as the most self-evident components of Christian teaching concerning the relation of the magistrate to the ultimate source of his authority in God."[27] Nevertheless, secularization of public policy is precisely what the U. S. Supreme Court requires through its "concocted" Lemon Test, which requires that every state statute must, first, "have a secular purpose; second, its principal or primary effect must be one that neither advances nor inhibits religion... and third, the statute must not foster an excessive government entanglement with religion."[28] At what point in its development did the Constitution mandate the secularization of state policies?

It is impossible to appreciate the U.S. Supreme Court's deviation from the original constitutional arrangement regarding religion without factoring in American federalism. Post-World War II Supreme Court decisions to the contrary notwithstanding, the framers did not agree to secularize national and state institutions. As a matter of historical fact, Christianity pervaded the politics of the period, especially at the state level. The framers were not irrational men; they would neither attempt the ratification of a national constitution that negated state policies toward religion, policies that varied from state to state and regionally, nor attempt to nationalize religious policies that would result in conflict between the national and state governments.[29] The historical evidence "is more than enough to demonstrate that a neutrality tending to become a hostility toward religion—an instrument for secularizing the public life—was not the purpose of any participant in the process of lawgiving."[30] The Supreme Court's First Amendment "wall of separation" is ahistorical and ideologically inspired.[31] For the objective analyst the intent of the framers' policy toward church and state is, Bradford maintained, readily discernible; those who claim otherwise are "both intellectually dishonest and absurd,"[32] not to mention creative.

Indeed, the original intent behind the First Amendment is readily discernible. Article Six ("no religious Test shall ever be required as a Qualification to any Office or public Trust under the United States") and the First Amendment ("Congress shall make no law respecting an establishment of religion, or prohibiting the free exercise thereof") are restrictions on the national government, not the states. "The truth about the limits marked off by the Establishment Clause and the exclusion of religious tests for officeholders in Article 6 is that they raise no wall of separation, only a check upon sectarian passions."[33] As Bradford points out, the national community did not confuse "freedom of religion with freedom from religion."[34] The framers "would not wish to live in a society that in no way identifies itself as a Christian community, which in its impious political character would invite the wrath of God. Neither did they wish to put their descendants in a situation where they cannot profess their Christianity in and through their work."[35] Thus, military chaplains, U.S authorized missions to "civilize the Indians," "In God We Trust" inscribed on currency, tax exempt status for churches, Sunday closing laws, government-sponsored days of prayer and thanksgiving, prayers in public schools, and state subsidies for religion, were not historically inconsistent with constitutionally sanctioned quasi-establishment through which the states were free to utilize public policy to nurture religious values, which in turn would facilitate the formulation of and compliance with public policy, while the national government deferred to and in some instances supported such state policies.

Bradford's analysis of First Amendment jurisprudence regarding church and state not only reveals that post-World War II constitutional law has deviated from original intent, but also the method and extent to which the nomocratic elements of the Constitution that were designed to secure popular control have been displaced by creative judicial teleocratic politics. Having liberated themselves from the restraints of original intent, the Court then proceeded *ultra vires* to impose their teleocratic preferences on the states. In other words, the nomocratic constitutionally established rules of political participation had been superseded by an inappropriate exercise of judicial review; by ignoring original intent the U.S. Supreme Court declared victory for proponents of secularization of state public policies by judicial decree.[36] Of course, the activist Court utilized the Constitution to claim legitimacy, with the justices (due to either intellectual dishonesty or incompetence) linking their opinions to the Constitution. Nevertheless, the end result is the same. The role of the states in public policy-making has been significantly diminished. Because post-World War II free exercise and establishment jurisprudence clears the constitutional decks for the Supreme Court to substitute its teleocratic principles for the more conservative principles that may have otherwise been sustained in the states, we can expect ongoing policy innovations promoting the former at the expense of the latter.[37]

Most of this post-World War II nation building at the expense of the states would have been neither politically nor constitutionally feasible had it not been for the academic rediscovery of the actions and rhetoric of Abraham Lincoln, the primary effect of which has been to merge the Constitution with a teleocratic interpretation of the Declaration of Independence. According to Bradford, Lincoln and his modern-day political managers are at center stage of these developments.

IV

Indisputable legitimacy for teleocratic-based judicial activism (both the conservative and liberal varieties) must hinge on an explicit constitutional provision or a teleocratic mandate sanctioning constitutional alterations by the federal judiciary. The Constitution lacks language that could be construed in either way; in fact, Article V establishes procedures for amending the Constitution, thereby implicitly precluding constitutional alterations by an activist Supreme Court. Nevertheless, a way has been found to circumvent the restrictive language of the Constitution. Through a commingling the Constitution with the rhetorical language of the Declaration of Independence, the role of the federal judiciary has been substantially enhanced as the guarantor of the Declaration's self-evident "Truths" of equality and unalienable rights.[38] Has American constitutional development experienced such a *coup de theatre,* and if so, by what means? To answer these questions Bradford directs our attention to Abraham Lincoln, sardonically identified as "Father Abraham."[39] Lincoln's teleocratic rhetoric provides much-needed aid and comfort for national reformers impatient with an essentially conservative nomocratic constitutional arrangement premised upon popular control within the respective states.[40]

Bradford's historical analysis makes clear that a series of events, with Lincoln at the center, made such a *coup* possible. Lincoln's importance stems not simply from his rhetoric, but from a convergence of his rhetoric, role as commander-in-chief, the Northern military victory, and his assassination. Within the context of American political mythology, the assassination facilitated the martyrdom of Lincoln, elevated his political rhetoric to the status of holy writ, and justified the Northern cause on messianic terms.[41] The significance of the military victory is saliently noted by considering the unthinkable, a Confederate victory. There is nothing like success to confirm the righteousness of the victors' cause and the methods used to achieve it. But it is Lincoln's rhetoric that is most interesting and important, because it laid the theoretical tracks for the subsequent derailment of the original constitutional order.[42]

In the wake (and political security) of a major military victory, President Lincoln outlined his political eschatology in the Gettysburg Address. This Periclean address is a masterpiece of American political rhetoric and marks a watershed of U.S. constitutional development, legitimizing the view that the Declaration has constitutional status. It postulates as settled significant questions that were anything but settled, or even worse, settled in the opposite direction. Questions such as, did the Declaration establish a new nation, or was it simply the unanimous declaration of thirteen sovereign states? Were these sovereign states (or nation) "conceived in Liberty" and destined to grow into a nation "dedicated to the proposition that all men are created equal," and if so in what manner and to what extent? What is the status of this "proposition" vis-à-vis the Constitution and the federalism that it was designed to secure? Does the "new birth of freedom" made possible by a Northern military victory justify the carnage of "a great civil war," past and forthcoming? Specifically, what did Lincoln mean by "to be dedicated to the unfinished work" and "the great task that remains before us"? Presumably he was not simply referring to achieving an end to the Civil War, as is indicated by the wording "that *that* nation might live" as opposed to "that *this* nation might live." The nation Lincoln had in mind was yet to be established (the "new birth of freedom"), but once established the fulfillment of the "proposition" to which he was dedicated was assured. Bradford designates Lincoln's proposition and its implementation as the "heresy of equality," the touchstone of contemporary activism in the policy area of fundamental rights.[43]

Bradford's view of Lincoln is disputatiously revisionist because it runs counter to myths that shield Lincoln the politician from public scrutiny, which in turn protect the teleocratic "equality" policy agenda. Nevertheless, Bradford was steadfast in his analysis of Lincoln the politician, stressing Lincoln's break with the original Constitution and the consequential innovations on and departures from the traditional constitutional order. According to Bradford, Lincoln changed the "character of our country," and not necessarily for the better:

> Of course, nothing that we can identify as part of Lincoln's legacy belongs to him alone. In some respects the Emancipator was carried along with the tides. Yet a measure of his importance is that he was at the heart of the major political events of his era. Therefore what signifies in a final evaluation of this melancholy man is that many of these changes in the country would never have come to pass had Lincoln not pushed them forward. Or at least not come so quickly, or with such dreadful violence. I will emphasize only the events that he most certainly shaped according to his relentless will, alterations in the character of our country for which he was clearly responsible.... The major charges advanced here, if proved, are sufficient to impeach the most famous and respected of public men.[44]

The significance of Bradford's attempt to expose as a political fraud the leading prophet of the teleocratic Constitution should not be overlooked. By discrediting Lincoln, he questions the legitimacy of national unenumerated rights that emanate from the equality abstraction.

Bradford's indictment of Lincoln is threefold: First, Lincoln's commitment to the abolitionist movement was primarily a partisan tactic to destroy the Democratic party in the North, in order to catapult the northern-based Republican party into national prominence, thereby enhancing the electoral prospects for the first Republican (and sectional) president. Lincoln's "assertion that the equality clause of the Declaration of Independence was the *father of all moral principles among us*" and its contrived application to the enslaved African Americans provided the constitutional and moral legitimacy he needed to effectively drive a partisan wedge between the Northeast, South, and to a lesser extent the West.[45] Lincoln's personal opinions about and his actual public policies toward African Americans are evidence, according to Bradford, that partisan politics were behind Lincoln's high-sounding rhetoric; in other words, there was a wide divide between his rhetoric and his policy agenda that cannot be simplistically explained away by rationalizing Lincoln as a man ahead of his time and constrained by insurmountable political and social obstacles. His claim that a nation half free and half slave cannot endure in spite of an historical record to the contrary, the Black Codes of his home state Illinois, the racist policies of his northern electoral base, his support for recolonization of African Americans to Liberia, the selective emancipation and the plight of freedmen overall (Lincoln, at the Hampton Roads Conference in 1865, is quoted as saying they can "root, hog, or die") all give an empty ring to his rhetoric of universal human rights. As Bradford poignantly remarked, that "for the sake of such vapid distinctions he urged his countrymen to wade through seas of blood."[46] Although destroying the northern wing of the national Democratic party was a shrewd and successful campaign tactic, the ethical ramifications of his shrewd political maneuvers should not be overlooked. Lincoln was well aware that northern and southern Democratic partisan ties were instrumental in keeping the Union intact, but yet he methodically cut away at those ties for Republican partisan gains, pushing the country incrementally closer to the bloody experience of civil war.

Second, in light of his alleged demagoguery, can one reasonably conclude that Lincoln's obsession with the pursuit of power for a just cause and the "seas of blood" that flowed during his tenure were justifiable consequences of the "new birth of freedom" he alluded to in the Gettysburg Address? Or, was there a more mundane motive behind Lincoln's policies with the ensuing civil war unexpectedly getting out of hand?[47] There can be little question that Lincoln and his Republican supporters had a mundane public policy agenda that overshadowed the rhetoric and legacy of their tenure in power. That agenda was Hamiltonian, insofar as it required a substantial transfusion of power from the states to the national government, in order for the latter to more effectively promote the pace of development toward a commercial empire and the corresponding opportunities for personal and national gains that such rapid commercial development entailed. The politically contentious issues of internal improvements, the national bank, and protectionism all made giant strides on behalf of national supremacy during the Lincoln Administration. In fact, the Gilded Age can be traced to the political economy of those Republicans who controlled the national government in the early 1860s:

> It is customary to deplore the Gilded Age, the era of the Great Barbecue. It is true that many of the corruptions of the Republican Era came to a head after Lincoln lay at rest in Springfield. But it is a matter of fact that they began either under his direction or with his sponsorship. Military necessity, the "War for the Union," provided an excuse, an umbrella of sanction, under which the essential nature of the changes made in the relation of government to commerce could be concealed.[48]

Lincoln's rhetoric in the Gettysburg Address reveals a Republican party committed to the fulfillment of Hamilton's dream of a commercial empire. The emergence of the commercial empire within the conceptual framework of Lincoln's incorporation of the Declaration into the Constitution (or vice versa), would result in the political millennium he alludes to in the Gettysburg Address. Lincoln had good reason to be optimistic. During the Republican party's war and post-war dominance, the use of government as a means toward commercial expansion and personal aggrandizement was shifted into overdrive.

Third, Lincoln's expansive interpretation of presidential powers made him the most imperial president in American history, thereby setting a dangerous precedent for predisposed successors. The incarceration of approximately twenty thousand political prisoners, the closing of over three hundred newspapers, the interruptions of state legislatures, the blockade of the South, the unilateral suspension of habeas corpus, explicit and implicit defiance of the Supreme Court, the creation of West Virginia, the property seizures, and the electioneering and voting irregularities, have all been rationalized as necessary war measures. However, such rationalization would ring hollow if the stated purpose was partisan aggrandizement. Bradford believes that there is ample evidence against Lincoln to support this charge. Consider Bradford's claim that Lincoln's partisan manipulations of commanders in the fields of battle were motivated by partisan politics. The evidence indicates that "in this role the image of Lincoln grows to be very dark—indeed, almost sinister.... Thousands of Northern boys lost their lives in order that the Republican Party might experience rejuvenation, to serve its partisan goals."[49]

Bradford's scrutiny of Lincoln must be distinguished from the issue of race. His censure of Lincoln is not that he necessarily went too far in adjusting the plight of African Americans, but that his rhetoric was that of the demagogue, using a subject class for expedient political gain, bypassing the nomocratic constitutional process that, perhaps, could have more effectively dealt with the peculiar institution and its long-term aftermath. The country as a whole, African Americans included, would have been better served in the short and long term had the South been permitted to resolve on its own terms the political, social, economic, and religious dimensions associated with the slavery issue.[50] But an incremental approach to the peculiar institution was not conducive to the Republican party's partisan interests in splitting the Democratic party along sectional lines, thereby incorporating the Northern remnants into their own ranks. In other words, Lincoln and his co-Republicans were disingenuous on the slavery issue in order to primarily achieve implementation of their economic (as opposed to social) public policy agenda:

> But the point is that Lincoln's commitment was precisely of the sort that the North was ready to make—while passing legislation to restrict the flow of Negroes into its own territories, elaborating its own system of segregation by race, and exploiting black labor through its representatives in a conquered South. Lincoln's double talk left part of the country with a durable heritage of pious self-congratulation...Left it with the habit of concealing its larger objectives behind a facade of racial generosity, of using the Negro as a reason for policies and laws which make only minimal alterations in his condition; and also with the habit of seeming to offer a great deal more than it is truly willing to give.[51]

The rationale behind Republican policies toward African Americans, North, South, and West, becomes discernible if, and only if, we are willing to discard our "mass hypocrisy" toward Negroes. "Or to put matters another way, it would be well if we learned to say no more than we meant. For the alternative is to produce in the targets of our beneficence the kind of anger that comes with the receipt of a promissory note that contains, as one of its terms, the condition that it need never be paid. Better than this would be a little honest dealing, whatever its kind."[52]

Obviously, current difficulties with race in America have many of their roots in intractable power politics; but if we are to formulate effective remedies for these difficulties we must begin with the historical, as opposed to the mythological, politics of Lincoln and his co-Republicans. Bradford's analysis of events makes it quite clear that the traditional rule of law was dealt a serious blow by power politics of the period, as opposed to the Mason-Dixon Line being simply a division between moral and immoral social systems.

V

Lincoln's impact on the rule of law is most discernible in constitutional law, especially as manifested in the judicial phenomenon of selectively incorporating provisions of the Bill of Rights into the Fourteenth Amendment. Because Fourteenth Amendment privileges or immunities, due process, and equal protection standards apply to all the states equally ("no State shall..."), whatever the Supreme Court decides is a Fourteenth Amendment protection automatically standardizes the policies of all the states in regard to that protection, thereby displacing with national standards what could otherwise be State and regional diversity. Thus, the uniformity of public policy that results from selective incorporation is one answer to Lincoln's "house divided against itself" dilemma, insofar as state diversity is supplanted with national standards. The virtually unrestrained power of Congress to regulate the economy literally overwhelms state economic prerogatives.[53] However, in the absence of Congressional "necessary and proper" and "regulate interstate commerce" (Article I, section 8) powers, state police power prerogatives have been much more resistant to nationalization until, that is, the twentieth-century judicial distortions about the Fourteenth Amendment's historical meaning.

According to Bradford, the "hue and cry over equality of opportunity and equal rights leads, *a fortiori,* to a final demand for equality of condition,"[54] and only the national government has the jurisdictional range and means to logistically pursue and implement equal opportunity, equal rights, and equality of condition. So once the constitutionality of national standards is mandated, the national government can proceed to displace the reserved police powers of the states. This is not to say that Bradford challenged the historical Fourteenth Amendment guarantees,[55] but he did challenge the constitutionality and prudence of an "equality" based national public policy agenda. When Publius wrote in *The Federalist* #10 that protecting "the diversity in the faculties of men... is the first object of government," he was expressing a truism about which Bradford concurred. The national government was not constitutionally designed to be instrumental in an attempt to achieve equality; such attempts are destined to failure because people are naturally diverse and unequal in their faculties. The only remotely obtainable equality is that of condition because, as Bradford points out, you cannot have equal opportunity between unequals; those with different types and degrees of talents do not and can not have equal opportunities. Equal opportunity is only possible among equals:

> Let us have no foolishness indeed. Equality as a moral or political imperative, pursued as an end in itself—Equality, with the capital "E"—is the antonym of every legitimate conservative principle. Contrary to most Liberals, new and old, it is nothing less than sophistry to distinguish between equality of opportunity (equal starts in the "race of life") and equality of condition (equal results). For only those who are *equal* can take advantage of a given circumstance. And there is no man equal to any other, except perhaps in the special, and politically untranslatable,

> understanding of the Deity. *Not intellectually or physically or economically or even morally. Not equal!* [56]

Lincoln's rhetorical commitment to "Equality" and the corresponding necessity of a strengthened Union was espoused in a 4 July 1861 speech that epitomizes his usefulness to contemporary egalitarians. As quoted by Jaffa, "Lincoln defined the cause of the Union...to maintain in the world

> that form, and substance of government, *whose leading object* is, to elevate the condition of men—to lift artificial weights from all shoulders—to clear the paths of laudable pursuit for all—to afford all, an unfettered start, and a fair chance, in the race of life.[57]

Lincoln's rhetoric provides much needed umbrage for those who want the force and might of the national government to be put into motion in the quest for equality. To appreciate Bradford's consternation with egalitarianism, one needs only to consider how these "artificial weights from all shoulders" are to be lifted. The mere attempt would require an instrumental national government of elites, functioning as Platonic guardians at war with the original federal constitutional arrangement that does not sanction nationalistic social engineering over unenumerated rights. Moreover, if Bradford is correct and equal opportunity is one step removed from equality of condition, then the cause of Lincoln's Union is a far cry from Publius's "first object of government" to "protect the diversity of faculties in men...from which the rights of property originate."[58]

Bradford's understanding of the American commitment to equality is grounded in historical facts and not abstractions. He cautioned against taking the Declaration's "all men are created equal" phrase out of its historical and textual contexts. These contexts make evident the nomocratic origins of the Declaration, through which everything in the "sequence appeals to the *consensus gentium* of sensible men (common reasonableness but not philosophy) and to English law."[59] Americans were pressing for their rights as English subjects and wanted to be treated on an *equal* basis with their English counterparts. In essence, the American Revolution was a political response to a constitutional crisis within the English Common Law tradition. The textual context of the Declaration makes clear that the Americans perceived King George III as the innovator at war with English constitutional precedent; in short, English policy toward the colonies was tyrannical. As a result "these commonwealths must file an official bill of divorcement, designed to the pattern of a countersuit in an action already initiated on the other side."[60] The same holds true for the South's 1860-65 reaction to Lincoln's "cause of the Union"; the southern states' secession documents were consistent with this common law tradition.

However, if Lincoln and his latter-day disciples have their way in asserting that the Declaration has constitutional status, and that its "all men are created equal" phrase is a constitutional mandate for the national government to ameliorate circumstantial inequality and its effects, which presumably obstructs equal opportunity, at that point the constitutional order will enter into a full-blown teleocratic paradigm. All nomocratically generated policies would have to be judicially tested in the crucible of the "Cult of Equality," a standard that makes a nomocratic constitutional order virtually impossible. As we have been instructed, Americans do not involve themselves in the political process in the pursuit of equality, but due to the connections subsisting between their passions, opinions, and self-love.[61] If Publius and Bradford are correct, then Lincoln and Jaffa must be erroneous in their assertions that equality is the central principle of our political culture. By raising these issues Bradford calls into question the causes and effects of the American Civil War, the legitimacy of Fourteenth Amendment incorporation policies, and subsequent judicially sponsored *sub rosa* egalitarianism, all of which have been and continue to be instrumental in overturning the original federal model premised upon states' rights.

The issue of constitutional federalism aside, the establishment of a unitary system of government "dedicated to the proposition that all men are created equal" raises an important collateral issue: Can a distorted version of the Declaration's equality proposition be realized? Bradford thinks not: "Trying to preserve property, secure tranquillity, and promote equal rights, all at the same time, insures that none of these purposes will be accomplished. And insures also a terrible, unremitting tension, both among those in power and among those whose hopes are falsely raised.[62]

VI

According to Bradford, the "unremitting tensions" are just now beginning to intensify, and thus the heightened relevance of the U.S. Supreme Court. Even though, as the nomenclature suggests, Reconstruction involved the antebellum regime and its postbellum replacement, the task of identifying an approximate date and the individuals responsible for the new regime is much more elusive and not necessarily proximate to the latter half of the nineteenth century. Bradford concluded that for fifty years judicial interpretations of the Civil War Amendments and civil rights laws were, in their cumulative effect, consistent with the "old antebellum Constitution.... Despite the alteration that they made in the balance of American federalism, the Reconstruction amendments and early civil rights laws did not change the Constitution of the United States into a teleocratic instrument: a law with endlessly unfolding implications in the area of personal rights."[63] Some radical Republicans made rhetorical overtures about converting the U.S. Constitution into a "teleocratic instrument," but were "successfully resisted by individuals who doubted that such proposals could be reconciled to the American tradition of limited constitutional government."[64] Substantial change to the American tradition of limited constitutional government was to come later, when Reconstruction was reconstructed with "inventions and concoctions of the High Court."[65] It is the ongoing judicially orchestrated reconstruction that relies so much on Lincoln's teleocratic rhetoric for its constitutional legitimacy.[66]

Bradford substantiates his understanding of what can be called protracted Reconstruction by analyzing events as "a sequence, an order in time as well as causality."[67] As manifested in their constitutional amendments, statutory laws, and Supreme Court decisions, the mainstream Civil War Republicans who dominated American politics did not have to resort to teleocratic justifications to pursue and implement their public policy agenda; due to the fact that they controlled the government, nomocratic processes effectively served their public policy agenda. To a significant extent the Thirteenth, Fourteenth, and Fifteenth Amendments were tactical instruments in the Republican party's strategic arsenal to maintain national political hegemony. The historical evidence is irrefutable that section one of the Fourteenth Amendment was originally designed to protect the 1866 Civil Rights Act from judicial nullification and congressional repeal. The act stipulates that "inhabitants of every race shall have the same right to make and enforce contracts, to sue, to be parties and give evidence, to inherit, purchase, lease, sell, hold and convey personal property, and to full and equal benefit of all laws and proceedings for the security of persons and property."[68] The amendment was not ratified as a conduit of rights to be tapped into at the Court's discretion in order to overturn American federalism; its ratification was simply the attempt to secure the extension of existing rights to a recently recognized class of citizens. Not even the touchstone of judicial activism, the Fourteenth Amendment, confers the right to vote to the freedman. It merely reduces the basis of representation in proportion to the number of freedmen whose voting rights were being abridged (Indians not taxed and ex-Confederates excluded). The amendments were not the product of teleocratic aspirations for unspecified abstract rights of man, through which the U.S. Bill of Rights were to be made applicable to the states, but rather designed to protect blacks from the type of discrimination that precluded them from enjoying existing constitutional guarantees and being loyal Republicans. Nevertheless, twentieth-century Fourteenth Amendment selective incorporation theory rejects the obvious for the ideologically expedient, in order to make way for teleologically based constructions:

> The modern rejection of the Court's 1875-1925 position on personal rights and equal protection has been the cutting edge in the transformation of the United States Constitution into an ostensibly teleocratic fundamental law. These readings have become the models for other distortions dealing with things beyond the freedman and his descendants.[69]

The "things beyond" that Bradford had in mind are manifested by the scenario of constitutional federalism being trumped by the application of the Lincolnian equality proposition and contemporary Fourteenth Amendment jurisprudence. The examples are legion. Simply consider pre-World War II state policies on religion, pornography, firearms, criminal justice, privacy, and elections, all of which have felt the impact of judicial distortions about what is constitutionally national and state public policy prerogatives. Bradford's concern over the power shift from the states to the national government is not trivial. At issue is the very essence of popular control constrained by the national and state constitutions. As was the case in Lincoln's day, nomocratic constitutionalism has its deepest roots in Southern soil, therefore, it is to the South that we must turn if we are to understand the course of constitutional developments and whether a recovery of the original Constitution is feasible and, for that matter, wise.

VII

Bradford spoke eloquently for the South,[70] not to the hostile exclusion of the rest of the nation, but on the behalf of southern and national interests. He was convinced that the best hope for a constitutional national republic hinged on the survival of southern constitutional principles.[71] Bradford's southern conservatism is neither atavistic nor nostalgic; it is the product of thoughtful analysis grounded in a concern for the public good. He was convinced that the South's nomocratic method of formulating public policy was being unconstitutionally undermined by nationalistic teleocratic principles. If allowed to continue unimpeded, the South as the locus of conservatism would soon cease to exist, with the end result being the triumph of barbarism over the entire nation, that is the arbitrary rule of elites in contradistinction to popular control through rule of constitutional law. Thus, his clarion call to keep the South's conservative nomocratic constitutionalism intact transcended the South; it was a nonideological summons to protect the Republic from the sort of centralization that historically results in oligarchy or tyranny (the personification of barbarism), both of which are anathema to constitutional federalism. For Americans, the means for avoiding tyranny is compliance with the nomocratic Constitution, which was designed to procedurally curtail the governing opportunities of national elites, or, to be more precise, would-be tyrants.

Because it inherently adheres to established customs and laws, as opposed to avant-garde teleocratic agendas in which the ends justify unconstitutional means, southern conservatism provides a useful benchmark in measuring the course of American constitutional development. Consider a nineteenth-century historical example, the unwillingness of southern states to plan, finance, and construct the internal improvements that northern states were busily pursuing. Even when the series of antebellum southern commercial conventions made the solid case that internal improvements were in the best "economic" interest of the region, southerners by and large were uninterested. A commitment to commercial empire building presupposes a teleocratic vision of society and government's role in fulfilling that vision. Southerners had a vision of society and government's role, but both were grounded in the familiar *is* as opposed to the unfamiliar *ought.*[72] Thus, their tolerance for modifying the Constitution in order to accommodate government planned and financed economic projects was constrained by their commitment to the society with which they were familiar and devoted, and their conservative reluctance to expand the powers of government. The most effective way to secure society as they knew it was to limit the powers of the national government through a federal system that deferred to the policy preferences of the respective states, in contradistinction to an elitist unitary model through which policy innovations could be pushed forward by a strong centralized national government, the policy preferences of the states notwithstanding. Because southerners were realists about human nature and political power, and skeptical about both, they were very reluctant to combine the two in such a way that potentially placed their regional political, economic, social, and cultural arrangements at risk.

From outside the region this may appear to be a teleocratic component to southern constitutional principles, insofar as the commitment to an established way of life is an overriding concern. But the South's commitment was not the product of ideology; it was patrimonial, handed down from generation to generation. Perhaps this does, in most instances, result in a *conserv*atism that is inclined to sustain the *status quo,* but not necessarily. For example, the pro-slavery "positive good" rhetoric of Calhoun, Hammond, Bledsoe, Fitzhugh, and others appears to be teleocratic. However, these arguments were reactions to teleocratic challenges by northerners. Southern pro-slavery arguments were responses in kind, responses that would never have been articulated had abolitionists not forced the issue. But even the pro-slavery arguments were shielded behind the assumption that slavery was good for southern society, the African Americans included. Slavery was a legal, social, and cultural reality in the Antebellum South, and in many ways persisted *de facto* for several generations after Appomattox, circumstances that confirm Southern conservatism and Northern politics. But one should not automatically assume that Southerners were incapable of resolving the slavery issue on their own terms, through their own nomocratic governing procedures. Not only were there strong currents in favor of institutional slavery's continuation, but for manumission too. This is evidenced by the facts that the Confederate States of America (C.S.A.) Constitution (1861-65) allowed each state to resolve the slavery issue on their own terms, allowed admission to the Confederacy of free States, and sanctioned C.S.A. legislation that granted freedom to slaves as compensation for service in the C.S.A. military. Could southerners have unilaterally, at their own pace, and without the devastation of the Civil War ended slavery and still be conservative? Bradford did acknowledge southern conservatism's "various incarnations and the fact that there are many durable features of the Southern configuration which are not persistently conservative in their impact on the region's behavior—features such as populism, a warlike disposition, a love of leisure, etc."[73] Thus, the answer would have to be a qualified yes, based upon the circumstances and pace of such a fundamental change (as is evidenced by New Orleans, where freedmen had incrementally tied into the commercialism of the region to such an extent that many of them were prosperous slave owners). As Bradford's political credo concedes, contingencies arise that require modification of the traditional social order. Southerners confronting the peculiar institution on their own terms could have been one such contingency eventually resulting in fundamental changes in regard to this specific area of public policy, without an abandonment of their overriding commitment to tradition. It was outside northern interference that toughened their resolve on the slavery issue and interrupted what might have been a nomocratic, albeit protracted but more genuine, southern solution to a national problem.

Much the same could be said about the long-term impact of U.S. Supreme Court teleocratic activism. Bradford attributed past and present southern resistance to outside interference to their commitment to corporate liberty, acknowledged as the most fundamental component of southern culture and defined as a community's prerogative to govern itself according to what it perceives to be in its best interest, as opposed to coercion from external national interests. Corporate liberty has deep roots in American politics. It was the foundation from which colonial Americans viewed the 1776 *Unanimous Declaration of the Thirteen United States of America*[74] and southerners four score and four years later when they opted for secession. The commitment to corporate liberty emanates from the presupposition "that man is a social being, fulfilled only in the natural associations built upon common experience, upon the ties of blood and friendship, common enterprises, resistance to common enemies, and a common faith,"[75] the very definition of *societas*. Government exists for the sake of *societas*, not to remake it according to some ideological blueprint. As Bradford insightfully reminds us, minimal government interference into the established relations of *societas* is not the equivalent of minimal checks on social interaction in which people are free to brutalize and oppress one another. Religion, specifically Protestantism, was the dominant force that keeps antisocial behavior in check within the respective communities. The "presence of a powerful (if pluralistic) Protestant establishment" in the South provided the parameters of acceptable behavior. To a significant extent southern churches functioned as the socializing agents. One merely has to consider the respective functions of churches in black and white southern communities to appreciate their influence. Moreover, contemporary public policies that are not sanctioned by the southern brand of Protestantism have serious *de facto* implementation difficulties in the region, as gay rights, abortion, and gun control controversies make clear.

For individuals the degree and intensity of social feelings among the different levels of corporate life vary, ranging from the family, the neighborhood, city, county, state, nation, and international alliances. Social feelings would be the strongest at the family level and weakest at the more remote international level. Each level is tied to the others, but those ties are consensual and not coercive. The neighborhood is a community of families, the city is a community of neighborhoods, the county is a community of neighborhoods and cities, the state is a community of counties, the nation is a community of states, and international alliances are communities of nations. The ties that bind the different levels together are not commitments to abstractions, such as Lincoln's *the Union at all cost*. Rather, the ties are grounded in acknowledged common interests that are sustained as the best practical way to promote the welfare of the voluntary interconnected communities and the individuals therein. For Americans, corporate liberty is at the core of these associations. This is why southerners consistently adhered to states' rights and secession and why the Confederacy left the slavery issue to the states. States' rights allowed a state to avoid a coercive national will, with secession providing states with a way out of a national association that proved to be counterproductive to interests of any or all parties. Not even the republican form of government was supported in the South because of its appeal as an abstraction. According to Bradford, the South continued to be republican "undogmatically, coincidentally republican, according to some notion of what is good for the regime, useful in protecting its cohesive force—but not abstractly republican, according to the authority of a principle to be honored, regardless of consequences."[76]

The same was true for the South's commitment to the Union; when continued membership in the Union was perceived to be counterproductive, southerners did what for them was logical and constitutional, they dissolved the association through secession.

A clearly identifiable southern version of *societas* began to take shape circa 1800; prior to that time the North and South shared common experiences. However, in the 1800s the rapid growth in Evangelical denominations "had sealed off the South from the influence of Yankee dialectics, values understood apart from their embodiment in a specific order."[77] "Yankee dialectics" led northern politics in one direction, while evangelism anchored southern politics to a somewhat more static biblical tradition. For churches to play such a major role in the lives of southerners is perfectly consistent with southern conservatism. First, a southerner's religion is by and large inherited. Second, it is not the product of abstraction, but grounded in divine revelation. Third, it is not coercively binding; one may, if you will, secede from one church to another or to the privacy of one's home with or without patrimonial bible and tradition in hand. For southerners the First Amendment guarantees of separation and free exercise were necessary, not to make the national government hostile to the influences of religion on state public policies, but for preventing the type of national denominational dominance that the Church of England exercised in Great Britain and, to a much lesser extent, in some of her former colonies. The historical First Amendment arrangement between church and state precluded the national government from taking over the role of denominational religion, not to mention governmentally endorsed secular-humanism, both of which are anathema to southern conservatism's opposition to innovation, abstraction, and coercion.

To reiterate, nothing strikes at the core of southern corporate liberty and the *societas* from which it emanates as does the U.S. Supreme Court's contemporary jurisprudence of separation of church and state and unenumerated rights; more than any other judicial concoctions—rightly or wrongly—they facilitate remaking the South in the image of twentieth-century "Yankee dialectics."

VIII

Professor Bradford's constitutional theory is, indeed, reactionary to the extent that the original Constitution is axiomatic to his scholarship.

Because the original intent of the framers can be discerned by studying the drafting and ratification processes of the U.S. and state constitutions, he walks us through those events. Thus, with the skill of the ablest scholar and rhetorician, he draws from literature, history, and politics elements of America's constitutional tradition, a tradition premised upon "the determination to live free and to secure that freedom to an always vulnerable society."[78] If his analysis is sound, then the eventual impact of teleocratic jurisprudence will have a profound negative impact on traditional American constitutionalism and the freedom it was designed to secure. In his own words, "there is an organized campaign set in motion by the highest levels of political leadership, by the courts, the media and universities to swallow up the Constitution in a simplistic reading of the Declaration, to conflate the two documents, confuse their purposes, and employ the combination to transform the meaning of Union into something instrumental in its promotion, through the agencies of government, a wide variety of causes which seem, for the moment, worthy: the most cunning formula for political tyranny ever devised by the mind of man."[79] In other words, under the guise of expanding the application of fundamental rights, the prerogatives of popular control within the context of American federalism are being undercut by national elites, who in the process make shambles not only of the Constitution, but also the right of Americans to be self-governing. This, according to Ronald Dworkin, is not only desirable, but requisite to the establishment of the just society.

VIII
Ronald Dworkin: A Liberal's Affirmation for the Rule of Principle

Ronald Dworkin's recent book, *Life's Dominion,* is much more than mere polemics about abortion, euthanasia, and individual freedom. It is, significantly, a forthright presentation regarding the direction U.S. Supreme Court jurisprudence has taken, and subsequently should take, in modernizing American constitutionalism in the policy area of unenumerated rights. His constitutional law modernization is contingent upon the establishment of constitutional norms that accommodate national uniformity in the policy area of fundamental rights. For example, Dworkin observed that "abortion is tearing America apart. It is also distorting its politics, and confounding its constitutional law."[80] If, indeed, the abortion issue is "tearing America apart" and "distorting its politics," the U.S. Constitution must be inflaming the political firestorm, not necessarily because of any inherent deficiency therein, but because it is the touchstone from which political opponents legitimatize their respective positions on fundamental rights, in this case the right to procure an abortion versus the right to life of the fetus. Obviously, the U.S. Supreme Court's role is pivotal, intended or unintended, in legitimating and facilitating political victory for those factions whose political objectives coincide with the Court's articulation of what constitutes a constitutionally guaranteed fundamental right. If the Supreme Court authoritatively decides that the right to procure an abortion is constitutionally protected, opponents of abortion lose constitutional cover for their public policy preferences on the issue, and must either amend the Constitution or look for legitimacy elsewhere, such as higher law, thereby dismissing the Constitution itself as a "pact with hell," following the course taken by radical antebellum abolitionists. Nevertheless, at the center of the debate is the U.S. Constitution and the manner and extent of its impact on public policy. What is significant about Dworkin's legal scholarship is the light it sheds not only on the jurisprudential bases of established constitutional law, but also on future constitutional developments. Just as Pound, Cardozo, Frank, and others blazed trails that the Warren and subsequent Courts traveled down,[81] Dworkin is providing similar service for the Court as it enters the twenty-first century. As M. E. Bradford forewarned, the nomocratic Constitution is being displaced by a teleocratic alternative. Dworkin's scholarship not only makes the development quite evident, but also more probable.

IX

In the chapter titled *The Constitutional Drama,* Dworkin asked the rhetorical question, "What kind of constitution should America have?"[82] His words are well chosen. In this constitutional drama the antagonists are the champions of two distinctively different constitutions, what Dworkin denotes as the constitution of *detail* in contradistinction to a constitution of *principle*. These two distinctively different constitutions are the equivalent of Bradford's nomocratic and teleocratic constitutions, respectively. The constitution of principle is an open-ended document, to be modified by deference to abstractions that promote the treatment "of all citizens with equal concern and respect." According to Dworkin, the Constitution "lays down general, comprehensive moral standards that government must respect but that leaves to statesmen and judges to decide what those standards mean in concrete circumstances. What the due process and equal protection clauses actually mean, on this view of the Constitution, depends on the best, most accurate understanding of liberty and equal citizenship."[83] The constitution of detail is constrained by an originalism and limited to the specific expectations of the framers who "wrote and voted for" it, and is merely a "collection of independent historical views and opinions unlikely to have great unity or even complete consistency." In Dworkin's mind the constitution of principle is exhilarating, while the constitution of detail is stagnant.[84]

To his credit, Dworkin does not shy away from openly acknowledging the instrumental role U.S. Supreme Court justices have in delineating the constitution of principle:

> The Supreme Court will have to decide, which means that the justices must answer intractable, profound questions of political morality that philosophers, statesmen, and citizens have debated for many centuries with no prospect of agreement. It means that the rest of us must accept the deliverances of a majority of the justices, whose insights into these great issues does not seem spectacularly special... This form of government gives very great power to judges. For all practical purposes, the federal courts, and finally the Supreme Court, have the last word about what rights the Constitution affirms and protects, and what the national and state governments therefore cannot do.[85]

According to Dworkin, fears that the constitution of principle model thwarts American federalism and its counterpart, republican constitutionalism, are misplaced. The less noble constitution of detail presents the most serious threat to American constitutionalism and to maintain the contrary is illusory: "The narrow, detailed conception of our Constitution is not even an option for contemporary America, and pretending to adopt it would provide no real check on judges' powers to impose their own convictions on the law, but only the dangerous illusion of such a check."[86]

Drawing from constitutional law on abortion, Dworkin directs our attention to three Reagan and Bush appointees—Justices Sandra Day O'Connor, Anthony Kennedy, and David Souter—for the appropriate jurisprudential vision requisite to giving life and substance to the abstract constitution of principle. Analyzing Dworkin's elevation and endorsement of their jurisprudence through the eyes of their colleague Justice Scalia—whom Dworkin criticizes as "the most radically conservative member of the present Court"[87]—provides insight into the jurisprudential direction the Court has adopted.

Applying the rational basis test, Scalia would have upheld all five provisions of the Pennsylvania Abortion Control Act (18 Pa. Cons. Stat. 3203-3220 [1990]).[88] However, Dworkin's praise for Justices O'Connor, Kennedy, and Souter was not due to their rejection of the spousal notification provision, but the jurisprudential bases of their refusal to overturn *Roe* v. *Wade*. Basing the decision on the "principles of institutional integrity and the rule of *stare decisis*"[89] is, according to Dworkin, tantamount to declaring judicial independence from the constitutional moorings of judicial review. Consider the manner and extent to which Justice Scalia's reasoning contravenes the majority's reasoning, and therefore draws Dworkin's indignation.

First, Scalia takes seriously the political question doctrine. He maintained that "the permissibility of abortion, and the limitations upon it, are to be resolved like most important questions in our democracy: by citizens trying to persuade one another and then voting." He acknowledges that abortion raises significant liberty issues in both the absolute and personal senses, but those are not necessarily justiciable issues. The pertinent issue is whether or not it is "a liberty protected by the Constitution." He is certain that it is not. Because it is not a liberty protected by the U.S. Constitution, it is by constitutional design relegated to the political process. Moreover, and perhaps most problematical for Dworkin's judicial scheme of fundamental rights, Scalia dismisses his personal "views concerning the concept of existence, of meaning, of the universe, and the mystery of human life," as irrelevant to his responsibilities as a Supreme Court Justice. Unlike the Court majority, Justice Scalia is not willing to "succumb" to the temptation to "systematically" eliminate checks upon the Court's power, in order to accommodate constitutional law to the policy preferences of the justices' concepts of liberty and justice.[90]

By applying his jurisprudence to fundamental rights, Justice Scalia proceeds to dismantle the Court's opinion. Because *Roe* is based on the philosophical abstraction that the fetus is merely potential human life, the most crucial question is left begging: "There is no way to determine that as a legal matter; it is in fact a value judgment."[91] Dworkin, on the other hand, maintains that "the crucial issue in the constitutional controversy is not whether a fetus is a person within the meaning of the Constitution, but whether states have a legitimate power to dictate how their citizens must respect the inherent value of life. Since any competent interpretation of the Constitution must recognize a principle of procreative autonomy, states do not have the power simply to forbid abortion altogether."[92] One way or the other the law will endorse some vision of the inherent value of life. Justice Scalia contends that value judgments of this nature belong in the political arena and are nonjusticiable, whereas Dworkin insists that the U.S. Supreme Court should impose his understanding of procreative autonomy, which includes the prerogative of abortion, which in turn may supersede the rights of the fetus that a state may or may not choose to respect. This is why Dworkin supports *Roe* and the direction it takes American jurisprudence. Answering by default the issue of when human life begins, *Roe*'s "reasoned judgment" that the right to abortion "inheres in liberty because it is among a person's most basic decisions; involves a most intimate and personal choice; it is central to personal dignity and autonomy; it originates with the zone of conscience and belief; it is too intimate and personal for state interference; it reflects intimate views of deep and personal character; it involves intimate relationships and notions of personal autonomy and bodily integrity; and it concerns a particularly important decision," all of which may, according to Justice Scalia, just as readily be applied to "homosexual sodomy, polygamy, adult incest, and suicide," thereby negating state laws that constrain consensual conduct in these areas of intimate relationships as well.[93] Dworkin would not only concur with Justice Scalia, but encourage the Court to remove these issues from the grasp of popular control and through judicial activism "answer these profound questions of morality."[94]

The joint opinion in *Casey* acknowledged its affinity with Dworkin's jurisprudence when it failed to maintain that *Roe* was a "correct application of reasoned judgment," but upheld the 1973 decision on *stare decisis et quieta non movere* grounds. The court opinion states that "Liberty finds no refuge in a jurisprudence of doubt.... After considering the fundamental constitutional questions resolved by *Roe*, principles of institutional integrity, and the rule of *stare decisis*, we are led to conclude this: the essential holding of *Roe* v. *Wade* should be retained and once again reaffirmed."[95] Although the Court's reaffirmation is qualified with a new standard, the undue burden test that state regulations must not have the "purpose or effect of placing a substantial obstacle in the path of a woman seeking an abortion of a nonviable fetus,"[96] its underlying purpose was social and economic gender equality:

> [T]o refuse to face the fact that for two decades of economic and social developments, people have organized intimate relationships and made choices that define their views of themselves and their places in society, in reliance on the availability of abortion in the event that contraception should fail. The ability of women to participate equally in the economic and social life of the Nation has been facilitated by their ability to control their reproductive lives. The Constitution serves human values, and while the effect of reliance on *Roe* cannot be exactly measured, neither can the certain cost of overruling *Roe* for people who have ordered their thinking and living around that case be dismissed.[97]

According to Justice Scalia, if the joint opinion's reasoning were the modus operandi in 1954, *Plessy* v. *Ferguson* (1896) would still be a permanent part of constitutional law.[98] In other words, to uphold *Roe* on the basis that women have become accustomed to the abortion option, would have been tantamount to upholding *Plessy* for similar reasons—people have become accustomed to segregation and ordered their lives accordingly. Moreover, overruling *Roe*'s central holding that women have a constitutional right to abortion up to and in some cases beyond viability is not synonymous with outlawing abortion. To the contrary, states would be free to establish their abortion policies, and it is only logical to conclude that a state's abortion policy would be a consequence of how people have "ordered their thinking and living" and their "traditions and consciences." However, deferring to the states is not consistent with Dworkin's model of "giving great power to judges." This is where Justice Scalia and Dworkin part company; According to Dworkin, because Justice Scalia is reluctant to expand the power of the U.S. Supreme Court beyond its constitutional limits, he is working against integrity in law, the essence of which "is principle, governed most profoundly not by an ad hoc list of detailed rules but by an ideal."[99]

X

In a peculiar way Dworkin is correct. Justice Scalia's jurisprudence does diminish the integrity in law, because he is not theoretically consistent. The chink in Justice Scalia's jurisprudential armor is his willingness to bow to Dworkin's "ideal principle" in some hard cases, but not in others. Consider *Brown* v. *The Board of Education.* Acknowledging that the framers' opinions of the Fourteenth Amendment's equal protection clause were well represented by the majority opinion in *Plessy* v. *Ferguson,* Dworkin rhetorically asked, "[I]n light of these opinions held by the authors of the equal protection clause, what does the clause mean today?"[100] Dworkin provides four responses that progressively give judges more discretion (i.e., power). The first is closest to originalism, in that the clause only provides blacks with remedies for breach of contract; the second forbids any serious discrimination against blacks; the third forbids any serious racial discrimination against blacks, whites, or anyone else; whereas the fourth "establishes a general principle of equality that affirms the genuine equal citizenship for all Americans.... in spite of what the authors themselves may have thought or would have approved."[101] Only the first is consistent with originalism, and Dworkin soundly rejects it:

> The first reading is a reductive one. It supposes that we respect the authority of the Constitution's authors by deciding issues as we believe they would have decided them in our shoes, today, if they had lived so long and by some bizarre miracle had changed none of their moral opinions in the meantime. This reductive thesis entails that the Supreme Court's landmark decision in *Brown* was a flat mistake, because we know that the authors of the equal protection clause did not believe that it outlawed explicit racial segregation in public schools.[102]

Dworkin maintains that the "most powerful argument against the reductive reading is the near-universal acceptance of the *Brown* decision." Dismissing the reductive approach as "unloved and unsupported," Dworkin instructs us that the three remaining approaches are "progressively more abstract, and progressively assign judges more and more responsibility for judgment." Then, rhetorically he asks, "If someone accepts originalism but rejects the first, reductive account of what it means for the equal protection clause, can he stop short of accepting the fourth, most abstract account?"[103] No, according to Dworkin, because in order to replace the framers' intent with some substantive content, the judge must rely on replacement abstractions. Thus, for Justice Scalia—and anyone else—to rely on original intent, as it pertains to unenumerated rights is "bogus." He looks forward "to the day when a judge would be embarrassed to appeal to those concepts as a scientist would be to appeal to phlogiston or bodily humors or ghosts."[104] In short, the essence of Justice Scalia's jurisprudence differs with Dworkin's in degree, that is, in what manner and to what extent should the judge conform constitutional law to his ideals, in contradistinction to should the judge ever establish such conformity.

XI

Central to Dworkin's rights jurisprudence is his refusal to constitutionally uphold popular control. He acknowledged that "one wants to say, in the United States for example, that the 'people' are sovereign. But this means almost nothing, and in itself provides no test for determining what the 'people' have commanded, or distinguishing their legal from their moral or social commands."[105] In effect, there are no such tests for the judiciary, unless justices accept the status quo as manifested in custom and statutory laws as embodiments of what the people command. Whereas such tests conform to Bradford's nomocratic constitutionalism, they may be inconsistent with Dworkin's idealized Constitution of principle and the role of the justices in articulating and elevating to constitutional status the tenets thereof. The elevation of these tenets is commensurate to lawmaking. For example, if the Supreme Court elevates some "novel right-of-privacy"[106] to the status of constitutional law, it asserts "in a shorthand way, that others have actual or hypothetical legal obligations to act or not to act in certain ways."[107] Is this not the very essence of law by judicial fiat?

According to Dworkin, the Constitution's principles are to be discovered and articulated by the justices, and in the hard cases—such as the articulation of unenumerated rights—it is an exercise in political theory.[108] However, a fundamental flaw of his jurisprudence is the failure to distinguish political theory from ideology. Perhaps this explains his inattention to the prospects of judicial tyranny. In his own words, "I begin with the idea of a political aim as a generic political justification. A political theory takes a certain state of affairs as a political aim if, for that theory, it counts in favor of any political decision that the decision is likely to advance, or to protect, that state of affairs, and counts against the decision that it will retard or endanger it."[109] In a footnote he adds, "A complete political theory must also recognize two other distinctions.... The first is the distinction between rights against the state and rights against fellow citizens. The former justify a political decision that requires some agency of the government to act; the latter justify a decision to coerce particular individuals.... The second distinction is between universal and special rights."[110] Integrally linking the "discovery of rights" to a political theory "that takes a certain state of affairs to be its political aim" is the very essence of ideology.[111] Thus, the power to implement an ideological agenda—detached from popular control—is anathema to government accountability. This is precisely what Dworkin supports, as he commends the Supreme Court for elevating its ideology to the status of constitutional law, thereby necessitating the rejection of popular control over the articulation of unenumerated rights when the latter obstructs the political aims of the former.

Notes

1. For example, the "switch in time that saved nine" and Justice Stone's famous footnote number four in U.S. v. Carolene Products Co. (304 U.S. 144 [1938]) demonstrate the importance of politics.
2. Utilizing Dworkin's scholarship in this manner is not meant to imply a lack of scholarly diversity inconsistent with Bradford's, or vice versa. The scholarly diversity regarding unenumerated rights is plentiful and complex. Nevertheless, on balance Bradford's scholarship is representative of a systematic conservatism, while Dworkin similarly represents liberalism. Where other scholarship falls on the continuum between Bradford's and Dworkin's juridical perspectives is more digressive than fundamental to the task at hand, which is discerning the relevance of popular control in the articulation and implementation of constitutional rights. For a current survey of scholarly debate over constitutional theory, see Earl M. Maltz, *Rethinking Constitutional Law: Originalism, Interventionism, and the Politics of Judicial Review* (Lawrence: University Press of Kansas, 1994).
3. *The Federalist*, #47.
4. This is not an overstatement. Even Justice Powell acknowledged that "a unique feature of the United States is the federal system of government guaranteed by the Constitution and implicit in the very name of our country. Despite some genuflecting in the Court's opinion to the concept of federalism, today's decision effectively reduces the Tenth Amendment to meaningless rhetoric when Congress acts pursuant to the Commerce Clause" [Garcia v. San Antonio Metropolitan Transit Authority 469 U.S. 559 (1985)]; according to Justice O'Connor, "Because virtually every state activity of a private individual, arguably 'affects' interstate commerce, Congress can now supplant the states from the significant sphere of activities envisioned for them by the Framers" (ibid., 585). There is also the impact of "selective incorporation," discussed *supra* and *infra*.
5. See Justice Peckham's court opinion in Lochner v. New York, 198 U.S. 45 (1905) for a classic example of substantive due process.
6. Garry Wills, "The Words That Remade America," *The Atlantic Monthly* (June 1992), 68.
7. M. E. Bradford, *Original Intentions On The Making Of The United States Constitution* (Athens: The University of Georgia Press, 1993), 16.
8. Ibid., xi–xii.

9. As discussed *infra,* Ronald Dworkin's *Life's Dominion: An Argument About Abortion, Euthanasia, and Individual Freedom* makes this quite evident. Dworkin also acknowledges two distinct constitutions, a constitution of *principle* (i.e., teleocratic) and a constitution of *detail* (i.e., nomocratic). Dworkin does not hesitate in applauding those justices who adhere to the constitution of principle, referring to supporters of the constitution of detail (Justices Scalia, Rehnquist, and Thomas) as unintelligent and unimaginative revisionists (see ibid., chap. 5, 118–47).
10. Dahl's contention that "thus to affirm that the Court supports minority preferences against majorities is to deny that popular sovereignty and political equality, at least in the traditional sense, exist in the United States; and to affirm that the Court ought to act in this way is to deny that popular sovereignty and political equality ought to prevail in this country" (Dahl, "Decision-Making in a Democracy: The Supreme Court as a National Policy-maker," *Journal of Public Law* 6 [1957], 283), fails to consider that the Court has a constitutional responsibility to guarantee certain minority and majority rights, such as those noted in Article I, sections nine and ten, and the Bill of Rights. Protecting such rights do not contravene popular sovereignty if the Court is essentially safeguarding "against the effects of occasional ill humors in the society" as opposed to substituting its "own pleasure to the constitutional interests of the legislature" (see *The Federalist,* #78).
11. For a traditional view of American federalism, see John C. Calhoun's "A Discourse on the Constitution and Government of the United States," in *Union and Liberty: The Political Philosophy of John C. Calhoun,* Ross M. Lence, ed. (Indianapolis, Ind.: Liberty Fund Press, 1992), 79–284.
12. Bradford, *Remembering Who We Are: Observations of a Southern Conservative* (Athens: The University of Georgia Press, 1985), 22–23.
13. Bradford, *Intentions,* 12.
14. Bradford used the word "comic" in the sense that Madison should have known better, especially when the intended or unintended effects of his actions could have been disastrous; for an explanation the word's meaning, see H. W. Fowler, *A Dictionary of Modern English Usage,* 2nd ed. (New York: Oxford University Press, 1965), 96.
15. Bradford, *Intentions,* 8.
16. Ibid., 7.
17. Ibid., 9.
18. Ibid., 42–86.
19. Ibid., 42.
20. Ibid, 35–36.
21. See Glenn A. Phelps, *George Washington and American Constitutionalism* (Lawrence: University Press of Kansas, 1993), chap. 4.
22. See *The Federalist Papers,* #10.
23. Bradford, *Intentions,* 12-13.
24. Ibid., 13.
25. Ibid., 88–89.
26. The range of Bradford's scholarship on the lives of the framers is second to none; based upon his erudite analysis, I am convinced that his numbers are reliable. See his *A Worthy Company* (Westchester, Ill.: Crossway Books, 1982).
27. Bradford, *Intentions,* 89.
28. Lemon v. Kurtzman, 403 U.S. 602 (1971), 613.

29. Quoting James McClellan, Bradford refers to this arrangement as quasi-establishment: "[I]t would appear there were basically three patterns of church-state relations in late-eighteenth-century America: quasi-establishment of a specific Protestant sect, as seen in most of New England; quasi-establishment of the Protestant religion, as seen throughout the nation; and the disestablishment of all religion, as seen in Rhode Island and Virginia" (Bradford, *Intentions,* 96). Quasi establishment usually took the forms of tacit and/or explicit support for religion without the required "credal acquiescence to the faith" (Ibid., 95-96).
30. Ibid., 93.
31. Ibid., 97-100. The "wall of separation" was elevated to constitutional status in Everson v. Board of Education of Ewing Township, 330 U.S. 1 (1947).
32. Bradford, *Intentions,* 98.
33. Bradford, *Against the Barbarians and Other Reflections on Familiar Themes* (Columbia: The University of Missouri Press, 1992), 77.
34. Bradford, *Intentions,* 100.
35. Ibid., 101.
36. It is significant that the Supreme Court does consider secular-humanism to be a type of religion, but without belief in the existence of God; see Torcaso v. Watkins, 367 U.S. 488 (1961).
37. This is only one aspect of the larger edifice of nation-building that moves us closer and closer to a unitary system of government. Other important aspects that diminish the policy prerogatives of the states include nationalistic interpretations of Congressional commerce powers and other variations of Fourteenth Amendment selective incorporation theories. For example, see Richard A. Epstein, *Takings: Private Property and the Power of Eminent Domain* (Chicago, Ill.: University of Chicago Press, 1985).
38. The success of judicial activism in the policy area of fundamental rights depends not only on the development of Supreme Court constitutional law, but also, and perhaps more importantly, through the status of the Declaration in our political culture, which in turn provides the stage from which the Court may more effectively rationalize its activism. Regarding the latter, great gains have been made. Consider the 1991 edition of *The Constitution of the United States and The Declaration of Independence,* published by the Commission on the Bicentennial of the United States Constitution. In its foreword, the late Chief Justice Warren Burger maintained that "this Constitution was not perfect; it is not perfect today even with amendments, but it has continued longer than any other written form of government. It sought to fulfill the promises of the Declaration of Independence of 1776, which expressed peoples' yearning to be free and to develop the talents given them by their Creator." (Published by the Commission on the Bicentennial of the United States Constitution, Thirteenth Edition, Washington, DC, 1991, foreword). In other words, the Declaration is the instrument with which the Constitution is moved closer to perfection.
39. Bradford's reference to "Father Abraham" is not new. Perceived as their American Moses leading them out of slavery into the promised land of freedom, emancipated African Americans initially made the biblical connection. But Bradford's meaning goes beyond that particular event to the realm of the theoretical, where an apotheosized Lincoln leads his followers from the nomocratic constitutional paradigm into a teleocratic one.
40. For example, Graham Walker, in his attempt to find constitutional legitimacy for his teleocratic *moral realism,* speculated that "*Moral Realism,* as I use the term

here, regards the good, whatever it may be, as a reality whose existence is independent of human artifice. That independent reality might be taken as ultimately located, as the American Declaration has it, either in Nature or Nature's God—or perhaps elsewhere. Whatever its locus, the good can be authoritative for human beings and human communities precisely because it is a reality independent of their manipulation. Human caprice or self-interest form neither its existence nor its essential character" (Graham Walker, *Moral Foundations Of Constitutional Thought: Current Problems, Augustinian Prospects* [Princeton University Press, 1990], 24-25). Walker equates conventionalism with nihilism, with the latter being the actuating premise of the former (ibid., 25). According to this view, Bradford's preference for a nomocratic constitutional order is deontological, relative, and in the end nihilistic, because it tolerates varying standards of the public good. However, Walker's theory has several insufferable qualities; it is hubristic insofar as it pretends to have a monopoly of virtue in discerning—albeit with the assistance of St. Augustine—the public good, and it is inherently tyrannical insofar as its notion of the public good is to be the authoritative one. Both qualities are repugnant to American republicanism.

41. See the writings of Harry V. Jaffa, a devoted disciple of an apotheosized Lincoln, especially *Crisis of the House Divided* (Chicago, Ill.: University of Chicago Press, 1982) and *How to Think About the American Revolution* (Durham, N.C.: Carolina Academic Press, 1978).
42. The metaphor is applicable to "The Declaration of Independence: A Derailment," in chapter 5 of Willmore Kendall's and George W. Carey's *The Basic Symbols of the American Political Tradition* (Baton Rouge, La.: LSU Press, 1970). Regarding the authors' thesis, Bradford admitted that "though I agree with Kendall/Carey that there is a distance between the Declaration and the Constitution of 1787, and that silence on equality in the latter reflects a conscious choice. I agree also with Professor Jaffa that the two are not in conflict" (Bradford, *A Better Guide Than Reason: Studies in the American Revolution* [La Salle, Ill.: Sherwood Sugden & Company Publishers, 1979], 41). Nevertheless, Bradford is in agreement with Kendall and Carey that Lincoln, by distorting the meanings of and relation between the two documents, was instrumental in the derailment of the American political tradition.
43. There are innumerable manifestations of Lincoln's impact on Americans' worldview. James Q. Wilson provides us with a recent one; see the chapter titled "The Universal Aspiration," in *The Moral Sense* (New York: The Free Press, 1993), 191-221.
44. Bradford, *Remembering,* 143-44.
45. Ibid., 145.
46. Ibid., 144-45.
47. Bradford agreed with historian Charles W. Ramsdell that Lincoln hoped for a military conflict, due to all the associated political and economic opportunities; however, the scale and extent of the conflict that ensued is another matter (see *Remembering,* 153-55).
48. Bradford, *Remembering,* 146.
49. Ibid., 150-51. Bradford attributed the loss of approximately 100,000 lives to Lincoln's partisan rejection of peace in 1864; the rejection was the result of partisan plans to sustain the Republican party's political hegemony (see *Remembering,* 151).
50. Commenting on Robert W. Fogel's and Stanley L. Engerman's *Time On The Cross: The Economics of Negro Slavery* [Boston, Mass.: Little, Brown and Co.,

(1974)], Bradford wrote: "But the ability, character, and acquired skills displayed by the slave in helping produce a prosperous and stable South are, his condition aside, a more durable inheritance than a hundred abortive rebellions or a thousand damaged mules. And, along with the evidence of slave family life, these qualities are not only a reason for ordinate pride but also an augury of good prospects yet awaiting him in the culture he helped to build" [*National Review*, "Time On The Cross: Debate," (28 March 1975), 341]. See my *The Confederate Constitution of 1861: An Inquiry Into American Constitutionalism* (Columbia: The University of Missouri Press, 1991) for a discussion about the constitutional issues at stake and the south's understanding of the principles of 1776 and 1789, an understanding that also could be interpreted as "an augury of good prospects" for African Americans absent the American Civil War. We will never know, and to maintain the contrary with absolutism is nothing more than intellectual arrogance. According to Bradford, "Blacks are sometimes Southern conservatives—even though they call it something else. But race, of course, continues to matter among Southerners, white, black and brown. We all know that Charles Roland of the University of Kentucky told us the truth about our world when he argued a few years ago that the color line still exists—though not in a way easily accessible to correction by statute or exhortation" (Bradford, *The Reactionary Imperative: Essays Literary and Political* [Peru, Ill.: Sherwood Sudgen & Publishers, 1990], 130).

51. Bradford, *Remembering*, 145-46.
52. Ibid., 146.
53. See National Labor Relations Board v. Jones & Laughlin Steel Corporation 301 U.S. 1 (1937) for an important development in precedent that granted the Congress approximate plenary power to regulate interstate commerce.
54. Bradford, *Guide*, 30.
55. Bradford agreed with Raoul Berger's conclusions in *The Fourteenth Amendment and the Bill of Rights* (Norman: University of Oklahoma Press, 1989) regarding the historical account of the Fourteenth Amendment's due process and equal protection guarantees.
56. Bradford, *Guide*, 29. This chapter was in response to an old liberal, the neoconservative Professor Harry Jaffa; specifically his "Equality as a Conservative Principle," in *Loyola of Los Angeles Law Review*, VIII (June, 1975), 471—505, subsequently included as chap. 2 in *How to Think About the American Revolution* (Durham, N.C.: Carolina Academic Press, 1978), 13-48. Professor Jaffa did not mince his words:

> The idea of equality, as expressed in the Declaration, is the key to the morality of "the laws of nature and of nature's God." It is this natural law which the Constitution—and the regime of which the Constitution is a feature—is designed to implement. The abandonment of the idea of Equality is perforce an abandonment of that morality and that constitutionalism. It is perforce the abandonment of the "ought" for the "is." It would be the abandonment of that higher law tradition which is the heart of that civility—and that Conservatism—which judges men and nations by permanent standards. As we propose to demonstrate, the commitment to Equality in the American political tradition is synonymous with the commitment to those permanent standards. Whoever rejects the one, of necessity rejects the other, and in that rejection opens the way to the relativism and histori-

cism that is the theoretical ground of modern totalitarian regimes (ibid., 19).

Obviously, Jaffa applauds Lincoln's role in raising, then and now, the "Cult of Equality" consciousness.

57. Ibid., 34 (emphasis not in the original).
58. *The Federalist,* 10. Jaffa painted a veneer over the incompatibility between Lincoln's contrived "leading object" for the national government and Publius's "first object of government." He wrote: "We saw that Madison reflected the doctrine of Equality, when he attributed the need for constitutional government, and constitutional morality, to the difference between men and angels. But he reflected no less when, in the tenth *Federalist,* he put as the 'first object of government, the protection of different and *unequal* faculties of acquiring property'" (ibid., 4). Jaffa's attempted reconciliation between Lincoln's and Publius's versions of the national government's primary responsibility is far from convincing.
59. Bradford, *Guide,* 37.
60. Ibid., 39.
61. See *The Federalist,* #10.
62. Guide, 53.
63. Bradford, *Intentions,* 104.
64. Ibid., 106.
65. Ibid., 105.
66. I am not convinced that had Lincoln not been assassinated, that he would have been a moderate Republican toward the conquered Confederacy. Scholars point to Lincoln's second inaugural address (4 March 1865) as evidence of his moderation, where in the closing paragraph he begins with the words "With malice towards none, with charity for all." But, the address is a rhetorical masterpiece. For example, throughout the address he indicts the South for the war and its horrors, even though he said "but let us judge not, that we be not judged." Moreover, he intimates that more suffering may be justified: "Yet, if God wills that it [this mighty scourge of war] continue until all the wealth piled by the bondsman's two hundred and fifty years of unrequited toil shall be sunk, and until every drop of blood drawn with the lash shall be paid by the sword, as was said three thousand years ago, so still it must be said, *The judgments of the Lord are true and righteous altogether.*" These are not words of moderation.
67. Bradford, *Intentions,* 108.
68. Ibid., 124.
69. Ibid., 129–30.
70. One must be circumspect when referring to the South. The South is not necessarily "solid" in all respects. There always has been and with increasing rapidity continues to be political, social, and economic diversity within the South. Nevertheless, the term does resonate with a solidarity that is not exclusively tied to the race question. Actually, the latter may be as much a product of what makes the South unique than vice versa, as is evidenced by the fact that southern African Americans are southerners too. According to Bradford's reading of Richard Beale Davis's *Intellectual Life in the Colonial South, 1585–1763,* 3 vols. (Knoxville: University of Tennessee Press, 1978), "The South thought and acted in its own way before the peculiar institution was much developed within its boundaries" (*Imperative,* 118). For our purposes references to the South include those states of the former Confederacy that had the common experience of resisting what

they perceived to be hegemonic national policies designed to subject them to northern industrial, fiscal, and social interests; this states' rights political/constitutional mindset epitomizes southern states' determination to be self-governing (see *The Confederate Constitution of 1861,* inter alia). As was the case with slavery in the antebellum South and civil rights thereafter, their common Confederate experience was a consequence and not the cause of the Southern political identity, although it certainly solidified that identity from perspectives inside and outside the region. Sectional disagreements over tariffs, internal improvements, western lands, slavery, commerce, civil rights, religion, abortion, and firearms have incrementally hardened southern sectional identity, both within and outside of the South. But Bradford was aware that southern identity is waning, due in part to the institutionalized national Leviathan, the demographic shifts of a highly mobile society organized along *Gesellschaft* principles as opposed to *Gemeinschaft,* the mega entertainment industry through which northeast and west coast values are consumed in southern living rooms, and the transformation of the southern economy at the expense of its former agrarian base. All of these compete with southern Protestantism and patrimonial culture as socializing ties that bind southerners together within and between their respective communities. To the extent that nonsouthern influences dominate the socialization of southerners, to that extent the South will continue to loose its sectional identity.

71. For some such a position is political heresy, because they equate the South with racist and corrupt politics. Obviously, Bradford was not only aware of such charges but was also personally targeted by his adversaries. A case in point, Bradford was President Reagan's initial nominee to chair the National Endowment for the Humanities, until neoconservatives in and at the door of the Reagan administration smeared him as a racist in order to place one of their own, William Bennett, in his stead. See Samuel Francis' *Beautiful Losers: Essays on the Failure of American Conservatism* (Columbia: University of Missouri Press, 1993), 116–17.
72. Jaffa refers to this as "perforce the abandonment of the 'ought' for the 'is'" (see *supra,* note 56); a conservative southerner would respond that the *is* and the *ought* are, for the most part, synonymous.
73. Bradford, *Reactionary,* 116.
74. It amazes me how scholars from across the political spectrum interpret the Declaration of Independence as substituting one unitary form of government—Great Britain—with another—The United States. The last paragraph of the Declaration without question stipulates that the states are "FREE AND INDEPENDENT" with "full Power to levy War, conclude Peace, contract Alliances, establish Commerce, and do all other Acts and Things which INDEPENDENT STATES may of right do." It was only logical for Article Two of the Articles of Confederation (1781) to confirm the sovereignty of the states, which in turn was consistent with the states' corporate liberty.
75. Bradford, *Reactionary,* 140.
76. Ibid., 127.
77. Ibid., 126.
78. Bradford, *Intentions,* 3.
79. Ibid., 220.
80. Ronald Dworkin, *Life's Dominion: An Argument About Abortion, Euthanasia, And Individual Freedom* (New York: Alfred A. Knopf, 1993), 4.
81. See chap. 3, *supra.*
82. Dworkin, *Life's Dominion,* 118.

83. Ibid., 119.
84. Ibid., 119.
85. Ibid., 120. In 1977 Dworkin concluded that "the various branches of the professional approach to jurisprudence failed... [because] they ignored the crucial fact that jurisprudential issues are at their core issues of moral principle, not legal fact or strategy... if jurisprudence is to succeed, it must expose these issues and attack them as issues of moral theory" (*Taking Rights Seriously* [Cambridge: Harvard University Press, 1977], 7).
86. Dworkin, *Life's Dominion,* 124.
87. Ibid., 132.
88. Planned Parenthood of Southeastern Pennsylvania, et al. v. Casey, 60 LW 4795 (1992), 4836. The Court upheld four of the five, overturning the provision that required a married woman to notify her husband that she is procuring an abortion, while upholding the statute's definition of a medical emergency, requiring a woman to give her informed consent with a minimum twenty-four-hour waiting period, requiring a minor to obtain the informed consent of one of her parents (with provisions for a judicial by-pass), and requiring abortion providers to report pertinent data—names and addresses of women who had abortions—to the state. See chapters 4 and 5, *supra.*
89. Casey, 4798.
90. Ibid., 4836.
91. Ibid., 4836.
92. Dworkin, *Life's Dominion,* 168.
93. Casey, 4837; citations and quotation marks omitted.
94. Dworkin, *Life's Dominion,* 120.
95. Casey, 4798.
96. Ibid., 4837.
97. Ibid., 4801.
98. Ibid., 4803.
99. Dworkin, *Life's Dominion,* 146-47.
100. Ibid., 139.
101. Ibid., 139-40.
102. Ibid., 140.
103. Ibid., 141.
104. Ibid., 144-45.
105. Dworkin, *Taking Rights Seriously* (Cambridge: Harvard University Press, 1977), 18.
106. Dworkin, *Life's Dominion,* 14.
107. Dworkin, *Taking Rights,* 17.
108. Ibid., 104.
109. Ibid., 91.
110. Ibid., 94.
111. See Donald S. Lutz, *A Preface To American Political Theory* (Lawrence: The University Press of Kansas, 1992), 7-17, for a discussion about the difference between political theory and ideology.

8

Prescriptive Thoughts on Reviving the Nomocratic Constitution

Discussions on the correctness or incorrectness of U.S. Supreme Court jurisprudence in the area of rights can go on indefinitely.[1] Nevertheless, refusing to denounce the Constitution as a dead letter, even though I am convinced that it is quickly becoming such,[2] I suggest that we turn to the Founding Era—especially the Antifederalists—in an attempt to re-invigorate popular control and the traditional constitutional rule of law. By restoring two important traditional linchpins of the original American constitutional order, popular control and a viable American federalism, steps toward the restoration of the original constitutional order can be taken.

Admittedly, popular control is difficult to measure and should not be confused with public opinion. Popular control is more precisely *consensus ad idem,* defined as "an agreement of parties to the same thing; a meeting of the minds."[3] The public holds the U.S. Supreme Court in high esteem and assumes that its decisions are firmly grounded in the Constitution. The Court perpetuates this myth[4] and thereby sustains public acquiescence to their policies, but not *consensus ad idem.* One way to remedy the problem of popular control is to institutionally augment its authority over judicial review. As the framers were well aware, the nomocratic Constitution was held together by the external and internal checks and balances; these key components of American constitutionalism functioned to maintain government accountability to the governed. Thus, if the problem is the U.S. Supreme Court exercising the prerogatives of judicial review in a manner inconsistent with constitutional popular control and federalism, one solution is to meaningfully augment the states' control over the U.S. Supreme Court. Historically, several solutions have been proffered, such as judicial elections, limited terms, and modification of the Court's jurisdiction. The advantages and disadvantages of these solutions are well known, and none of them will necessarily result in a reinvigorated federal system. My solution takes a different tact. As Madison cautioned:

> [T]he great security against a gradual concentration of the several powers in the same department consists in giving to those who administer each department the necessary constitutional means and personal motives to resist encroachments of the others. The provision for defense must in this, as in all other cases, be made commensurate to the danger of attack. Ambition must be made to counteract ambition. The interest of the man must be connected with the constitutional rights of the place.[5]

A Madisonian solution to an unconstitutional nationalistic exercise of judicial review by the U.S. Supreme Court would be to empower the states with the constitutional means to secure their constitutional place in the federal system. Accordingly, an innovative nomocratic procedure through which a majority of state chief judicial officials have the prerogative to judicially review and overturn U.S. Supreme Court decisions, could restore the states to their constitutional roles in the American federal system and reinvigorate popular control. Consider the effects of the proposed constitutional amendment:

> When a national majority of each State's chief judicial official declares a decision by the U.S. Supreme Court to be inconsistent with the U.S. Constitution, the said decision shall thereby be negated and precedent restored. The States' designated chief judicial officers shall convey their declarations to the U.S. Solicitor General, who in turn will notify the Chief Justice of the U.S. Supreme Court to take appropriate measures consistent with this amendment.

A state's "chief judicial official" would be determined by each state. It could be the state attorney general, a sitting judge on the state's highest court, or a newly created position. For example, terms of office among the state chief judges and justices vary, but whether or not they have terms for life, placed on the bench by partisan elections, nonpartisan elections, gubernatorial appointment, legislative election, or merit selection and retention plan,[6] state judges are—or through changes in the states' selection process can be made to be—more accountable to states' interests. This accountability will significantly enhance American federalism in several ways.

First, overturning a controversial U.S. Supreme Court decision can be done more expeditiously and competently. The states would collectively have the wherewithal to effect U.S. Supreme Court policy without resorting to a cumbersome amendment process or the national congress that is significantly detached from states' interests.[7] Second, the proposed amendment would have a chilling effect on the U.S. Supreme Court, to the extent that cognizance of having their poorly reasoned and presumably activist decisions overturned by a majority of the states' chief judicial officials, would make them somewhat more circumspect in issuing such decisions in the first place. Moreover, the absence of a timetable to which state judges must comply, broadens the scope for state intervention both retrospectively and prospectively, which in turn would support Publius's attempt to augment the legislature's "mature deliberations" by "a series of particular discussions" in ascertaining the meaning of law.[8] Third, the heightened role of state judges in the articulation of national jurisprudence could lead to heightened interests in the states regarding the staffing of their respective chief judgeships.[9] This, in turn, could conceivably reinvigorate political participation at the state level while simultaneously enhancing states' rights vis-à-vis the national government.

Neither the pace of development for judge-made law nor its corresponding impact on popular control is admitted in a straightforward fashion (for reasons discussed *supra*), if at all. Models of judicial behavior to tell us what we know by common sense: That judicial *activism* is a powerful prerogative and when exercised to overrule a state law or policy, popular control has been dealt a setback. This is not to say that the prerogative of judicial review may never be appropriately exercised, but when premised upon penumbras and emanations, which in turn are utilized to rewrite the Ninth Amendment or any other constitutional provision, in order to "constitutionalize" the U.S. Supreme Court's policy preferences on rights, then the prerogative of judicial review has been misused, or more precisely, the U.S. Supreme Court has usurped the policy prerogatives of the states. Convinced that Dworkian overemphasis on rights detracts from the most fundamental of rights—the right to be self-governing—my proposal is a republican remedy toward restoring American constitutionalism to its nomocratic principles, by providing the states with the requisite constitutional authority and opportunity to directly check the political prerogatives of the U.S. Supreme Court, thereby indirectly checking national centralization of political power. In other words, it is deference to state sovereignty. This is not to say that my proposed amendment would result in a reactionary sort of juridical originalism; but it would heighten popular control over unenumerated rights jurisprudence, and to that extent a significant portion of originalism would be recovered.

I am convinced that this is an originalist approach to a nonoriginalist-generated constitutional crisis. However, this is by no means a settled question. For example, Professor Maltz recently concluded that "state sovereignty cannot be regarded as the definitive expression of the framers' interpretive intent that should guide modern constitutional analysis." Maltz claims that state sovereignty did not necessarily survive the Philadelphia Convention intact. Citing James Wilson, he maintains that it is very plausible that the framers subordinated the states to the national government, and that the Constitution should be interpreted accordingly. Moreover, even if state sovereignty did survive the Philadelphia Convention, "the victory of the Union armies and subsequent adoption of the Reconstruction Amendments represented a clear repudiation of Confederate constitutional opinion. Thus, whatever its historical significance, the concept of state sovereignty should not be the touchstone for the supplemental evidentiary rules necessary to originalist theory."[10] Even if Maltz's conclusions are correct—practically speaking they are, historically and theoretically they are not[11]—Article V of the Constitution provides us with the means to adjust the balance of power between the national and state governments in favor of the latter. Today, the issue is more than legitimacy—such as is the corpus of post-World War II rights jurisprudence in the strict sense constitutional?—but also one of accountability, such as should the U.S. Supreme Court be made more accountable to the states and the popular sovereignty embodied therein? In the words of Publius,

> It has been frequently remarked that it seems to have been reserved to the people of this country, by their conduct and example, to decide the important question, whether societies of men are really capable or not of establishing good government from reflection and choice, or whether they are forever destined to depend on their political constitutions on accident and force. If there be any truth in the remark, the crisis at which we are arrived may with propriety be regarded as the era in which that decision is to be made; and a wrong election on the part we shall act may, in this view, deserved to be considered as the general misfortune of mankind.[12]

We too, are confronted with a choice as the twenty-first century draws near. We can acquiesce to being governed by national elites—and in the case of unenumerated rights a national judicial elite—or support republican remedies for the ongoing concentration of political power at the national level.

Notes

1. This prescriptive chapter is, in part, a product of *A New Constitutionalism: Designing Political Institutions For A Good Society*, ed. Stephen L. Elkin and Karol Edward Soltan (Chicago: The University of Chicago Press, 1993). In essence, it is time once again that political scientists more readily complement their descriptive analyses with prescriptive remedies. Also see Mark C. Smith, *Social Science in the Crucible: The American Debate Over Objectivity and Purpose, 1918–1941* (Durham, N.C.: Duke University Press, 1994).
2. As Ronald Dworkin used to his advantage (see chap. 7, *infra*), even legal scholars with solid conservative credentials are willing to wax and wane on the hard cases. For example, "*Brown* was a great and correct decision, but it must be said in all candor that the decision was supported by a very weak opinion. Those two facts, taken together, have caused an enormous amount of trouble in the law" (Robert H. Bork, *The Tempting of America: The Political Seduction of the Law* [New York: The Free Press, 1990], 75). Walter Berns was more forthright in his assessment of *Brown*: By the 1960s the "prevailing view was that the Supreme Court justices could not be bound by the original understanding of a constitutional provision or by the intent of its framers, even if that understanding or intent could be unearthed from the rubble of those old words. The good judge, according to this view, does not engage in the hopeless and, more to the point, irrelevant task of trying to ascertain the 'true meaning of the equal protection clause. He does what Justice William O. Douglas was praised for doing: he raises the question of what is good for the country and seeks 'to translate his answers...into constitutional law'" (*Taking The Constitution Seriously* [New York: Madison Books, 1992], 216-17).
3. *Black's Law Dictionary*, 6th ed., ed. Joseph R. Nolan, et al, (St. Paul, Minn.: West Publishing Co., 1990).
4. See Richard Neely, *How Courts Govern America* (New Haven, Conn.: Yale University Press, 1981), chap. 1, 1-22, for a discussion about the myth and operational system disparities.
5. *The Federalist*, #51.
6. See Lawrence Baum, *American Courts: Process And Policy*, 3rd. ed. (Boston: Houghton Mifflin Company, 1994), 114-30.
7. Recall Justice O'Connor's claim that due to the direct election of U.S. Senators (i.e., the Seventeenth Amendment), Senators are more accountable to national interest groups than to their respective states; see Justice O'Connor's dissent in Garcia v. San Antonio Metropolitan Transit Authority, 469 U.S. 528 (1985).
8. According to Madison, "All new laws, though penned with the greatest technical skill and passed on the fullest and most mature deliberations, are considered as more or less obscure and equivocal, until their meaning be liquidated and ascertained by a series of particular discussions and adjudications" (*The Federalist*, #37).

9. It stands to reason that if the U.S. Supreme Court is made to be somewhat less supreme, and a portion of that supremacy is shifted to the states, interests in the state courts would be enhanced. I am convinced that one of the consequences of Supreme Court activism is a general decrease in political participation, because Americans intuitively sense that in the final analysis the unelected life tenured U.S. Supreme Court justices will have the final say.
10. Earl M. Maltz, *Rethinking Constitutional Law: Originalism, Interventionism, and the Politics of Judicial Review* (Lawrence: University Press of Kansas, 1994), s29.
11. There is ample evidence that the Reconstruction Amendments were necessitated by the context of state sovereignty, and that they were specific curtailments of state powers that emanated from state sovereignty; moreover, Chief Justice Chase expressed a truism when in 1869 he opined that "the Constitution, in all its provisions, looks to an indestructible Union, composed of indestructible States" (Texas v. White, 19 L.Ed. 227). This postbellum decision, written by an arch nationalist, certainly acknowledged the states to be viable units in the federal arrangement. In light of his previous statements, it is curious that Maltz concurs: "In short, a consistent application of the most plausible version of originalism would in essence turn contemporary constitutional jurisprudence on its head. Both the power-granting and rights-creating provisions of the Constitution would be confined to the narrow understanding of the framers. Federal power would face significant limitation; state governments, by contrast, would enjoy far greater freedom of action. Such a prospect is odious to most contemporary constitutional theorists. Thus, it is not surprising that they have launched vigorous attacks on the limitations that originalism would place on federal power and the restrictions it would impose on the federal courts in constitutional adjudication" (Maltz, *Rethinking Constitutional Law,* 36).
12. *The Federalist,* #1.

Selective Bibliography

Abraham, Henry J. *Freedom and the Court: Civil Rights and Liberties in the United States*, 5th ed. New York: Oxford University Press, 1988.

______. *The Judiciary: The Supreme Court in the Governmental Process*, 8th ed., Dubuque, IA: Wm. C. Brown Publishers, 1991.

Ackerman, Bruce. *Reconstructing American Law*. Cambridge, MA: Harvard University Press, 1984.

Abrahamson, Shirley. "Reincarnation & Reawakening: Long Forgotten By Civil Libertarians, State Courts Are Now Getting The Respect They Deserve," *Human Rights*, vol. 19, no. 1, 26, Winter 1992.

Agneshwar, Anand. "Ex-Justice Says He May Have Been Wrong," *National Law Journal*, vol. 13, Nov. 5, 1 (1990): p. 3.

Althouse, Ann. "How To Build A Separate Sphere: Federal Courts And State Power," *Harvard Law Review*, vol. 100, no. 4 (April 1987): 1485–1538.

Bamberger, Phylis. "Beware of the Dark Side of Constitutional Law," *Human Rights*, vol. 19, no. 1, 22, Winter 1992.

Barnett, Randy E., ed. *The Rights Retained By The People: The History and Meaning of the Ninth Amendment*, 2 vols. Fairfax, VA: George Mason University Press, 1989 and 1993.

Baum, Lawrence. *American Courts: Process and Policy*. Boston, MA: Houghton Mifflin Company, 1994.

Beard, Charles A. "The Supreme Court-Usurper Or Grantee?", *Political Science Quarterly*, vol. xxvii, no. 1 (March 1912): 1-35.

Berger, Raoul. *The Fourteenth Amendment and the Bill of Rights*. Norman, OK: University of Oklahoma, 1989.

______. *Federalism: The Founders' Design*. Norman, OK: University of Oklahoma Press, 1989.

______. "The Ninth Amendment," *Cornell Law Review*, vol. 66 (1980) 1–26.

______. *Government By Judiciary: The Transformation of the Fourteenth Amendment*. Cambridge: Harvard University Press, 1977.

Bertelsman, William O. "The Ninth Amendment And Due Process Of Law—Toward A Viable Theory Of Unenumerated Rights," *Cincinnati Law Review*, vol. 37 (1968): 777–796.

Bickel, Alexander M. *The Supreme Court And The Idea Of Progress*. New York, NY: Harper & Row, Publishers, 1970.

______. *The Least Dangerous Branch.* Indianapolis, IN: Bobbs-Merrill, 1962.

Bird, F.W. "The Evolution Of Due Process Of Law In The Decisions Of The United States Supreme Court," *Colombia Law Review*, vol. 13 (1908): 37–50.

Bonventre, Vincent Martin. "Beyond the Reemergence-Inverse Incorporation And Other Prospects For State Constitutional Law," *Albany Law Review*, vol. 53 (Winter 1989): 403–418.

Bork, Robert H. *The Tempting of America: The Political Seduction of the Law.* New York: The Free Press, 1990.

Bradford, M.E. *Original Intentions: On The Making And Ratification Of The United States Constitution.* Athens, GA: The University of Georgia Press, 1993.

______. *Against the Barbarians and Other Reflections on Familiar Themes.* Columbia, MO: The University of Missouri Press, 1992.

______. *The Reactionary Imperative: Essays Literary & Political.* Peru, IL: Sherwood Sugden & Publishers, 1990.

______. "The Authoritative Constitution: A Reading of the Ratification Debates", *Texas Tech Law Review*, vol. 21, no. 4 (1990): 2349–2374.

______. "Changed Only A Little: The Reconstruction Amendments And The Nomocratic Constitution of 1787," *Wake Forest Law Review*, vol. 24, no. 3, (1989): 573–598.

______. *Remembering Who We Are: Observations of a Southern Conservative.* Athens, GA: The University of Georgia Press, 1985.

______. *A Worthy Company.* Westchester, IL: Crossway Books, 1982.

______. *A Better Guide Than Reason: Studies in the American Revolution.* La Salle, IL: Sherwood Sugden & Company Publishers, 1979.

Brandeis, Louis and Warren, Samuel. "The Right to Privacy", *Harvard Law Review*, Vol. IV, No. 5., December 15 (1890) 193

______."The Living Law", *Illinois Law Review*, Vol. X, February 1916, No. 7, 461–471.

Brennan, William J. "The Bill Of Rights And The States: The Revival Of State Constitutions As Guardians Of Individual Rights," *New York University Law Review*, vol. 61, no. 4 (October 1986): 535–553.

Brest, Paul. "The Fundamental Rights Controversy: The Essential Contradictions of Normative Constitutional Scholarship," *The Yale Law Journal*, vol. 90 (1981): 1063–1109.

Call, Joseph L. "Federalism and the Ninth Amendment," *Dickinson Law Review*, vol. 64 (1960): 121–131.

Caplan, Russell L. "The History And Meaning Of The Ninth Amendment," *Virginia Law Review*, vol. 69, no. 2 (March 1983): 223–268.

Cardozo, Benjamin N. "Address before the New York State Bar Association Meeting, Hotel Astor, January 22, 1932," *New State Bar Association Report*, 1932:263.

______. *The Paradoxes Of Legal Science*. New York, NY: Columbia University Press, 1928.

______. *The Growth Of The Law*. New Haven, CT: Yale University Press, 1924.

______. *The Nature Of The Judicial Process*. New Haven, CT: Yale University Press, 1921.

Choper, Jesse H. "The Scope of National Power Vis-á-Vis the States: The Dispensability of Judicial Review," *The Yale Law Journal*, vol. 86 (1977): 1552–1621.

Collins, Ronald K. L. and Galie, Peter J. "Models of Post-Incorporation Judicial Review: 1985 Survey of State Constitutional Individual Rights Decisions", *Publius: The Journal of Federalism*, no. 16 (Summer 1986): 111–139.

Collins, Ronald K. L., Galie, Peter J. and Kincaid, John. "State High Courts, State Constitutions, and Individual Rights Litigation Since 1980: A Judicial Survey", *Publius: The Journal of Federalism*, no. 16 (Summer 1986): 141–161.

The Conference of Chief Justices: Report of the Committee on Federal-State Relations as Affected by Judicial Decisions, Adopted, August, 1958, Pasadena, California, 1958.

Corwin, Edward S. *Constitutional Revolution, Ltd.* Claremont, CA.: Claremont College, 1946.

______. *The "Higher Law" Background of American Constitutional Law*. Ithaca, NY: Great Seal Book, 1961.

______. "The Basic Doctrine Of American Constitutional Law," *Michigan Law Review*, vol. xii, no. 4 (1914): 247–276.

Cox, Archibald. *The Court And The Constitution*. Boston, MA: Houghton Mifflin Company, 1987.

Croly, Herbert. *The Promise of American Life*. New York: The Macmillan Company, 1911.

Curtis, Michael Kent. "Privileges Or Immunities, Individual Rights, And Federalism," *Harvard Journal of Law & Public Policy*, vol. 12, no. 1 (Winter 1989): 53-61.

Dahl, Robert. *Democracy And Its Critics*. New Haven, CT, Yale University Press, 1989.

______. "Decision-Making in a Democracy: The Supreme Court as a National Policy-maker," *Journal of Public Law*, no. 6, 279-295, 1957.

Davis, Richard Beale. *Intellectual Life in the Colonial South, 1585–1763*, 3 vols. Knoxville, TN: University of Tennessee Press, 1978.

DeRosa, Marshall L. *The Confederate Constitution of 1861: An Inquiry Into American Constitutionalism*. Columbia, MO: The University of Missouri Press, 1991.

De Tourtoulon, Pierre. *Philosophy In The Development Of Law*. New York, NY: The Macmillan Company, 1922.

Devlin, John. "Privacy and Abortion Rights Under the Louisiana State Constitution: Could *Roe* v. *Wade* be Alive and Well in the Bayou State?," *Louisiana Law Review*, vol. 51, (1991): 685-732.

Drake, Joseph. "The Sociological Interpretation Of Law," *Michigan Law Review*, vol. xvi (1918): 599-616.

Dunscomb, S. Whitney. "The Police Power and Civil Liberty," *Columbia Law Review*, vol. vi (1906): 93-101.

Dworkin, Ronald. *Life's Dominion: An Argument About Abortion, Euthanasia, And Individual Freedom* New York, NY: Alfred A. Knopf, 1993.

______. "Unenumerated Rights: Whether and How *Roe* Should Be Overruled," *University of Chicago Law Review*, vol. 59 (1992): 381-432.

______. *Taking Rights Seriously*. Cambridge, MA: Harvard University Press, 1977.

Dye, Thomas R. *American Federalism: Competition Among Governments*. Lexington, MA: Lexington Books, 1990.

Elazar, Daniel J. "Contradictory Trends in Contemporary American Federalism: Court, Congress and Centralization," *The Journal of State Government*, vol. 62, no. 1 (1989): 46-49.

Elkin, Stephen L. and Soltan, Karol Edward. *A New Constitutionalism: Designing Political Institutions For A Good Society*. Chicago: The University of Chicago Press, 1993.

Ely, John Hart. *Democracy and Distrust: A Theory of Judicial Review*. Cambridge, MA: Harvard University Press, 1980.

Ely, James W. *The Guardian Of Every Other Right: A Constitutional History of Property Rights*. New York: Oxford University Press, 1992.

Elliot, Jonathan, ed. *Debates on the Adoption of the Federal Constitution in the Convention Held at Philadelphia in 1787*, vol. V. New York, NY: Burt Franklin, 1888.

Epstein, Richard A. *Takings: Private Property and the Power of Eminent Domain*. Chicago: University of Chicago Press, 1985.

Evans, Stanton M. *The Theme Is Freedom: Religion, Politics, And The American Tradition*. Washington, DC: Regnery Publishing, Inc., 1994.

Farrand, Max, ed. *The Records of the Federal Convention of 1787*, 4 vols. New Haven, CT: Yale University Press, 1911.

Field, Martha A. "Abstention In Constitutional Cases: The Scope of the Pullman Abstention Doctrine," *University of Pennsylvania Law Review*, vol. 122, no. 5, (1974): 1071-1187.

Fishkin, James S. *The Dialogue of Justice: Toward a Self-Reflective Society*. New Haven, CT: Yale University Press, 1992.

Fleming, Thomas. "The Federal Principle," *Telos: A Quarterly Journal of Critical Thought*, no. 100 (Summer 1994): 17-36.

Fogel, Robert W. and Engerman, Stanley L. *Time On The Cross: The Economics of Negro Slavery.* Boston: Little, Brown and Co., 1974.

Fowler, Robert Ludlow. "The New Philosophies Of Law," *Harvard Law Review*, vol. xxvii (1914): 718–731.

Fowler, Robert Booth. *The Dance With Community: The Contemporary Debate In American Political Thought.* Lawrence, KS: The University Press of Kansas, 1991.

Francis, Samuel. *Beautiful Losers: Essays on the Failure of American Conservatism.* Columbia, MO: University of Missouri Press, 1993.

Frank, Jerome. *Law and the Modern Mind.* Garden City, NY: Anchor Books, 1930.

Frankfurter, Felix. "Twenty Years Of Mr. Justice Holmes' Constitutional Opinions," *Harvard Law Review*, vol. xxxvi, no. 8 (June 1923): 909–939.

Friedelbaum, Stanley H. "Reactive Responses: The Complementary Role of Federal and State Courts," *Publius: The Journal of Federalism*, Winter, 33–50 (1987).

Fuller, Paul. "Is There A Federal Police Power?" *Columbia Law Review*, vol. iv (1904): 563–588.

Gardner, James A. "The Failed Discourse Of State Constitutionalism, *Michigan Law Review*, vol. 90, no. 4 (February 1992): 761–837.

Graglia, Lino A. "Judicial Activism: Even on the Right Its Wrong", *The Public Interest*, vol. 95 (Spring 1989): 57–74.

Grano, Joseph D. "Deconstructing the Constitution," *Academic Questions*, (Winter 1988-89): 10–21.

Grey, Thomas C. "Do We Have an Unwritten Constitution?", *Stanford Law Review*, vol. 27 (1975): 703–718.

______. "The Uses of An Unwritten Constitution", *Chicago-Kent Law Review*, vol. 64, no. 1 (1988), 211.

Haines, Charles Grove. *The Revival of Natural Law Concepts.* Cambridge, MA: Harvard University Press, 1930.

______. "The Law Of Nature In State And Federal Judicial Decisions," *Yale Law Journal*, vol. xxv (1916): 618–657.

Hall, Arnold Bennett. *Popular Government: An Inquiry into the Nature and Methods of Representative Government.* New York, NY: The MacMillan Company, 1921.

Hall, Margaret E. and Patterson, Edwin W. *Selected Writings of Benjamin Nathan Cardozo.* New York: Fallon Publications, 1947.

Hamilton, Alexander, Madison, James, and Jay, John. *The Federalist Papers*, Clinton Rossiter, ed. New York: New American Library, 1961.

Hand, The Honorable William Brevard and Neuhaus, Richard John. *American Education on Trial: Is Secular Humanism a Religion? The Opinion of Judge*

W. Brevard Hand in the Alabama Textbook Case. Washington, DC: Center for Judicial Studies, 1987.

Hunter, James Davison. *Culture Wars: The Struggle To Define America*. Basic Books, 1991.

Hyman, Harold M. "Federalism: Legal Fiction and Historical Artifact?", *Brigham Young University Law Review*, (1987): 905-925.

Isseks, Samuel Shepp. "Jurisdiction Of The Lower Federal Courts To Enjoin Unauthorized Action Of State Officials," *Harvard Law Review*, vol. 40 (1927): 969-988.

Jaffa, Harry V. *Crisis of the House Divided*. Chicago: University of Chicago Press, 1982.

______. *How to Think About the American Revolution*. Durham, NC: Carolina Academic Press, 1978

Kahn, Ronald. *The Supreme Court and Constitutional Theory, 1953–1993*. Lawrence, KS: University Press of Kansas, 1994.

Kent, Irvin M. "Under The Ninth Amendment What Rights Are The 'Others Retained By The People'?", *The Federal Bar Journal*, vol. 29 (1970): 219-237.

Kelley, James F. "The Uncertain Renaissance of the Ninth Amendment," *The University of Chicago Law Review*, vol. 33 (1966): 814-836.

Kelsey, Knowlton H. "The Ninth Amendment of the Federal Constitution," *Indiana Law Review*, vol. xi, no. 4 (April 1936): 309-323.

Kendall, Willmore. "Equality: Commitment or Ideal?" *The Intercollegiate Review: A Journal of Scholarship and Opinion*, vol. 24, no. 2, Spring 1989, pp. 25-33.

Kendall, Willmore and Carey, George. *The Basic Symbols of the American Political Tradition* (Baton Rouge, LA: Louisiana State University Press, 1970.

Kennedy, Walter B. "Functional Nonsense And The Transcendental Approach," *Fordham Law Review*, vol. 5 (1936): 272-300.

Kincaid, John. "The State and Federal Bills of Rights: Partners and Rivals in Liberty", *Intergovernmental Perspective*, Fall 1991, Vol. 17, No. 4.

______. "A Proposal to Strengthen Federalism," *The Journal of State Government*, vol. 62, no. 1 (1989): 36-45.

______. "State Constitutions In A Federal System," *The Annals of The American Academy of Political and Social Science*, vol. 496 (March 1988): 12-22.

______. "The New Judicial Federalism", *Journal of State Government*, vol. 61, no. 5 (1988): 163-169.

Kincaid, John and Schechter, Stephen L. "The State of American Federalism," *Publius: The Journal of Federalism. 1985*, no. 16 (Summer 1986): 1-15.

Kirk, Russell, ed. *The Assault on Religion: Commentaries on the Decline of Religious Liberty*. New York: University Press of America, 1986.

Kirven, Gerald. "Under The Ninth Amendment, What Rights Are The 'Others Retained By The People'?" *South Dakota Law Review*, vol. 14 (Winter 1969): 80–91.

Krabbe, H. *The Modern Idea Of The State*. New York: D. Appleton and Company, 1922.

Lasser, William. *The Limits of Judicial Power: The Supreme Court in American Politics*. Chapel Hill, NC: The University of North Carolina Press, 1988.

Lence, Ross M., ed. *Union And Liberty: The Political Philosophy of John C. Calhoun*. Indianapolis, IN: Liberty Press, 1992.

Lien, Arnold J. *Concurring Opinion: The Privileges or Immunities Clause of the Fourteenth Amendment*. St. Louis, MO: Washington University Studies, 1957.

Llewellyn, Karl N. "Some Realism About Realism-Responding to Dean Pound", *Harvard Law Review*, vol. 44, (1931): 1222–1256.

______."A Realistic Jurisprudence—The Next Step," *Columbia Law Review*, vol. xxx, no. 4 (April 1930): 431–465.

Lutz, Donald S. *A Preface To American Political Theory*. Lawrence, KS: The University Press of Kansas, 1992.

______.*The Origins of American Constitutionalism*. Baton Rouge, LA: Louisiana State University Press, 1988.

______."The United States Constitution as an Incomplete Text," *The Annals of the American Academy of Political and Social Science*, vol. 496 (March 1988): 23–42.

______.*Popular Consent and Popular Control: Whig Political Theory in the Early State Constitutions*. Baton Rouge: Louisiana State University Press, 1980.

Malcolm, Joyce Lee. "The Right of the People to Keep and Bear Arms: The Common Law Tradition," *Hastings Constitutional Law Quarterly*, vol. 10:285, Winter (1983)

Maltz, Earl M. *Rethinking Constitutional Law: Originalism, Interventionism, and the Politics of Judicial Review*. Lawrence, KS: University Press of Kansas, 1994.

______."Individual Rights And State Autonomy," *Harvard Journal of Law & Public Policy*, vol. 12, no. 1 (Winter 1989): 163–192.

McAffee, Thomas B. "The Original Meaning Of The Ninth Amendment," *Columbia Law Review*, vol. 90 (1990): 1215–1320.

McDowell, Gary L. "Rediscovering Federalism? State Constitutional Law And The Restoration Of State Sovereignty," *Rutgers Law Journal*, vol. 21 (1990): 797–818.

______.*Curbing The Courts: The Constitution And The Limits Of Judicial Power*. Baton Rouge, LA: Louisiana State University Press, 1988.

McDonald, Forrest. *Novus Ordo Seclorum: The Intellectual Origins of the Constitution*. Lawrence, KS: the University Press of Kansas, 1985.

Meyer, Hermine Herta. *The History And Meaning Of The Fourteenth Amendment: Judicial Erosion of the Constitution Through the Misuse of the Fourteenth Amendment.* New York: Vantage Press, 1977.

Mitchell, Lawrence E. "The Ninth Amendment and the Jurisprudence of Original Intention," *The Georgetown Law Journal*, vol. 74 (1986): 1719-1742.

Neely, Richard. *How Courts Govern America.* New Haven, CT: Yale University Press, 1981.

Newman, Jon O. "Restructuring Federal Jurisdiction: Proposals to Preserve the Federal Judicial System," *The University of Chicago Law Review*, vol. 56, no. 2 (Spring 1989): 761-777.

O'Brien, David M. *Storm Center: The Supreme Court in American Politics*, 2 ed. New York: W.W. Norton & Company, 1990.

Osborne, David and Gaebler, Ted. *Reinventing Government: How the Entrepreneurial Spirit is Transforming the Public Sector.* Reading, MA: Addison-Wesley Publishing Company, Inc., 1992.

Patterson, Bennett B. *The Forgotten Ninth Amendment: A Call For Legislative and Judicial Recognition of Rights Under Social Conditions of Today.* Indianapolis: The Bobbs-Merrill Company, Inc., 1955.

Paust, Jordon J. "Human Rights and the Ninth Amendment: A New Form of Guarantee," *Cornell Law Review*, vol. 60 (1975): 231-267.

Perry, Michael J. *The Constitution, The Courts, And Human Rights: An Inquiry into the Legitimacy of Constitutional Policymaking by the Judiciary.* Yale University Press, 1982. 39.

Phelps, Glenn A. *George Washington and American Constitutionalism.* Lawrence, KS: University Press of Kansas, 1993.

Pound, Roscoe. *Finding Law Through Experience and Reason: Three Lectures.* Athens, GA: University of Georgia Press, 1960.

______. *Social Control Through Law.* New Haven, CT: Yale University Press, 1942.

______. *Contemporary Juristic Theory.* Claremont, CA: Claremont College, 1940.

______. "The Call For A Realist Jurisprudence," *Harvard Law Review*, vol. 44 (1931): 697-711.

______. *Law and Morals.* Chapel Hill: The University of North Carolina Press, 1926.

______. "The Theory of Judicial Decision," *Harvard Law Review*, vol. xxxvi, no. 6 (April 1923): 641-662 and 940-959.

______. "A Theory of Social Interests", *Papers and Proceedings, Fifteenth Annual Meeting, American Sociological Society*, vol. xv (1920): 16-45.

______. "Interests of Personality," *Harvard Law Review*, vol. xxviii, no. 4, (1915):343-365.

______."Courts and Legislation," *The American Political Science Review*, vol. vii, no. 3 (1913): 361-383.

______."Common Law and Legislation", *Harvard Law Review*, vol. xxi, no. 6 (1908): 383-407.

______."Mechanical Jurisprudence", *Columbia Law Review*, vol. viii, no. 8 (1908): 599-623.

Pressman, Steven. "Protecting Rights In State Courts," *Editorial Research Reports*, May 27, 1988: 274-282.

Quade, Vicki. "State Courts: The Next Frontier For Civil Liberties," *Human Rights*, vol. 19, no. 1, 14, Winter 1992.

Rapaczynski, Andrzej. "From Sovereignty To Process: The Jurisprudence Of Federalism After Garcia," *The Supreme Court Review*, vol. 8 (1985): 341-419.

Redlich, Norman. "Are There Certain Rights Retained By The People?", *New York Law University Review*, vol. 37 (1962): 787-812.

Reeves, Mavis Mann. "State Activism as a Balance in Preserving Federalism," *The Journal of State Government*, vol. 62, no. 1 (1989): 20-24.

Riker, William H. "Six Books in Search of a Subject-Or Does Federalism Exist and Does It Matter?", *Comparative Politics*, vol. 2 (1969): 135-146.

Sandoz, Ellis. *A Government of Laws: Political Theory, Religion, and the American Founding*. Baton Rouge: Louisiana State University Press, 1990.

Sayre, Paul. *The Life of Roscoe Pound.* Iowa City: State University of Iowa, 1948.

Schreiber, Harry N. "Federalism And Legal Process: Historical And Contemporary Analysis Of The American System," *Law & Society Review*, vol. 14, no. 3 (Spring 1980): 663-722.

Simon, Yves R. *The Tradition of Natural Law: A Philosopher's Reflection.* New York: Fordham University Press, 1992.

Solimine, Michael E. and Walker, James L. "State Court Protection Of Federal Constitutional Rights," *Harvard Journal of Law & Public Policy*, vol. 12, no. 1 (Winter 1989): 127-162.

Spitzer, Robert J. *The Politics Of Gun Control.* Chatham, NJ: Chatham House Publishers, Inc., 1995.

Stammler, Rudolf. "Fundamental Tendencies In Modern Jurisprudence," *Michigan Law Review*, vol. 21, no. 6 (April 1923): 623-654.

Story, Joseph. *Commentaries On The Constitution Of The United States*, 3 vols. New York: DaCapo Press, 1970.

Thorpe, Francis Newton. *The Federal and State Constitutions: Colonial Charters, and Other Organic Laws of the States*. Washington: Government Printing Office, 7 vols. (1909).

Tribe, Laurence H. and Dorf, Michael C. *On Reading the Constitution.* Cambridge, MA: Harvard University Press, 1991.

U.S. Department of Justice, Office of Legal Policy. *Report to the Attorney General. Wrong Turns on the Road to Judicial Activism: The Ninth Amendment and Privileges or Immunities Clause.* September 25, 1987, Doc. J1.2: At 8/7.

Walker, Graham. *Moral Foundations Of Constitutional Thought: Current Problems, Augustinian Prospects*. Princeton: Princeton University Press, 1990.

Warren, Charles. *The Supreme Court in United States History, 1836–1918*, 2 vols. Boston: Little, Brown, and Company, 1926.

______."The New Liberty Under The 14th Amendment", *Harvard Law Review*, vol. 39(1925-1926): 431-465.

______."Legislative Judicial Attacks On The Supreme Court Of The United States," *The American Law Review*, vol. 47 (1913): 161-189.

______."A Bulwark To The State Police Power—The United States Supreme Court," *Columbia Law Review*, vol. xiii, no. 8 (1913): 667-695.

Wells, Michael. "The Role Of Comity In The Laws Of Federal Courts," *North Carolina Law Review*, vol. 60 (1981): 59-86.

Wickersham, George W. "The Police Power, A Product Of The Rule Of Reason," *Harvard Law Review*, vol. xxvii, no. 4 (1914): 297-316.

Wigdor, David. *Roscoe Pound: Philosopher of the Law*. Westport, CT: Greenwood Press, 1974.

Wildavsky, Aaron. *The Rise Of Egalitarianism*. Washington, DC: The American University Press, 1991.

Wills, Garry. *Lincoln At Gettysburg: The Words That Remade America*. New York: Simon & Schuster, 1992.

Wilson, Clyde N., ed. *The Essential Calhoun*. New Brunswick, NJ: Transaction Publishers, 1992.

Wilson, James Q. *The Moral Sense*. New York: The Free Press, 1993.

Wilson, Woodrow. "The Law And The Facts," *The American Political Science Review*, vol. v, no. 1, February (1911): 1-11.

Wood, Gordon S. *The Creation of the American Republic, 1776–1787*. Chapel Hill: University of North Carolina Press, 1969.

Wright, Benjamin Fletcher. *American Interpretations Of Natural Law: A Study in the History of Political Thought*. New York, NY: Russell & Russell, 1962.

Wright, Charles Alan. *The Law of the Federal Courts*. St. Paul, MN: West Publishing Company, 1983.

Selective Case Bibliography

Adair v. United States, 208 U.S. 161 (1908).
Baker v. Carr 369 U.S. 186 (1962).
Barron v. The Mayor and City Council of Baltimore, 8 L.Ed. 672 (1833).
Bowers v. Hardwick, 106 S.Ct. 2841 (1986).
Butchers' Benevolent Association of New Orleans v. The Crescent City Livestock and Slaughter-house Company, 21 L.Ed. 394 (1873).
Butchers' Union Slaughter-house and Livestock Landing Company v. Crescent City Live-Stock Landing and Slaughter-house Company, 111 U.S. 746 (1883).
Calder v. Bull 1 L.Ed. 648 (1798).
Champion v. Ames, 188 U.S. 321 (1903).
Chisholm v. Georgia, 1 L.Ed. 440, (1793).
Cohens v. Virginia, 5 L.Ed. 257 (1821).
Colgrove v. Green, 328 U.S. 549 (1946).
Cooley v. The Board of Wardens, 13 L.Ed. 996 (1851).
Corfield v. Coryell, 6 Fed. Cas. No. 546 (C. C. E. D. Pa.).
Davis v. Wechsler, 68 L.Ed. 143 (1923).
Dred Scott v. Sandford, 15 L.Ed. 691 (1857).
Eakin v. Raub, 12 Sergeant and Rawle (Pennsylvania Supreme Court) 330 (1825).
Eisenstadt v. Baird, 405 U.S. 438 (1972).
Evans v. Romer, 854 P. 2d 1270 (Colo. 1993).
Everson v. Board of Education of Ewing Township, 330 U.S. 1 (1947).
Fletcher v. Peck, 6 Cranch (10 U.S.) 87 (1810).
Furman v. Georgia, 408 U.S. 238 (1972).
Garcia v. San Antonio Metropolitan Transit Authority, 105 S.Ct. 1005 (1985).
Gibbons v. Ogden, 6L.Ed. 23 (1824).
Gitlow v. New York, 268 U.S. 652 (1925).
Golden v. Prince, Fed. Cas. No. 5509, Vol. 10 (1814) 542.
Gregg v. Georgia, 96 S.Ct. 2909 (1976).
Griswold v. Connecticut, 85 S.Ct. 1678, (1965).
Hammer v. Dagenhart, 247 U.S. 251 (1918).
Harris v. McRae, 448 U.S. 497 (1980).
Heart of Atlanta Motel v. United States, 379 U.S. 241 (1964).

Hodgson v. Minnesota, 110 S.Ct. 2926 (1990).
Katzenbach v. McClung, 379 U.S. 294 (1964).
Leisy v. Hardin, 34 L.Ed. 128 (1890).
Lemon v. Kurtzman, 403 U.S. 602 (1971).
Lochner v. New York, 198 U.S. 45 (1905).
Lucas v. South Carolina Coastal Council, 112 S.Ct. 2886 (1992).
Luther v. Borden, 48 U.S. 1 (1849).
McCulloch v. Maryland, 4 L.Ed. 579 (1819).
Marbury v. Madison 2 L.Ed. 60 (1803).
Martin v. Hunter's Lessee, 4 L.Ed. 97 (1816).
Meyer v. Nebraska, 262 U.S. 390 (1923).
Miller v. California, 413 U.S. 5 (1973).
Minersville School District v. Gobitis, 84 L.Ed. 1375 (1940).
Muller v. Oregon, 208 U.S. 412 (1908).
National Labor Relations Board v. Jones & Laughlin Steel Corp., 301 U.S. 1 (1937).
Ogden v. Saunders, 12 Wheat. (25 U.S.) 213 (1827).
Palko v. Connecticut, 82 L.Ed. 288 (1937).
Philadelphia v. New Jersey, 437 U.S. 617 (1978).
Planned Parenthood of Louisiana, Inc., et al. v. State of Louisiana (LA, 1991).
Planned Parenthood of Southeastern Pennsylvania v. Casey, 112 S.Ct. 2791 (1992).
Plessy v. Ferguson, 16 S.Ct. 1138 (1896).
Poe v. Ullman, 367 U.S. 497 (1961).
Presser v. Illinois, 6 S.Ct. 581 (1886).
Prigg v. Pennsylvania, 16 Pet. (41 U.S.) 539 (1842).
Railroad Commission of Texas v. Pullman Company, 85 L.Ed. 971 (1941).
Reynolds v. Simms, 377 U.S. 533 (1964).
Rochin v. California, 342 U.S. 165 (1952).
Roe v. Wade, 93 S.Ct. 705 (1973).
Rust v. Sullivan, 111 S.Ct. 1759 (1991).
Shapiro v. Thompson, 394 U.S. 618 (1969).
Smith v. Allwright, 321 U.S. 649 (1944).
Sojourner T., et al., v. Edwards, et al., U.S. Fifth Circuit, no. 91-3677 (1992).
Southern Pacific Co. v. Jensen, 244 U.S. 205 (1917).
Texas v. Johnson, 491 U.S. 397 (1989).
Texas v. White, 74 U.S. 700 (1869).
Torcaso v. Watkins, 367 U.S. 488 (1961).
Twining v. State of New Jersey, 211 U.S. 78 (1908).
U.S. v. Carolene Products Co., 304 U.S. 144 (1938).
U.S. v. Cruikshank, 92 U.S. 549 (1876).
U.S. v. Lopez, 63 LW 4343 (1995).

U.S. v. Miller, 307 U.S. 174 (1939).
U.S. v. Warin, 530 F. 2d. 104 (1976).
Webster v. Reproductive Health Services, 109 S.Ct. 3040 (1989).
Wesberry v. Sanders, 376 U.S. 1 (1964).
West Virginia State Board of Education v. Barnette, 87 L.Ed. 1628 (1943).
Zorach v. Clauson, 343 U.S. 306 (1952).

Index

For Product Safety Concerns and Information please contact our EU
representative GPSR@taylorandfrancis.com
Taylor & Francis Verlag GmbH, Kaufingerstraße 24, 80331 München, Germany

www.ingramcontent.com/pod-product-compliance
Ingram Content Group UK Ltd.
Pitfield, Milton Keynes, MK11 3LW, UK
UKHW022118190926
475702UK00013B/1520

* 9 7 8 1 1 3 8 5 1 6 5 0 2 *